THE DEEP STATE

ALSO BY MIKE LOFGREN

The Party Is Over

THE DEEP STATE

THE FALL OF THE CONSTITUTION
AND THE RISE OF A SHADOW
GOVERNMENT

Mike Lofgren

VIKING

VIKING
An imprint of Penguin Random House LLC
375 Hudson Street
New York, New York 10014
penguin.com

ISBN 978-0-525-42834-3

Printed in the United States of America
10 9 8 7 6 5 4 3 2 1

Set in Haarlemmer MT Std

This book is dedicated to
Joan Millicent Morris Lofgren
A mother and a teacher: To you I owe everything

CONTENTS

ACKNOWLEDGMENTS

I would like express my sincere thanks to Bill Moyers for his encouragement and advocacy of this project from its very inception. Bill's suggestion to write an essay on the Deep State was the acorn from which the oak took root. Gratitude is owed to Chuck Spinney and Brian O'Malley, two firm friends and former fellow travelers with me in the government. Their observations over the years helped me crystallize and polish the concept of the Deep State. Thanks also to Andrew Cockburn, Ray McGovern, Tom Drake, Winslow Wheeler, Andrew Feinstein, and Bill Binney for their valuable assistance at critical stages. To former colleagues and bosses who provided me with an endless stock of practical knowledge about the way government really works: well, you know who you are! In hindsight, all my governmental experiences were enlightening, if not always as edifying as a Parson Weems fable at the time they actually occurred. Joy de Menil, the editor of this book, worked tirelessly with me to structure the narrative into a coherent whole. Bridget Matzie, my agent, was an unwavering supporter throughout the project. And, of course, none of this would have been possible without a loving and totally supportive family: Alisa, Laura, and Eric.

INTRODUCTION

For twenty-eight years I was a congressional employee with an interesting and challenging but by no means remarkable career on Capitol Hill as a staff member and national defense analyst for the House and Senate budget committees. I began my tenure as a mainstream Republican in the early days of the Reagan presidency. By the end of my career I considered myself a resolute nonpartisan, and increasingly viewed all political ideologies as mental and emotional crutches, or substitute religions: for leaders, a means of manipulating attitudes and behaviors; for the rank and file, a lazy surrogate for problem solving and a way of fulfilling the craving to belong to something bigger than oneself.

My first perception of this ideological syndrome came in the mid-1990s, when Republicans had taken over the majority in the House of Representatives for the first time in forty years. It was an exciting time, to be sure, but a tumultuous one. Speaker of the House Newt Gingrich, the Robespierre of the Republican revolution, employed chaos, polarization, and scapegoating as the means of carrying out a divide-and-rule strategy. It worked for a time, but I saw in retrospect that it was a technique that crippled the legislative branch so that it could no longer work effectively. It did not help that many Republican congressmen were too busy lasciviously ogling the sordid details of Kenneth Starr's report on the Monica Lewinsky affair to notice that an obscure extremist group called al-Qaeda had blown up two of our embassies in Africa.

The real wake-up call for me came during that surreal period between the terrorist attacks of September 11, 2001, and the invasion of Iraq in March 2003. If there was any point in our post–World War II history that called for careful analysis of the facts and rational responses that would serve the nation's long-term security interests, this was surely it.

Instead, a clique of neoconservative ideologues both inside and outside the George W. Bush administration, abetted at every step by the mainstream news media, acted as carnival barkers for the most destructive and self-defeating policies since Vietnam, and maybe since the eve of the Civil War. A majority of politicians on Capitol Hill, along with a sizable portion of the American people, ambled around like sleepwalkers on the edge of a precipice, unaware of the danger the ideologues were luring them into. When the House Administration Committee instructed the institution's cafeterias to rename French fries "freedom fries" because the government in Paris stubbornly remained unmesmerized by the Bush administration's arguments for war in the Middle East, I recognized that the People's House had hit intellectual rock bottom.

Still, I told whoever would listen that the "slam dunk" evidence of Saddam Hussein's weapons of mass destruction was weak and that by invading Iraq the United States might be purchasing its very own West Bank on steroids—not that my objections changed anyone's mind. Later, when the invoices began to pile up—the total bill for Iraq summed up to a nice, round one trillion dollars, excluding debt service—I attempted, from my position on the Budget Committee, to reconcile this extravagance, as much as the numbers would allow, with the rote statements of representatives and senators that deficit spending was a sign of an out-of-control government and a national moral blot that would impoverish our children.

Parallel to these developments, the American economy was mutating into a casino with a tilted wheel. Ably assisted by politicians, whom I began to see less and less as leaders and more and more as corporate errand boys, the titans of Wall Street constructed a heads-I-win-tails-you-lose economic system based on Ponzi schemes, asset stripping, and rent extraction. The inevitable result was the economic meltdown of 2008. The eventual solution to that catastrophe was not national reconstruction but a bailout of the financial institutions that had caused the disaster in the first place. They soon returned to record profitability and market dominance as the rest of the country experienced the slowest recovery since the Great Depression.

The twin shocks of 9/11 and the Great Recession seem mentally to have unhinged a portion of the American people and much of the political class. The following years were consumed by crazy arguments about the president's birth certificate, death panels, and voters shouting that the government must get its hands off their government-provided Medicare. By 2011, when a new crop of Tea Party freshmen had taken their seats in Congress and announced that their first priority was to drive the country into a sovereign debt default, I decided I'd had enough. The circus was being run from the monkey cage, and it was time to move on.

Back in private life, I wrote about the rightward lurch of the Republican Party and the intractable gridlock on the Hill in a book titled *The Party Is Over: How Republicans Went Crazy, Democrats Became Useless, and the Middle Class Got Shafted*. Perhaps I can claim a modest amount of credit for helping to launch the now-thriving cottage industry of political pundits noticing the nuttiness of the present-day Party of Lincoln with the mortified distaste of an Anglican bishop confronted by a tribe of cannibals. That said, I was hardly ready to launch myself into the arms of the Party of Jefferson and Jackson. That crowd had serious problems, too.

Shortly after finishing the book, I began to feel that I had dealt with the symptoms—lurid symptoms, to be sure—rather than fundamental causes. Diseases always manifest themselves as symptoms, but these should not be confused with the underlying cause of the malady. America's politics were broken, but so were its economic engine and its supposedly bipartisan foreign policy. Social indicators of human development such as life expectancy and maternal mortality showed that America was slipping in comparison with other developed countries. Economic inequality was growing. Infrastructure was getting rickety. Educational policy was confused and ineffectual. The Tea Party, as gaudy and irrational as its anger might be, was merely one among several warning signs of a deep-seated dysfunction in the way American society was run at the very top.

Anyone who has spent time on Capitol Hill will occasionally get the feeling when watching debates in the House or Senate chambers that he or she is seeing a kind of marionette theater, with members of Congress reading carefully vetted talking points about prefabricated issues. This impression was particularly strong both in the run-up to the Iraq War and later, during the mock deliberations over funding that ongoing debacle. While the public is now aware of the disproportionate influence of powerful corporations over Washington, best exemplified by the judicial travesty known as the *Citizens United* decision, few fully appreciate that the United States has in the last several decades gradually undergone a process first identified by Aristotle and later championed by Machiavelli that the journalist Edward Peter Garrett described in the 1930s as a "revolution within the form." Our venerable institutions of government have outwardly remained the same, but they have grown more and more resistant to the popular will as they have become hardwired into a corporate and private influence network with almost unlimited cash to enforce its will.

Even as commentators decry a broken government that cannot marshal the money, the will, or the competence to repair our roads and bridges, heal our war veterans, or even roll out a health care website, there is always enough money and will, and maybe just a bare minimum of competence, to overthrow foreign governments, fight the longest war in U.S. history, and conduct dragnet surveillance over the entire surface of the planet.

This paradox of penury and dysfunction on the one hand and unlimited wealth and seeming omnipotence on the other is replicated outside of government as well. By every international metric of health and living standards, the rural counties of southern West Virginia and eastern Kentucky qualify as third-world. So do large areas of Detroit, Cleveland, Camden, Gary, and many other American cities. At the same time, wealth beyond computation, almost beyond imagining, piles up in the money center of New York and the technology hub of Palo Alto. It piles up long enough to purchase a $95,000 truffle, a $38 million vintage Ferrari GTO, or a $179 million Picasso before the balance finds its way to an offshore hiding place.

These paradoxes, both within the government and within the ostensibly private economy, are related. They are symptoms of a shadow government ruling the United States that pays little heed to the plain words of the Constitution. Its governing philosophy profoundly influences foreign and national security policy and such domestic matters as spending priorities, trade, investment, income inequality, privatization of government services, media presentation of news, and the whole meaning and worth of citizens' participation in their government.

I have come to call this shadow government the Deep State. The term was actually coined in Turkey, and is said to be a system composed of high-level elements within the intelligence services, military, security, judiciary, and organized crime. In John le Carré's recent novel *A Delicate Truth,* a character in the book describes the Deep State as "the ever-expanding circle of non-governmental insiders from banking, industry and commerce who were cleared for highly classified information denied to large swathes of Whitehall and Westminster." I use the term to mean a hybrid association of key elements of government and parts of top-level finance and industry that is effectively able to govern the United States with only limited reference to the consent of the governed as normally expressed through elections.

The Deep State is the big story of our time. It is the red thread that runs through the war on terrorism and the militarization of foreign policy, the financialization and deindustrialization of the American economy, the rise of a plutocratic social structure that has given us the most unequal society in almost a century, and the political dysfunction that has paralyzed day-to-day governance.

Edward Snowden's June 2013 exposure of the pervasiveness of the National Security Agency's surveillance has partially awakened a Congress that was asleep at the switch and has ignited a national debate about who is really in charge of our government. At the same time, a few politicians, most notably Elizabeth Warren of Massachusetts, are beginning to argue that the American economy is rigged. But these isolated cases have not provided a framework for understanding the extent of the shadow government, how it arose, the interactions of its various parts, and the extent to which it influences and controls the leaders whom we think we choose in elections. This book, based in large part on my experiences and observations while in public service, aims to provide that framework.

My reflection on our shadow system of government has come only after my retirement in 2011 and my physical withdrawal from Washington, D.C., proper and the institutions located there. Unlike the vast majority of Capitol Hill strivers who leave the place for greener pastures, I had no desire to join a lobbying shop, trade association, think tank, or consultancy. But I did have a need to see in perspective the events I had witnessed, and I came to realize that the nation's capital, where I lived and worked for more than half my lifetime, has its own peculiar ecology.

To look upon Washington once again with fresh eyes, I sometimes feel as Darwin must have when he first set foot on the Galapagos Islands. From the Pentagon to K Street, and from the contractor cube farms in Crystal City to the public policy foundations along Massachusetts Avenue, the terrain and its people are exotic and well worth examining in a scientific manner. The official United States government has its capital there, and so does our state within a state. To describe them in the language of physics, they coexist in the same way it is possible for two subatomic particles to coexist in an entangled quantum state. The characteristics of each particle, or each governmental structure, cannot fully be described independently; instead, we must find a way to describe the system as a whole.

1

BELTWAYLAND

Rome lived on its principal till ruin stared it in the face. Industry is the only true source of wealth, and there was no industry in Rome. By day the Ostia road was crowded with carts and muleteers, carrying to the great city the silks and spices of the East, the marble of Asia Minor, the timber of the Atlas, the grain of Africa and Egypt; and the carts brought out nothing but loads of dung. That was their return cargo.
— Winwood Reade, *The Martyrdom of Man* (1871)

If I wanted to go crazy I would do it in Washington because it would not be noticed.
— Attributed to Irvin S. Cobb, in *Respectfully Quoted: A Dictionary of Quotations Requested from the Congressional Research Service* (1989)

Imperial City on the Potomac Swamp

Like ancient Rome, Washington, D.C., is an imperial city. The capital of the United States produces laws, Supreme Court decisions, regulations in the *Federal Register,* circulars from the Office of Management and Budget, a trillion dollars of contracts a year, gossip, scandal, and punditry. All of these products are not dung—well, not exactly—but their value has in recent years become increasingly questionable.

First, a point of clarification: the city is usually not called "Washington" except by out-of-towners. It is "D.C." or "the District" to the locals. Despite this convention, some congressmen who have held office for decades still affect a folksy, fake-populist cant in their jeremiads against the city they have operated in most of their adult lives and perpetually run for reelection while deploring "those pointy-headed bureaucrats in Washington."* A few years ago, there was a fad among Republican politicians to denounce any spending their constituents or K Street contributors didn't like as "Washington spending."

Sometime during the 1980s, the Beltway, the sixty-four-mile-long Interstate highway encircling the capital, came to be used as shorthand for the political culture of Washington. "Inside the Beltway" gradually became the description of an out-of-touch, undoubtedly liberal, elitist snob and the political philosophy he adhered to. Although the actual Beltway had been completed by the mid-1960s, the Reagan administration represented the first mass influx of political operatives who self-consciously viewed themselves as political outsiders and made their aversion to a supposed Beltway mind-set a proud talking point, despite the large number of them, like Michael Deaver and Kenneth Duberstein, who remained in Washington for decades to cash in. It was during the Reagan years that a largely phony inside-the-Beltway/outside-the-Beltway distinction took hold in the minds of Washington's political operatives. "Beltwayland" as a state of mind was born. It is significant that it was born in the hypocrisy of visceral opponents of Washington's culture who made the nation's capital their permanent headquarters.

John F. Kennedy famously quipped that Washington was a town of "Northern charm and Southern efficiency." When he said that, more than fifty years ago, he may have been right. Ever since the cornerstone of the Capitol was laid in 1800, similar comments have abounded. Before the Second World War, prior to the widespread use of air conditioning, members of the British diplomatic service stationed in Washington received an extra salary allowance for the presumed rigors of serving in a tropical duty station. The soon-to-be Capital of the Free World might as well have been a colonial outpost in Burma or the Gambia in the eyes of Foreign Office mandarins. During the first year of World War II (just before American entry into the war, a critical time when the British could have

---

* The more flamboyantly antielitist among them will pronounce it "Warshington."

been expected to be doing their utmost to woo American support), the British ambassador in Washington, Lord Lothian, found the whole tenor of the town so off-putting that he did his utmost to avoid the wretched place altogether: "He had little interest in anyone in Washington: a boring and provincial town, he thought. He associated with almost no one but the socialites of New York, Newport, and Palm Beach."[1]

Fortunately, his death in December 1940 released Lord Lothian from having to serve the crown in the fetid miasma of the Potomac's tidal swamps.

Despite the vast expansion of government during and after the Second World War, the nation's capital remained at the time of Kennedy's presidency surprisingly small and parochial. London, Paris, or Berlin it was not. It may not even have been Stockholm, since it didn't have so much as a subway system and had only begun building an international airport at the end of Eisenhower's second term.

No one could ignore the fact that Washington lay below the Mason-Dixon Line during the era when racial segregation sputtered to its inglorious end. The city's manners, mores, and "peculiar institutions," like racial segregation, all had a southern flavor. This was unsurprising, as the powerful committee chairmen of the House and the Senate were mostly geriatric southern Dixiecrats. House and Senate committees directly ruled the city with scant regard for the wishes of its citizens. Mississippi senator Theodore Bilbo, chairman of the Committee on the District of Columbia, once told a delegation of black civic leaders from the District that the only realistic prospect for their race was to repatriate to Africa (note that this incident occurred not in the 1850s but after World War II!). Modern memory has tended to blur the fact that Sam Ervin, the Senate Judiciary Committee chairman whose role in the Watergate hearings made him a liberal hero, was also a staunch segregationist. In response to the 1954 *Brown v. Board of Education* ruling by the Supreme Court, Ervin drafted *The Southern Manifesto,* a document urging defiance of federal desegregation efforts; the vast majority of southern senators and representatives signed it.

Watergate and the Rise of 24/7 Politics

Times were changing in America, and soon Washington would be changing with it. While the city began to shed much that was old, rustic, and retrograde, this was not unalloyed progress in view of what it was to become. The Capital of the Free World was gradually exchanging the southern, small-city provincialism of contemporary Richmond for the more indefinable provincialism of a burgeoning metropolis producing little else than politics as blood sport and a governing elite intent on conducting perpetual and lucrative wars on one thing or another, whether drugs or terrorism. The 1970s were a key transition period in this metamorphosis.

In 1971, the city acquired the Kennedy Center, the upstart town's claim to being a national beacon of arts and culture almost (but not quite) on a par with New York. Adjacent to the Kennedy Center was the Watergate complex, significant not only for its size (which threatened to breach local height restrictions) and contemporary architectural brutalism, but also for its political symbolism. President Nixon's bugging of the Democratic National Headquarters in that building instituted the politics of 24/7 scandal, accelerated the concentration of national media in Washington, and inaugurated the coming decades of heavily polarized, ideological political parties in America. A crucial adjunct to this politicization was the rise of the tax-exempt foundation, which would soon become the farm team and temporary holding pen for the burgeoning class of operatives who would come to garrison the Deep State.

Foundations have of course existed ever since enactment of the federal income tax law of 1913 gave America's tycoons an incentive both to dodge taxes and bypass state laws forbidding wills that seek to establish a perpetual inheritance. For the most part, these early foundations engaged in medical research, education, charitable work, and other do-gooding. There were naturally exceptions, such as the right-wing American Enterprise Institute (founded in 1938) and the left-wing Institute for Policy

Studies (established in 1963), but by and large the foundation world was a staid and genteel one, and not overtly partisan.

That changed in the 1970s with the rise of the politically focused foundation. The Greater Washington area is now home to over sixteen hundred foundations of various kinds; the hordes of gunslinging grantsmen who try to maintain a façade of scholarly disinterest are functionally as much a part of the ecosystem of the town as the lobbyists on K Street. A new threshold of sorts was crossed in 2013 when Jim DeMint (R-SC), with four years still remaining in his Senate term, resigned from office to become president of the Heritage Foundation, not only because he could exert more influence there than as a sitting senator (or so he claimed—which, if true, is a sad commentary on the status of most elected officials), but also because he would no longer be limited to a senator's $174,000 statutory annual salary.

By the 1980s, the present Washington model of "Beltwayland" was largely established. Contrary to widespread belief, Ronald Reagan did not revolutionize Washington; he merely consolidated and extended preexisting trends. By the first term of his presidency, the place even had its first openly partisan daily newspaper, the *Washington Times,* whose every news item, feature, and op-ed was single-mindedly devoted to harping on some conservative bugaboo or other. The *Times* was the first shot in a later barrage of openly partisan media. Some old practices lingered on, to be sure: Congress retained at least an intermittent bipartisanship until Newt Gingrich's speakership ended it for all time. But the foundation had been laid by 1979, when the C-SPAN cameras were allowed into the House Chamber, and the cement was drying fast.

Washington had long since shed the aura of being a sleepy southern town. In 1960, even the rural areas in Maryland north of the capital were culturally southern. By 1983, when I arrived in Washington, many observers reckoned the border of Dixie to lie roughly along the Occoquan River, about twenty miles south of Washington. Now the cultural border is at least as far south as the line of the Rappahannock River near Fredericksburg, more than fifty miles south of the city.

The town was physically changing, too. It was less the growth of the government itself than the metastasizing spread of contractors, lobbyists, media organizations, and think tanks feeding off the government that created contemporary Beltwayland. The District of Columbia proper has a population of 659,000, and is only the twenty-second-largest city in the country, having recently enjoyed modest growth after a steady drop in population since 1950. But the Washington Metropolitan Area, the region around the Beltway, has added two and a half-million people since 1970, making it the seventh-largest metropolitan area in the United States. Tysons Corner, a sprawl of shopping malls and office parks along the Virginia portion of the Beltway, has more office space than anywhere else between New York and Atlanta.

Like other office parks around the D.C. suburbs, but unlike most of the rest of the nation, it also has its own covert CIA facilities camouflaged in plain sight, housed in the usual drab and depressing office barracks that everywhere deface the American landscape. The National Security Agency and many of the other covert arms of the state whose existence many Americans consider quasi-mythical and exotic also have their quota of cheerless satellite offices around the Beltway, where the reality of the daily commuting routine reduces Hollywood's fantasies of glamorous espionage to a dismal watercooler joke. This is the Deep State at its most numbingly banal.

As Washington expanded, its center of gravity shifted as well. It has long been a part of Republican lore that the town is dominated by the so-called Georgetown elite: a coterie of wealthy liberals who dwell in the west end of town in a historic neighborhood of nineteenth-century houses holding posh dinner parties, salons, and klatches where they socialize, network, and generally conspire to undermine the real America beyond the Beltway.

At one time there may have been some truth to this notion of a dominant liberal elite, particularly after then-senator John F. Kennedy purchased a Georgetown town house in the 1950s. One has only to think of the influential columnists Joseph and Stewart Alsop; Katherine Graham, the wealthy publisher and owner of the *Washington Post;** Ben Bradlee, the *Post*'s editor during the Watergate scandal; and many others to know that once upon a time there really was a liberal establishment. But Georgetown as a political state of mind was already in decline by the 1980s, and by the time of the death of its most illustrious soiree hostess, Pamela Churchill Harriman, in 1997, it was as defunct as the Romanov dynasty, despite the occasional outburst of right-wing indignation at the Georgetown liberal elite.

Besides, Georgetown had too many elegant but cramped town houses with inadequate wiring, tasteful but worn Persian carpets, and an aura of ever-so-slightly shabby gentility characteristic of the traditional Eastern Establishment. Who needed that when you could buy a brand-new 12,000-square-foot McMansion with cast-stone lions guarding the front gate, a two-and-a-half-story-tall great room, and a home cinema with built-in FSB ports? If that sounds more like the jumped-up suburb of a Sunbelt city like Houston or Atlanta than the traditional, old-money atmosphere of Georgetown or Beacon Hill or the Philadelphia Main Line, it is because that is precisely what the new neighborhoods of the reigning establishment have become.

Up the George Washington Parkway in Virginia, across the Potomac from Georgetown and its shabby-chic semidetached Federal houses lies McLean, where by the late 1970s the growing new elite was already settling in on former pasturage near the CIA's headquarters. It became the mecca of the moneyed new class: some Democrats (mega-fund-raiser and Virginia governor Terry McAuliffe is one such resident, as is Zbigniew

---

* On one occasion during the late 1980s, I happened to be in the headquarters of the CIA and noticed a poster on the wall announcing that Katherine Graham would be the speaker at an event for employees in the CIA's auditorium. A pillar of the so-called adversarial press being invited to a secure facility to address members of the intelligence community is something that ideologues of both political parties may have a hard time assimilating into their worldview, but it explains why Beltway insiders regard the *Post* as "the CIA paper." In fact, many members of the "Georgetown Set" were CIA officials like Frank Wisner or James Angleton.

Brzezinski), but overwhelmingly they are Republican officeholders of the better-heeled sort (a former employer of mine, Senator Judd Gregg of New Hampshire, was one), consultants, lobbyists, lawyers, fund-raisers, pollsters, and the occasional venture capitalist. The roster includes such luminaries as Colin Powell, Newt Gingrich, and GOP megalobbyist Ed Rogers.

McLean is also desirable real estate for executive-level contractor personnel, whose work is ostensibly the technocratic administration of national security programs, but who in practice constitute part of a distinctive American political class. All of these people—politicians, their handlers, lobbyists, contractors—are much the same as the political "new class" that Yugoslavian dissident Milovan Djilas wrote about in 1957 when he described the rising Communist Party bureaucracy as a clique of self-interested strivers who had become a privileged bureaucracy that enjoyed great material benefits from their positions. The pillars of Beltwayland's establishment, the squirearchy of McLean, often make their living denouncing the evil ways of Washington. So it is that former Nixon speechwriter Pat Buchanan periodically issues jeremiads bemoaning the fate of Western civilization and the white working class from his manse in McLean.

A bit further north and back across the Potomac River from McLean lies the similarly well heeled commuter dormitory of Potomac, Maryland. It is politically more evenly divided than McLean, with roughly equal parts Democrats and Republicans, but the social dynamic remains much the same. Both suburbs are the residential headquarters of the nouveau riche class of political operatives, lobbyists, and contractors who do well by doing good—for their clients and shareholders, if not the country.

Across Beltwayland, similar communities of political interest have managed to coalesce, from deep blue Takoma Park in the Maryland suburbs, which still declares itself a nuclear-free zone, to the deep scarlet developments of McMansions in Loudoun County, in the shadow of the Blue Ridge Mountains. Loudoun is now the richest county per capita in the country. To the east of Washington lies Prince George's County, the richest county per capita in the country with a majority black population. It is usually considered impolitic to point this out, but Prince George's County might as well be Vladivostok as far as the prime operators of the Beltway rackets are concerned. It is too facile to ascribe this merely to racism, as Washington's political classes tend to be oblivious to anything that dwells outside the template of their own careerism. Muncie, Indiana, is not much on their radar screen, either.

The McMansion as Symbol of the Deep State

My own neighborhood lies near the Potomac River five miles south of Alexandria, Virginia, and it is symptomatic both of the economics of Greater Washington and of its association with the military. Its eponym is Fort Hunt, a former military facility that played a key cameo role in World War II and the early cold war. During the war it served as the secret interrogation center for captured U-boat officers (and was known only as Post Office Box 1142), and during a brief period immediately after the war it was a holding pen for important German military and civilian personnel who preferred to give themselves up to the U.S. Army rather than submit to the tender mercies of the Soviets. Wernher von Braun, the father of the all-American space program,* and General Reinhard Gehlen, the head of German military intelligence whose hyperbolic estimates of Soviet forces helped mentor his American counterparts in the art of threat inflation, were both guests of the facility.

Fort Hunt is one of the innumerable current and former bases, forts, and other military properties that dot the D.C. metro area. I do hate to

---

* Satirist Tom Lehrer immortalized von Braun, the developer of the Nazis' V-2 rocket, thus:

> Some have harsh words for this man of renown,
> But some think our attitude
> Should be one of gratitude;
> Like the widows and cripples of old London town
> Who owe their large pensions to Wernher von Braun.

sound flippantly critical of my neighborhood—it is actually idyllic in the old-fashioned manner. There are ice cream trucks in the summer, local parades on the Fourth of July, and so forth. It's almost like the anachronistic town in the *Twilight Zone* episode in which the harried executive imagines going back to the warm, friendly community of his youth. But looks can be deceiving. These days you can hardly throw a brick in the Fort Hunt neighborhood without hitting a retired army colonel or navy captain. It is so dependent on government spending that if the Treasury collapsed tomorrow, grass would be growing in the streets within a few weeks. There is also a high percentage of intact, two-parent households in Fort Hunt, which is undeniably a good thing. Those who bray about "family values" and "traditional mores" fail to consider that the modern American economy is increasingly unable to deliver the stable, well-paid jobs, medical insurance, and family leave that make such a way of life possible. Ironically, the despised federal government is one of the remaining employment sources supporting the family structures that conservatives claim to uphold. The neighborhood, with its 1950s split-levels, is as relentlessly middle class as *Leave It to Beaver*'s fictional town of Mayfield, but a mile or so north, closer to the Potomac views, the better-heeled new class is taking root.

The properties there were allotted in the 1920s, and a surprising number of the houses are quite modest in scale. Or were, a few years ago: one by one, they are being razed. In their place have arisen the stereotypical McMansions that have irrupted across the country in eczematous patches ever since the savings and loan deregulation of the early 1980s. The structures resemble the architecture of the Loire Valley, Elizabethan England, or Renaissance Tuscany as imagined by Walt Disney. As with McMansions everywhere, the new owners could have gotten a much sounder design for the same price or less, but they prefer the turrets, porte cochères, and ill-proportioned Palladian windows that they bought, and they accent the whole monstrous ensemble with the obligatory Range Rover in the driveway.

It tells one something about the raw, nouveau riche tastes of the contractors, lobbyists, and corporate lawyers who make up the New Class that they seem to possess a demonic lust to make whole neighborhoods gauche and hideous. They are like Shelley's Ozymandias proclaiming "Look on my works, ye Mighty, and despair!" The bloated, sprawling tastelessness of their dwellings is commensurate with the metastasizing growth in and around Washington of the Deep State's own facilities: elephantine structures, raw and uncompromising in their ugliness.

Within a week of my arrival in Washington back in 1983, the landlord of my basement apartment on Maryland Avenue told me, "Democrats live in Maryland, Republicans live in Virginia." The reality at present is a bit more complex, but it remains broadly true. In his 2004 book *The Big Sort: Why the Clustering of Like-Minded America Is Tearing Us Apart,* Bill Bishop theorized that in the last thirty years or so, Americans have been sorting themselves into homogeneous communities: people will choose the neighborhood that best fits their beliefs and lifestyle politics.

A 2014 Pew poll concurred, finding both heightened levels of ideological polarization and increasingly different lifestyle choices based on political identification.[2] Another survey found that even consumer brand preference has become ideological, whether the choice is cars or laundry detergents.[3] Beltwayland, which makes its living from the care and feeding of contending political cultures in addition to housing the growing contingent of contractors and fixers that the Deep State produces, is Bishop's "big sort" in microcosm—but with increased ideological intensity and heightened stakes for our national future.

Empires Don't Run on Autopilot

Beltwayland contains other peculiarities as a result of being the capital of the sole remaining superpower. Many novels and insider exposés of Washington feature, as a kind of isn't-this-decadent-and-aren't-you-envious bit of authorial conceit, the lavish soirees of Georgetown, Capitol Hill, and points in between as an ironic counterpoint to the rest of America sinking into postindustrial squalor. According to this trope, Alan

Greenspan, Andrea Mitchell, Colin Powell, Sally Quinn, and all the other players of the game seem to exist on truffles, smoked salmon, and Dom Pérignon; that is, when they're not forming a conga line in the back garden of some stately Georgetown mansion. There may be some truth to that picture, but not a lot.

One will notice that most of the characters in these sybaritic sagas of Washington are either elderly, turfed out of their former positions of power, or in the fortunate position of having subordinates do the actual work. A global empire does not run itself. Imperial administrators are too busy to dance in conga lines; that is a job for aging administrators emeriti, or for appointed figureheads who are the mouthpieces of the administrative bureaucracy. With respect to socializing, Washington is actually a dead boring town—there is just too much work to do (granted, some of it is make-work). I have called some of the D.C. suburbs commuter dormitories, for that is what they truly are. With the possible exception of Zürich, I have never seen any "international" city where people go to bed so early. In many of the quieter suburbs, you could fire an artillery piece down the street after sunset and not hit anyone. Why?

In many agencies, the mania for the 7 A.M. or 8 A.M. staff meeting prevails; this practice may derive by osmosis from the heavy presence in Washington of the armed forces and their early-morning work routines. And while the House and Senate have much more relaxed starting times for their official sessions (which can, however, stretch far into the night), before the session, members of Congress are usually attending working breakfasts (which may be fund-raisers) or giving speeches. Who on earth wants to go see a politician speak at 8 A.M.? You do, if you are a lobbyist who needs to be seen there. It is quite the opposite of the atmosphere in imperial Britain described by author Len Deighton: even in 1940, at a time of the greatest peril in the country's history, it was difficult to find anybody at the Foreign Office before eleven in the morning. The contrast between the two cultures is the difference between the languid self-confidence of aristocracy and the anxiety and elbows-out eager-beaverism of the rising careerist class.

It is perhaps these work schedules, combined with the self-important workaholic's sense that anything other than his career is a waste of time, that account for Beltwayland's having a social tenor that combines Puritan Salem with Moscow during the Stakhanovite era of the Soviet Union. All the great intellectual capitals of the past had their playful, bohemian side requiring more or less frivolous socializing: the salons of Paris, the cafés of Vienna, Bloomsbury London. While FDR's Brain Trust and Kennedy's New Frontiersmen were reputed to have kept up a semblance of this attitude, those days are long gone and whatever extracurricular socializing I encountered at the beginning of my career was pretty much extinguished by the time of its conclusion.

The reasons for this may have something to do with the triumph of the ideologue and his killjoy spirit, but are almost certainly related to the rise of more or less obligatory "events"—fund-raisers and receptions in honor of this or that bogus person, program, or cause. These affairs, which mingle the tedium of work with the unease and frozen embarrassment of awkward social engagements, have, by sucking up the time that would otherwise be devoted to informal mingling with friends and colleagues, effectively killed private socializing.

Hollywood for Ugly People

Other than possibly Manhattan, Hollywood, and Silicon Valley, there is no other large concentration of people in the United States with as high a quotient of careerist strivers as in Beltwayland. It is said that "Washington is Hollywood for ugly people," and Beltwayland has its own peculiar celebrity culture in a kind of parody of Hollywood. The inside-the-Beltway newspaper *Politico* is the town's version of TMZ, and it reports on the area's political sham celebrities with the same kind of guileless gush and gossipy dishing that would have given Hedda Hopper or Louella Parsons a run for their money in the old days of the Hollywood studio system. *Politico* has always been good at the small stuff: If Harry Reid said something snarky about Ted Cruz, or vice versa, it is certain to be the day's headline. But in dealing with major legislation or matters of war and peace, not so much.

The higher purpose of *Politico* is to help Beltway denizens maintain the illusion that the bubble they live in is the only reality. And just as a visitor to the Los Angeles Basin will notice that he is in a kind of city-state, cut off from the rest of the country and possessing no geographic center, an alert observer will detect the same dynamic in Beltwayland: a diffuse megalopolis no longer centered on an urban core, possessing rhythms separate and distinct from ordinary national life, and obsessed with the presentation of image.

For different types of celebrity, there are different accoutrements. The social movers and shakers of Hollywood and New York have their own styles, but these do not translate well to their counterparts within the Beltway. However gauche and gaudy they may be at home (and as we have seen, their private homes often exhibit what H. L. Mencken called "a libido for the ugly"), the personnel of the Beltway have to tone it down at work. An Armani suit would never do; it is important that one look the part of a sober servant of the people, or humble petitioner of a servant of the people,* even if the only people one is serving are plutocrats. Therefore, Brooks Brothers or Nordstrom will do just fine: they are as much a civilian uniform as the Class A Service Dress that generals and admirals wear when they testify on Capitol Hill.

One does occasionally see a lobbyist in an ostentatiously expensive suit and decked out with a Rolex or other such vulgar finery. This is, however, the exception, because those he is lobbying, with their high-status and objectively quite powerful but (relatively) low-paying jobs do not like to be reminded of their comparative penury; a gross difference in material status objectifies the bottom line a little too explicitly and hints uncomfortably at the quid pro quo between the lobbyist and the lobbied. It like-

---

* Lobbyists naturally base their low calling on high principles: lobbying, they claim, is the constitutionally guaranteed right of a citizen to petition for redress of grievances.

wise raises the question as to whether the lobbyist's clients are receiving the best return on their investment.

The same applies to one's choice of car: no Ferraris or Bentley Continentals such as one might see in Hollywood or Palm Beach—generally, at most one will see a Lexus or a Mercedes in suitably muted colors, although if the owner is an elected official, he had better get an American car so as to keep up his relentless "man of the people" routine. Almost two decades ago, when Pat Buchanan had political ambitions, reporters asked him why, if he was such a fierce protectionist, he owned a Mercedes. In any case, the truly prestige ride in Beltwayland is to be driven in a convoy of identical black Chevrolet Suburbans: this type of motorcade conveys a low-key but intimidating clout transcending the power of the merely moneyed glitterati elsewhere.

Washington was once a relatively egalitarian city: with top salaries limited by the government GS scale, everyone working in and around government had some money, but not so much as to create the yawning social chasms that have always been visible in New York or Los Angeles. While all political pretenses are partly sham, there was at least the ghost of a reality to the "public service" ethos that motivated the New Deal and the New Frontier. In theory at least, the young intern in a congressional office was the social peer of a high-ranking government official, and they might refresh themselves at the same watering holes.

I remember at the dawn of my political career occasionally spending an evening with the pleasant fellows in the grill room of the Capitol Hill Club, an adjunct of the Republican National Committee.* Bob Michel (then House minority leader), Guy Vander Jagt, and Phil Crane were in regular attendance, as were a few Democrats. The conversations then were amiable, good-humored, and, while political, tended not to be com-

---

* The Capitol Hill Club has always managed to maintain an ambiance about thirty years behind whatever the present date is, perhaps in keeping with Republican social policy. In the early 1980s, it looked like a social club from the Eisenhower era, complete with funeral-home furniture and matriarchal women with corsages and big hats.

batively ideological. But the infusion of vast amounts of money into Beltwayland has increased social distances; in any case, politicians are now
too busy raising money and nervously looking over their shoulders to do
much after-hours socializing. In addition, the rise of a humorless, dogmatic puritanism among Republicans makes the prospect of quaffing a
refreshment with Michele Bachmann or Ted Cruz as socially awkward as
it is unlikely.

Camouflage Chic

As the seat of government and location of the headquarters of the armed
forces, Washington has always had a large military contingent. Its presence is impossible to ignore. Now that it is regulation to wear camouflage
uniforms as ordinary stateside service dress—is the rationale that an ISIS
terrorist may emerge from behind the potted palm at the Washington
Hilton?—this post-9/11 convention leads to some incongruous Washington scenes. It has always amused me to see an officer in camouflage dress
and desert boots, briefcase in hand, queuing up to board the No. 101 Fairfax Connector bus en route to the Pentagon for grueling duty preparing
PowerPoint slides for his general's budget presentation. A desert camouflage uniform would not render the wearer particularly inconspicuous in
an urban setting. Wouldn't Brooks Brothers be the ultimate stealth clothing on K Street or Pennsylvania Avenue?

However that may be, it is an inescapable fact that Washington is
unique among capital cities of the so-called free world in the ubiquity of
its military presence. I have never seen anything comparable elsewhere
except in East Berlin in 1974 and Moscow in 1979. The extent to which
Washington has become a garrison town makes an ironic counterpoint to
the widespread myth that the city is some kind of radical-liberal Gomor-
rah. Its genuine vices are of an altogether different kind.

The growing militarization of Beltwayland has yet to end. This process might have been expected to slacken when the Berlin Wall fell, but the
opposite has been true. Beginning in the 1990s, an increasing number of

defense contractors, many of whom had been situated in Southern California, began to relocate their headquarters to Washington, D.C., and its suburbs so as to be closer to the political action. Lockheed, a defense and aerospace firm located on the West Coast, moved its headquarters to Bethesda, Maryland, in the D.C. suburbs, when it merged with Martin Marietta in 1995 to form Lockheed Martin. The merger, like those of many other military contractors at the time, should have been a scandal but wasn't: two years before, at Secretary of Defense William Perry's urging, Congress passed a provision allowing the merged companies to expense millions of dollars of merger costs on their contracts. (In other words, the taxpayer ended up footing the bill for what should have been in the companies' business interest to do in the first place.) Companies like Northrop Grumman and General Dynamics have followed suit in this migration to Beltwayland. Even British contracting giant BAE Systems, Inc., has an imposing satellite office in suburban Virginia, just across the Memorial Bridge from the monuments of Washington.

It is worth examining BAE Systems, Inc., and asking just how a foreign company not only got prime real estate in Rosslyn, Virginia, within sight of the Pentagon, but rapidly grew to become the sixth-largest contractor in America's military-industrial complex while being permitted to merge with domestic American companies specializing in extremely sensitive research and development work. London-based investigative journalist Andrew Feinstein told me that this de facto Deep State merger with a foreign entity grew out of the historical special relationship with the United Kingdom, and BAE's capacity to engage in deals that were either politically or legally barred to its American counterparts.

During the 1980s, the Reagan administration wanted to make a military sale of unprecedented size to Saudi Arabia, but Congress balked. As a reward for Prime Minister Thatcher's unrelenting diplomatic support of U.S. nuclear policy in Western Europe—which incited huge popular protests—the next-best thing was to let the British make the deal: BAE got most of the £45 billion Saudi deal. Six billion pounds of this sum consisted of "unauthorized commissions," meaning bribes, to the Saudi royals. Since the British hardware had U.S. technology, the Justice Department was forced to take notice and impose a settlement on BAE. The latter had to pay some derisory fines, but the blooming relationship of America's military-industrial complex with BAE was undeterred.[4] BAE Systems, Inc., the American subsidiary of British parent BAE Systems plc, incorporated on American soil in 1999.

A decade and a half after the Saudi affair, the Deep State sought yet another helping hand from across the pond. At frequent points during the run-up to the invasion of Iraq, the tongue-tied George W. Bush sorely needed the mellifluous double-talk of British prime minister Tony Blair, on the theory that nothing sells hideously awful policy as well as an Oxford accent (the American political class swoons on cue at gibberish delivered with Received Pronunciation). By a strange coincidence, from the moment of Blair's Iraq salesmanship onward, BAE Systems, Inc., grew rapidly.

Our stuffy British cousins are now really learning how to play the Washington game: in 2010 they chose Michael Chertoff to sit on the board of BAE Systems, Inc., and in 2012 they named him chairman of the board. While Chertoff displayed negligible administrative vision as Bush's secretary of homeland security, he did distinguish himself by turning his department's procurement system into a contractor-infested replica of the DOD's in only a couple of years. His postgovernment career has been a single-minded attempt to cash in personally on his bureaucratic creation and his own notoriety. Also on the board are former congressman Lee H. Hamilton, the vice chairman of the 9/11 Commission, and General Anthony C. Zinni, former commander of the U.S. Central Command, the regional military authority in charge of Middle East conflicts.

The Merchants of Death Go Madison Avenue

This seamless mixture of Mars and Mercury results in some picturesque Washington touches that could never have been glimpsed in Napoleonic

Paris or Wilhelmine Berlin, however militarized those capitals may have been. A visitor to the city might be surprised to find ads in the city's Metro system selling a fighter plane, or spot the huge sign on a telecom building near the Southeast-Southwest Freeway extolling the virtues of an aerial tanker aircraft. A reader of *National Journal* or *Congressional Quarterly* or *Politico* will discover full-page ads for the littoral combat ship.

A listener to WTOP news radio, the city's highest-rated radio station, will hear commercial spots hawking some homeland security gizmo that promises to make our daily lives even more inconvenient, while other spots solicit persons possessing top-secret/SCI clearances (which give them access to the most sensitive "code word" information) to join this or that Beltway contractor for a unique and fulfilling career. All of this weapon-mongering has become so ubiquitous that no one stops to think and ask one elementary question: why on earth?

It is not as if the commuter from Reston or the soccer mom in Fairfax City is going to plunk down $135 million to buy a shiny new F-35. The U.S. government is a monopsony for the contractors: the sole customer for their wares. Even overseas contracts must be duly authorized, as Congress has the right to prohibit the sale. Government purchases must be made according to applicable statute and according to the Federal Acquisition Regulations, subject to the availability of funds appropriated expressly for the purpose. So why is public advertising necessary?

Despite the formal ban on using contract revenues for advertising, the fungibility of money makes it difficult to interpret ads by a company that is dependent on the government for most of its revenue as anything other than the use of taxpayer dollars in a propaganda campaign for the purpose of pushing their wares in front of Washington's so-called opinion leaders. Whether they intended it or not, the contractors have succeeded in normalizing the abnormal by transforming the sale of a killer drone into the ethical equivalent of a *Mad Men* pitch for a new mouthwash brand.

All this shilling for implements of mayhem requires a corresponding quotient of hypocrisy. Every Memorial Day and Veterans Day, the major contractors take out full-page ads in the *Post* and many of the other political gazettes of the Beltway to salute and rhapsodize over America's soldiers in the required reverential tone. There is a sort of unwritten rule that the bottomless cynicism of a merchant of death must not expose itself too visibly, lest the rubes in the provinces catch on. Precisely because I was annoyed by that hypocrisy, I had always enjoyed talking to Ted, an independent defense consultant and former congressional staff member, as he refused to pretend that he was engaged in some sort of patriotic and holy calling. In the immediate aftermath of 9/11, Ted let on to me that he was on the lookout for business opportunities with the bigger contractors that might open up as a result of that attack.

A couple of weeks later, I was meeting with Ann, a Washington representative of Lockheed Martin, in the Budget Committee conference room. This was several months before most of us had learned to treat invocations of 9/11 as a cynical ploy to advance overtly political agendas, and consequently most people were a bit uncomfortable discussing the topic. After completing her pitch on how the contracting community could be helpful to the Hill during those trying times, Ann launched into a soliloquy about how mortifyingly tasteless some people were in trying to cash in on a horrific tragedy. Her voice resonant with indignation, she emphasized that one consultant had had the gall to ask her company about business opportunities as a result of 9/11! It was Ted, of course, and it was evident that she was attempting to burn his contacts on the Hill. Her performance was all the more bitterly ironic in retrospect: in 2002, the first full year after the terrorist attacks, Lockheed Martin's net sales increased by more than $2.5 billion. Like a Miss Manners of the military-industrial complex, the Lockheed Martin rep had undertaken to teach us the difference between proper and improper war profiteering.

The Flotsam of Foreign Intervention

Washington is in the business of running a global empire, and often enough its efforts misfire. The metropolitan area is therefore notable for its ethnic enclaves that have resulted from America's failed interventions abroad over the last fifty years. At the conclusion of the Vietnam War, Arlington was flooded with so many Vietnamese refugees who had backed the wrong horse—us—that one neighborhood became known as "Little Saigon." I once went with some Armed Services Committee colleagues to eat at a Vietnamese restaurant in Arlington that bore the telltale stigmata of America's botched crusade in Southeast Asia: on the walls were at least two dozen black-and-white photos taken upcountry of American advisers in tiger-stripe cammies and boonie hats posing with local Vietnamese friendlies. After the 1979 Iranian revolution, another group of exiles, this time speaking Farsi, washed up on the Virginia shore of the Potomac. Now in the 2010s, one of the biggest concentrations of expats voting in the Iraqi elections is in northern Virginia, where polling places are provided.

Northern Virginia may be a magnet for these groups in part because of the close proximity to the Pentagon and CIA headquarters; both agencies have helped many former host country operatives and translators find a new life in America. Nguyễn Ngọc Loan, the South Vietnamese National Police chief whose shooting of a Vietcong suspect in front of a camera during the Tet offensive became a famous, or infamous, Pulitzer Prize–winning photograph, lived out his days running a pizzeria in Arlington. Khalifa Hifter, a Libyan army officer who defected to the CIA in the 1980s, spent many of the succeeding years living in Falls Church and Vienna, Virginia. In 2014, he had returned to Libya and was trying to overthrow the same people who, with U.S. assistance, had just finished overthrowing Muammar Gaddafi.[5] Beneath its buttoned-down exterior, Washington, D.C., and its suburbs seethe with enough intrigue to rival World War II Casablanca, although it probably would not make as good a movie.

The War on Terror as a Washington Real Estate Scam

In the immediate aftermath of the September 11, 2001, terrorist attacks, I recall some informal discussion in Congress to the effect that Washington and its critical governmental nodes were too vulnerable to terrorist attacks. This was the time when there was a brief fad for "continuity of government" exercises, and Vice President Cheney, then a physical as well as political troglodyte, flitted between "secure, undisclosed locations" that were often underground. The proper institutional solution would have been to permanently disperse much of Washington's governmental operations to areas around the country: with secure, encrypted teleconferencing and other electronic aids, this plan was eminently feasible. Most other cities have cheaper real estate and living costs.

The problem was the same one defense contractors had solved by moving their headquarters to Washington: career-anxious generals and bureaucrats like to be physically, and not just electronically, close to the action. The newly created Department of Homeland Security, which rapidly became the third-largest cabinet agency, would certainly seem to have been a prime candidate for relocation: if any agency should have been concerned about terrorist attacks, DHS was it. And as a brand-new agency, it could start with a clean slate in thinking about its headquarters location. Yet it ended up in Southeast D.C., less than three miles from the Capitol Building. The kicker was that the property DHS took over was the site of a disused, dungeon-like insane asylum, Saint Elizabeths Hospital. Those readers who are tired of having their shampoo bottles confiscated at airports might ponder the cosmic justice in the location of DHS's headquarters, which is $1 billion over budget and ten years behind schedule.

This mania for physical proximity to the "decision makers" (and the purse strings they hold) is an abiding obsession of those who indulge in the Deep State's power games, much as the French aristocracy jockeyed to be in close attendance to the Sun King at the court of Versailles. It reached an apotheosis of sorts in the DOD's 2005 Base Realignment and Closure (BRAC) process. BRAC was supposed to *reduce* the excess military base infrastructure of the Department of Defense; yet Fort Belvoir, just fifteen miles south of D.C., along with a related site not far away, ended up with 30,000 *more* personnel as a result. So much for dispersal: Beltwayland already has some of the worst traffic in the country, yet the geniuses on the Army staff decreed that it was appropriate to jam-pack commuters into facilities with no commuter rail transportation astride the main automobile evacuation route from D.C. to points south. The whole notion that 9/11 would "change everything" was, at least insofar as the convenience of the heads of agencies and commands was concerned, a fraud. The fact that the whole scam managed to lift local real estate prices has been a collateral benefit to Beltwayland's numerous brokers and fixers.

That is not to say that nothing has changed. During the first few years after 9/11, Washington's neoclassical core was defaced by checkpoints, miles of hideous Jersey wall, and swarms of ninja-suited security squads. The city began to look less like Pierre l'Enfant's architectural vision of the neoclassical capital of a virtuous republic and more like cold war East Berlin. But what fascinated me most was to watch the reaction of tourists. A large number actually seemed impressed by the display: It was just like television, and there they were in real life, caught up in some drama out of a Tom Clancy novel or an episode of 24. It was something they could relate to via their media conditioning. One suspects the vast majority of Americans' acquiescence at airports and acceptance of surveillance can be traced to similar behavioral roots. If one is patted down or watched by the government, it is somehow reassuring to be worthy of all that trouble.

For all the bellyaching that goes on throughout the country about out-of-touch bureaucrats, corrupt and unresponsive government, and how much everyone hates Washington, these visible signs of our increasingly intrusive and overbearing government did not fall out of the sky upon an unsuspecting public. The Deep State, along with its headquarters in Washington, is not a negation of the American people's character. It is an intensification of tendencies inherent in any aggregation of human beings. If the American people did not voluntarily give informed consent to the web of unaccountable influence that radiates from Washington and permeates the country, then their passive acquiescence, aided by false appeals to patriotism and occasional doses of fear, surely played a role. A majority of Americans have been anesthetized by the slow, incremental rise of the Deep State, a process that has taken decades. But before turning to the rise of this powerful leviathan, let us consider exactly what it is.

2

WHAT IS THE DEEP STATE?

Unhappy events abroad have retaught us two simple truths about the liberty of a democratic people. The first truth is that the liberty of a democracy is not safe if the people tolerate the growth of private power to a point where it becomes stronger than their democratic State itself. That, in its essence, is fascism—ownership of government by an individual, by a group or by any other controlling private power. The second truth is that the liberty of a democracy is not safe if its business system does not provide employment and produce and distribute goods in such a way as to sustain an acceptable standard of living. Both lessons hit home. Among us today a concentration of private power without equal in history is growing.
—Franklin D. Roosevelt, message to Congress, April 29, 1938

The Visible State and the Invisible State

There is the visible United States government, situated in imposing neoclassical buildings around the Mall in Washington, D.C., and there is another, more shadowy and indefinable government that is not explained in Civics 101 or observable to tourists at the White House or the Capitol. The former is the tip of an iceberg that is theoretically controllable via elections. The subsurface part of the iceberg operates on its own compass heading regardless of who is formally in power.

During the last half-dozen years, the news media have been flooded with pundits decrying the broken politics of Washington. Conventional wisdom has it that partisan gridlock and dysfunction have become the new normal. That is certainly the case, and I have been among the harshest critics of this development. But it is imperative to acknowledge the limits of this critique. On one level, it is self-evident: in the domain that the public can see, Congress and the executive branch are hopelessly deadlocked in the worst manner since the 1850s, the violently rancorous decade preceding the Civil War.

Other than in the two-year period after his inauguration, when Democrats held both the House and the Senate, President Obama has not been able to enact most of his domestic policies and budgets. Because of incessant GOP filibustering, not only could he not fill the numerous vacancies in the federal judiciary, he could not even get some of his most innocuous presidential appointees into office. Democrats controlling the Senate during the 113th Congress responded by weakening the filibuster, but Republicans inevitably retaliated with other parliamentary delaying tactics.

Despite this apparent impotence—and defenders of the president are quick to proclaim his powerlessness in the face of ferocious Republican obstruction—President Obama can liquidate American citizens without due process, detain prisoners indefinitely without charge, conduct "dragnet" surveillance on the American people without judicial warrant, and engage in unprecedented—at least since the McCarthy era—witch-hunts against federal employees through the so-called Insider Threat Program. Within the United States, we are confronted with massive displays of intimidating force by militarized federal, state, and local law enforcement. Abroad, President Obama can start wars at will and engage in virtually any other activity whatever without so much as a by-your-leave from Congress, including arranging the forced landing of a plane carrying a sovereign head of state over foreign territory.

Despite their habitual complaints of executive overreach by Obama, the would-be dictator, we have until recently heard very little from congressional Republicans about these actions—with the minor exception of a gadfly like Senator Rand Paul of Kentucky. Democrats, save for a few mavericks like Ron Wyden of Oregon, are not unduly troubled, either—to the extent of permitting seemingly perjured congressional testimony by executive branch officials on the subject of illegal surveillance. The Constitution means one thing for most matters, but anything goes if someone in power invokes the sacred phrase "national security."

These are not isolated instances of a contradiction; they have been so pervasive that they tend to be disregarded as background noise. During the time in 2011 when political warfare over the debt ceiling began to paralyze the business of governance in Washington and the Treasury juggled accounts to avoid breaching the statutory limit on public debt, the United States government somehow scraped together $1 billion to overthrow Muammar Gaddafi's regime in Libya and, when the instability created by that coup spilled over into Mali, provide overt and covert assistance to French military intervention there. And at a time when there was heated debate about continuing meat inspections and civilian air-traffic control because of the budget crisis, our government was somehow able to raise $385 million to keep a civil war going in Syria and to pay at least £100 million to the United Kingdom's Government Communications Headquarters (GCHQ) to buy access to that country's intelligence (including its surveillance intercepts within the United States, which the NSA would be legally or constitutionally barred from collecting).[1]

Since 2007, two bridges carrying interstate highways have collapsed because of inadequate maintenance of infrastructure; during that same period of time, the government has spent $1.7 billion constructing a building in Utah that is the size of seventeen football fields. This mammoth structure is intended to allow the NSA to store a yottabyte of information, which is equal to 500 quintillion pages of text—basically, everything that has ever been written. The NSA needs that much storage to archive every single electronic trace you make.

An Evolution, Not a Conspiracy

Yes, there is another government concealed beneath the one that is visible at either end of Pennsylvania Avenue, a hybrid entity of public and private institutions ruling the country according to consistent patterns in season and out, tethered to but only intermittently controlled by the visible state whose leaders we nominally choose. Those who seek a grand conspiracy theory to explain the phenomenon will be disappointed. My analysis of the Deep State is *not* an exposé of a secret, conspiratorial cabal. Logic, facts, and experience do not sustain belief in overarching conspiracies and expertly organized cover-ups that keep those conspiracies successfully hidden for decades.

Belief in conspiracy as a systematic explanation for the functioning of a complex society is like belief in intelligent design, a pseudoscience which imagines that wisdom teeth, tonsils, and appendixes came about as the intentional result of a grand designer's infallible master plan. Mountains of empirical evidence teach us that those features arose by tiny degrees over eons as random adaptations to chance and necessity—and they are not always optimal designs: our eyes possess blind spots because they are wired backward. In the same way, mechanisms of social control evolved through historical circumstances, chance, and the peculiarities of human psychology. The Deep State, like a set of infected tonsils, is hardly an optimal design, but it became ascendant over our traditional representative democracy as a result of the gradual accumulation of historical circumstances.

Some on both ends of the political spectrum, but now mainly on the increasingly radical Right, routinely liken the prevailing governance of the United States to Nazi Germany or Stalinist Russia. Aside from trivializing historical crimes of unthinkable magnitude, such irresponsible hyperbole leads us away from proper diagnosis and cure. Given that the current cries of "Hitler!" from the Right have coincided with a Democratic presidency, we can safely infer political partisanship from the people who regard Barack Obama as a tyrant unique in the American experience but who were undisturbed by the same policies and trends under his immediate predecessor.

Likewise, many on the Left saw George W. Bush as a demonic figure when in reality he was a man out of his depth who came to the presidency at exactly the wrong time in history—a reprise of the hapless James Buchanan on the eve of the American Civil War. As the world's oldest constitutional republic in continuous existence, there remain many procedures, traditions, and habits of mind within the American body politic that have ensured, until now, the essential aspects of a free life for most of our citizens most of the time. The overall trends, however, should cause concern to us all. Rather than making ludicrous and politically self-serving historical comparisons to other nations in other epochs, we should ask which specific deformities in our own system created lamentable specimens like Bush and promoted them to power, and why a president with a personality so apparently different as Obama's should govern in a manner so similar to Bush on the big issues of national security, the economy, and the accountability of government to the people. My purpose with this book is to question the rationale of the game rather than attack the player who happens to be at bat in any given inning.

The Components of the Deep State

The Deep State does not consist of the entire government. It is a hybrid of national security and law enforcement agencies, plus key parts of the other branches whose roles give them membership. The Department of Defense, the Department of State, the Department of Homeland Security, the Central Intelligence Agency, and the Justice Department are all part of the Deep State. We also include the Department of the Treasury because of its jurisdiction over financial flows, its extensive bureaucracy devoted to enforcing international economic sanctions, and its organic symbiosis with Wall Street (as we shall see, the Treasury has quietly become the epicenter of a new form of national security operation, with some of its day-to-day execution outsourced to American financial institutions in almost the same way that the Pentagon has outsourced military logistics in war zones to contractors). All these agencies are coordinated by the Executive Office of the President via the National Security Council.

Certain key areas of the judiciary belong to the Deep State, like the Foreign Intelligence Surveillance Court (appointed by the chief justice of the Supreme Court), whose actions are mysterious even to most members of Congress. Also included are a handful of vital federal trial courts, such as the Eastern District of Virginia and the Southern District of Manhattan, where sensitive proceedings in national security cases are conducted.

The final government component (and possibly last in precedence among the formal branches of government established by the Constitution) is a kind of rump Congress consisting of the congressional leadership and some (but not all) of the members of the Defense and Intelligence committees. The rest of Congress, normally so fractious and partisan, is mostly only intermittently aware of the Deep State and, when required, usually submits to a few well-chosen words from its emissaries.

While the government may be obsequiously attentive to the desires of all corporate entities, this governmental complex I have described is even more intimately connected by a web of money, mutual goals, and careerism to specific and very powerful elements of corporate America. These elements include the military-industrial complex, Wall Street, and—surprising as it may sound to some—Silicon Valley (one former NSA insider told me the spy agencies are completely dependent on Silicon Valley's technology, communications backbones, and cooperation to even begin to perform their mission).

The Deep State does not consist only of government agencies. What is euphemistically called private enterprise is an integral part of its operations. In a special series in the *Washington Post* called "Top Secret America," Dana Priest and William Arkin described the scope of the privatized Deep State and the degree to which it has metastasized after the September 11 attacks.[2] There are now 854,000 contract personnel with top-secret clearances—a number greater than that of cleared civilian employees of the government. While they work throughout the country and the world, their heavy concentration in and around the Washington suburbs is unmistakable: since 9/11, thirty-three facilities for top-secret intelligence have been built or are under construction. Combined, they occupy the floor space of almost three Pentagons—about 17 million square feet. Seventy percent of the intelligence community's budget goes to paying contracts with private-sector companies.

The membrane between government and industry personnel is highly permeable: the director of national intelligence, James R. Clapper, was an executive of Booz Allen, the government's largest intelligence contractor. His predecessor as director, Vice Admiral Mike McConnell, is the current vice chairman of the same company. Booz Allen is virtually 100 percent dependent on government business (the Carlyle Group, a private equity firm with $189 billion in assets under management, owns a majority stake in Booz Allen's government business). These contractors increasingly set the political and social tone of Washington, just as they set the direction of the country, but they are doing it quietly, their doings unrecorded in the *Congressional Record* or the *Federal Register,* and they are rarely subject to congressional hearings.

Corporate Influence on the Deep State

Washington is the most important node of the Deep State, but it is not the only one. Invisible threads of money and ambition connect the town to other nodes. One is Wall Street, which supplies the cash that keeps the political machine quiescent and operating as a diversionary puppet show. Should the politicians forget their lines and threaten the status quo, Wall Street floods the town with cash and lawyers to help the hired hands remember their own best interests. It is not too much to say that Wall Street may be the ultimate owner of the Deep State and its strategies, if for no other reason than that it has the money to reward government operatives with a second career that is lucrative beyond the dreams of avarice— certainly beyond the dreams of a government salaryman.*

This inverted relationship is also true between the visible govern-

---

* The attitude of some members of Congress toward Wall Street was memorably expressed by Representative Spencer Bachus (R-AL), the incoming chairman of the House Financial Services Committee, in 2010: "In Washington, the view is that the banks are to be regulated, and my view is that Washington and the regulators are there to serve the banks."

ment and Silicon Valley, defined here in its broader sense to mean not only hardware and software companies, but the telecommunications backbones that enable these devices to work. Growing rapidly in the 1980s and 1990s, and then exploding in the twenty-first century, the Valley has far outstripped traditional smokestack industries as a generator of wealth and has created individual fortunes that easily rival those of Wall Street. Its research-and-development operations are vital to the operation of the Deep State—not only for its globe-spanning surveillance technology, but for the avionics, sensors, and guidance systems of every plane, ship, tank, missile, and drone that the military buys.

Accordingly, Congress has been as indulgent toward Silicon Valley as it has toward Wall Street: the Telecommunications Act of 1996 was a public auction of votes for money, and in return the industry received extraordinary leeway to abuse its market power over consumers, as any cable subscriber will attest. The Digital Millennium Copyright Act of 1998 upset the traditional understanding of copyright as a balanced legal protection afforded to creators for a finite period of time and skewed power in favor of the copyright holder to the point where fair use and competition have sometimes been threatened. The Stop Online Piracy Act, first introduced in Congress in 2011 and periodically reintroduced in modified form, would further shift the balance to copyright holders such that innocent computer users could unknowingly become criminals.

While nothing in America can rival the material opulence of Wall Street or Palo Alto in recent years, the center of gravity of the Deep State remains situated in and around the nation's capital. Washington's explosive expansion and consolidation around the Beltway would seem to make a mockery of the frequent pronouncements that national governance is breaking down. The institutions of the visible state may be dysfunctional, but the machinery of the Deep State has been steadily expanding. That this secret and unaccountable shadow government floats freely above the gridlock between both ends of Pennsylvania Avenue is the paradox of American governance in the twenty-first century: drone strikes, data mining, secret prisons, and Panopticon-like control* of citizens' private data thanks to the technology of Silicon Valley on the one hand; while the ordinary, visible institutions of self-government decline to the status of a banana republic.

The Deep State Is More Than Just the Military-Industrial Complex

The ruling structures of large and complex societies are never uniform. A coalition of dominant factions operates according to an unwritten (or even unspoken) agreement that wary cooperation is better than open strife, and that any clash of conflicting interests ought to be shelved—or at least hidden from public view—in favor of longer-term advantage. Critical analyses of the various components of the Deep State tend to view them as stand-alone entities rather than cooperating factions in a larger social environment. Ever since Eisenhower's critique of the military-industrial complex, whole libraries have come into print about American militarism and its impact on domestic politics. Likewise, harsh critiques of Wall Street and its periodic seizure of the political process in Washington go back to the nineteenth century.†

Silicon Valley, the newest of the three corporate sectors I have mentioned, has by contrast almost escaped attention as to its national political impact: admiring biographies of its hero-entrepreneurs and breathless futurologies of the wonders that the high-tech revolution will achieve

---

* The Panopticon was English philosopher Jeremy Bentham's design for a circular prison that would permit a single watchman to observe all of the inmates without their being able to know whether they were being watched or not. Ironically, Bentham, a philosopher of the utilitarian school, was a forerunner of the modern libertarian ideology that is so much in vogue among Silicon Valley tech moguls. Libertarian or not, Bentham said the Panopticon's purpose was to be "a mill for grinding rogues honest."

† What is old is often new again. In early 2014, French economist Thomas Piketty ignited a firestorm and a bestselling sensation with a book containing the revolutionary observation, backed by reams of data, that the rich tend to get richer and everyone else, not so much.

have been the literary staple so far. Critiques are usually limited to grousing about how the Valley's moguls are responsible for skyrocketing real estate prices in San Francisco, or wonderment over billion-dollar market capitalizations for apps that tell you when your pizza is cooked.

The March 2003 invasion of Iraq stimulated many more books and articles grappling with America's military-industrial complex and its baneful political consequences. The financial meltdown of September 2008 was followed by an avalanche of volumes describing in minute detail the chicanery of our largest financial institutions and their near immunity from accountability. In the wake of Edward Snowden's exposure of domestic surveillance by the NSA, much public debate has focused on the vast extent of that surveillance, how much Congress, the NSA's ostensible overseers, didn't know about it, and the ambiguous role of Silicon Valley.

Few have stood back to examine these seemingly separate stories as related and synergistic components of a much larger story: the transformation of the United States from a quasi–social democracy to a political oligarchy maintaining the outward form, but not the spirit, of constitutional government. My argument is that a different kind of governing structure has evolved that made possible both the rapacity of Wall Street and the culture of permanent war and constant surveillance. These superficially distinct phenomena are outgrowths of the same political culture, so they must be seen as related, just as a house cat and a leopard are related through a common ancestor.

The state within a state that promotes and benefits from militarism, a plutocratic boom-and-bust economy, and a comprehensive surveillance state is hiding in plain sight. Its operators pursue agendas that are hardly secret. That they are uncompromisingly self-seeking should hardly be surprising, nor is it evidence of a deep-laid plot. As the political scientist Harold Lasswell observed more than half a century ago, a society's leadership class consists of people whose "private motives are displaced onto public objects and rationalized in terms of public interest." It slightly misses the mark to fall back on traditional terminology and refer to the leaders of the Deep State simply and without elaboration as "the establishment."

All complex societies have an establishment, a social network committed to its own enrichment and perpetuation. In terms of its scope, financial resources, and sheer global reach, the American hybrid state is in a class by itself: sheer quantity can achieve a quality all its own. That said, it is neither omniscient nor invincible. The institution is not so much sinister (although it possesses menacing aspects) as it is relentlessly well entrenched. Far from being invincible, its failures—Iraq, Afghanistan, Libya; its manifest incapacity to anticipate, avert, or appropriately respond to the greatest financial crash since the Great Depression; even its curious blindness to the obvious potential for a hurricane to drown New Orleans—are routine enough that it is only its protectiveness toward its higher-ranking officials that allows them to escape the consequences of their frequent ineptitude.*

Far from being brilliant conspirators, the prevalence of mediocre thinking is what frequently makes the system's operatives stand out. We had better debunk an erroneous popular notion which holds that structures that arise from evolutionary processes are qualitatively "better" than the ones preceding them. The Deep State is a wasteful and incompetent method of governance. But it persists because its perverse incentive structure frequently rewards failure and dresses it up as success. Its pervasive, largely commonplace corruption and creation of synthetic bogeymen and foreign scapegoats anesthetize the public into a state of mind variously composed of apathy, cynicism, and fear—the very antithesis of responsible citizenship.

---

* Twenty-five years ago the sociologist Robert Nisbet described this phenomenon as "the attribute of No Fault. . . . Presidents, secretaries, and generals and admirals in America seemingly subscribe to the doctrine that no fault ever attaches to policy and operations. This No Fault conviction prevents them from taking too seriously such notorious foul-ups as Desert One, Grenada, Lebanon, and now the Persian Gulf." To Nisbet's somewhat dated list we might add 9/11, Iraq, Afghanistan, Libya, and Syria.

How Groupthink Drives the Deep State

How did I come to write about the Deep State, and why am I equipped to write it? As a specialist in national security with a top-secret security clearance, I was at least on the fringes of the world I am describing, if neither totally in it by virtue of full membership nor of it by psychological disposition. But like virtually every person employed by a bureaucracy—and it makes no difference whether that bureaucracy is in government or the private sector—I became partially assimilated by the culture of the institution I worked for, and only by slow degrees, starting just before the invasion of Iraq, did I begin fundamentally to question the reasons of state that motivate the people who are what George W. Bush would call "the deciders."

Cultural assimilation is partly a matter of what psychologist Irving L. Janis called "groupthink," the chameleon-like ability of people to adopt the views of their superiors and peers.[3] This syndrome is endemic to Washington: the town is characterized by sudden fads, be it biennial budgeting, grand bargains, or the invasion of countries that our citizens can barely locate on a world map. Then, after a while, all the town's cool kids drop those ideas as if they were radioactive. Just as in the military, everybody has to get on board, and it is not a career-enhancing move to question the mission. The universe of people who will critically examine the goings-on at the institutions they work for is always going to be small. As Upton Sinclair said, "It is difficult to get a man to understand something when his salary depends upon his not understanding it."

A more elusive aspect of cultural assimilation is the sheer weight of its boring ordinariness once you have planted yourself in your office chair for the ten thousandth time. Your workday is typically *not* some vignette from an Allen Drury novel about intrigue under the Capitol dome. Sitting and staring at the government-issue clock affixed to the off-white office wall when it's eleven in the evening and you are vowing never, ever to eat another slice of takeout pizza in your life is not an experience that summons the higher literary instincts of a would-be memoirist. After a while, a functionary of the state begins to hear things that, in another context, would be quite remarkable, or at least noteworthy, and yet they simply bounce off one's consciousness like pebbles off steel plate: "You mean the number of terrorist groups we are fighting is *classified*?"*

No wonder so few people are whistle-blowers, quite apart from the draconian retaliation whistle-blowing often provokes: unless one is blessed with imagination and a fine sense of irony, it is easy to grow immune to the often Kafkaesque strangeness of one's surroundings. To borrow the formulation of the inimitable Donald Rumsfeld, who bloviated about "unknown knowns," I didn't know all that I knew, at least until I had been a few years away from government to reflect upon it.

Key Turning Points

Although the problems I shall discuss have roots reaching back many decades before I came to Washington, I had the privilege to be present, in a small capacity, at a few key historical inflection points that locked in tendencies and habits of mind. I was handling a member of Congress's armed services portfolio when the Berlin Wall fell and, shortly after that, American forces defeated Saddam Hussein's army in the Persian Gulf War. A sense of euphoria bordering on hubris was palpable. Triumph in the cold war was supposed to mark, in the words of Francis Fukuyama's exuberantly silly essay of the time, "the end of history," the dawn of a Periclean age of unparalleled American might made even more attractive by American fast-food franchises straddling the globe (*New York Times* columnist Thomas Friedman bookended Fukuyama's essay with the even more shallow observation that no two countries with McDonald's restaurants had

---

* When the public-interest journalism site *ProPublica* asked the Department of Defense for a list of terrorist groups affiliated with al-Qaeda, a Pentagon official responded that disclosing such a list could cause "serious damage to national security." Apparently, the great strategists at the DOD think letting terrorist groups know that we know they exist would shake the security of our country to its foundations.

ever fought one another—a statement that was false even at the time he wrote it).

A few years later, when I was a staffer with the House Budget Committee, Federal Reserve Board chairman Alan Greenspan regularly gave testimony heralding the "New Economy," which would mysteriously conquer the business cycle and balance the federal budget while curing unemployment and inflation. The dot-com revolution, well under way as he uttered those pronouncements, was supposed to unleash a golden era of prosperity, creativity, and personal freedom. It didn't quite work out that way.

The September 11, 2001, terrorist attack and the botched response to it delivered a twofold lesson: first, perpetual intervention in conflicts abroad is likely to spawn what the CIA, the author of many such interventions since World War II, calls "blowback"—the unintended negative consequences of an intervention suffered by the party that intervenes. It is irrefutable that America's funding and arming a religious-based resistance to the Soviet invasion of Afghanistan created a Frankenstein's monster that little more than a decade later brought the war back to the United States. But we have largely been unwilling to connect the dots beyond that. Invading Iraq in 2003 spawned further instability in the Middle East, and more terrorist groups. Why is it that so few of our pundits have noted the obvious fact that the civil war in Syria and the rise of ISIS are the direct results of our actions in Iraq? Beyond that, the United States government's ham-fisted meddling in internal Ukrainian politics helped set in motion a predictable chain of events that has sparked a new cold war. Actions such as these have drained our treasury, reduced our international prestige, and destabilized large areas of the world.

Seven years after the attacks on the World Trade Center and the Pentagon, the idol of free-market dogma came crashing to the ground. All the imbecilities of 1980s and 1990s economic policy that had been masquerading as common sense—unregulated Wall Street speculation as the most efficient way to allocate capital; markets as self-correcting mechanisms; tax cuts that pay for themselves; a rising tide lifting all boats—were comprehensively discredited in a titanic blowout that erased

$12.8 trillion in wealth, equal almost to an entire year's gross domestic product. For the first time since the Great Depression, the raw material was at hand for national economic reform based on an empirical critique of the performance of free-market ideology over the previous thirty years.

We were at a historical turning point and yet history somehow failed to turn. The actual policy choices that followed the disaster of 9/11 and the invasion of Iraq on the one hand, and the 2008 financial meltdown and the collapse of the housing market on the other, were neither the choices that a dispassionate examination of the facts would have suggested, nor what dozens of public opinion polls implied the American people wanted. The American leadership class (in the broadest sense of that term: government elites, top business executives, corporate media management, newspaper editorial boards, "opinion leaders" everywhere) succeeded in bandaging together a top-down consensus that the failures could not have been predicted, no one in charge was to blame, and the malfunctions were isolated and episodic rather than a systemic moral corruption of America's leadership class. The disingenuous testimony of Condoleezza Rice, President Bush's national security adviser, to the 9/11 Commission that no one could have foreseen that someone would fly airplanes into buildings was echoed a half-dozen years later by one Wall Street executive after another trooping to the witness table on Capitol Hill and swearing under oath that selling no-documentation mortgages to people who couldn't pay them back seemed like a sound business model at the time.

Did "Hope and Change" Really Change Anything?

Some political observers assert that Barack Obama is measurably different from his predecessor. If that assertion is true, it would undercut the Deep State thesis that fundamental policy continuity exists regardless of which party controls the levers of government. Obama, they say, took over from the bungling and reckless Bush and saved an economy in free fall from collapsing. If one looks at superficial economic indices like the more than doubling of the Dow Jones average since early 2009, steady if tepid GDP growth, and a marked if hardly spectacular reduction in unemployment, their assertion appears correct.

A broader picture of the economy, however, paints a less favorable picture: national economic inequality is still increasing, GDP growth is outrunning wage growth, and an unreformed Wall Street is still creating highly leveraged markets that are as vulnerable to breakdown as the mortgage market of the 2000s. Even the stock market recovery has been deceptive: individual stock ownership has fallen to its lowest level since the 1990s,[4] much of the gain in equities is from cash-rich corporations engaging in the economically useless practice of buying back their own stock, and most of the trading volume comes from high-frequency traders frontrunning the market and skimming profits from all the hapless remaining investors.

Median pay for the top one hundred highest-paid CEOs at publicly traded companies in the United States reached $13.9 million in 2013, a 9 percent increase over the previous year, according to a new Equilar pay study for the *New York Times*.[5] Meanwhile, median household income has been stagnant or declining.[6] From that perspective, the Obama administration did not so much save the economy as stabilize the status quo by reforming a few of the worst aspects of the system it inherited while adopting a strategic change in tone. Obama kept the key features of the Deep State intact.

The same picture emerges from an examination of the Obama administration's national security policy. Analysts like those at the Democratic-leaning Center for American Progress lauded Obama's withdrawal of U.S. troops from the Iraq War he opposed as a senator. Later, when the security situation there sharply deteriorated, Republicans excoriated Obama for "losing" Iraq. Yet he merely executed the identical withdrawal on the same timetable that had been agreed to by his predecessor. Obama's military budget continued to increase during the first three years of his administration—he was actually spending more than the Bush administration had budgeted in its out-year planning documents. The administration's policies on drones, surveillance, and detention, accompanied by rhetorical flourishes about ending or cutting back on the prevailing practices, did little more than set in cement the most egregious practices of his predecessor.

What are we to make of this? That Obama was a more articulate Bush with better speechwriters? That the quadrennial circus called the presidential election campaign has a tendency to yield disappointing results? That all politicians are rogues and rascals? An alternative explanation lies at hand, even if it leads away from the political horse race, the tendency of politicians to disappoint us, and partisan enthusiasms and frustrations. This explanation focuses on institutions and their capacity to shape the behavior of the human agents who are tasked to lead them—even (or perhaps especially) self-anointed agents of change.

The American government, together with the corporations that make up its satellite and parasite organizations of contractors, campaign contributors, and influence peddlers, constitutes the largest and most complex institution the world has known. This institution has evolved into what sociologist Max Weber called an "iron cage." The cage is a metaphor representing the bureaucratization of society and its relentless pressure on individual actors to conform to the ingrained expectations of the organizations they work for.

Weber recognized that while bureaucracies are supposed to be based on rational decision making, actors within them end up behaving in an irrational manner. Modern societies create administrative structures such as law enforcement and courts to safeguard the lives and civil liberties of the law-abiding, but institutional logic impels those agencies to violate those same liberties because, officials insist, they must do whatever it takes to "keep us safe." It is equally true that the formal rules of a bureaucracy bar nepotism, bribery, or insider trading—so the institution evolves ever more subtle practices to allow legalized corruption, such as the creation of political action committees and quasi-charitable organizations.

At bottom, societies create bureaucratic structures to solve problems.

During the last dozen years, the Deep State has done a horrible job of averting or overcoming severe crises in the defense of the country and in ensuring a functioning national economy that serves the material needs of the great majority of citizens, not to mention preserving their liberties. But the shadow government has easily mastered the task of creating a fog of soothing propaganda to ensure its own perpetuation and aggrandizement while protecting the reputations and incomes of its senior players. More than that, it has kept virtually every single one of them out of jail. No one above the enlisted ranks ever served prison time for torture, atrocities, or the other crimes associated with an unprovoked and unjustified war, just as no senior Wall Street executive ever landed behind bars for the mortgage and securities frauds associated with the 2008 financial collapse.

How and why these circumstances arose, and where our system of unaccountable government is heading, is the subject of the following chapters.

3

BAD IDEAS HAVE CONSEQUENCES

Today we are engaged in a final, all-out battle between communistic atheism and Christianity. The modern champions of communism have selected this as the time, and ladies and gentlemen, the chips are down—they are truly down.
> —Senator Joseph McCarthy, speech in Wheeling, West Virginia, February 9, 1950

Look, if you think any American official is going to tell you the truth then you're stupid. Did you hear that? Stupid.
> —Arthur Sylvester, assistant secretary of defense for public affairs, speaking to U.S. correspondents in Saigon in 1965, as quoted by CBS News correspondent Morley Safer

World War II, the Atomic Bomb, and the Dawn of the Deep State

On the eve of World War II, the American state had great potential for world power. It was, after all, already by a significant margin the biggest economy in the world. But that potential was as yet unrealized. Our army was far from the most powerful ground force on the globe: it ranked seventeenth in the world, smaller than the armies of Romania or Sweden. Its equipment was woefully inadequate, and some senior officers still resisted converting their cavalry regiments from horses to tanks. There was no separate air force, and the Air Corps (which was subordinate to the Army) was inferior to the air forces of several other countries. The Navy was in somewhat better shape, managing a rough parity in capital ships with the United Kingdom, although many of its weapons and tactics were out of date.

Over the course of the war, the United States, through pluck, grit, and improvisation, built a military-industrial machine such as the world had never conceived possible. It constructed pipelines in Burma, airfields in the Arctic, swarms of aircraft, and a vast naval fleet a single temporary task force of which was larger than the entire British navy. German survivors of D-Day remarked in awe that the whole English Channel was so full of Allied ships that one could almost have walked dry-shod from one vessel to the other.

The crowning achievement of this new military colossus was the development, at breakneck speed, of the ultimate war-winning weapon and inverted guardian angel of the cold war: the atomic bomb. The attainment of workable nuclear weapons was almost certainly the Deep State's moment of conception. No other governmental project had been so large, and no other large project had ever been shrouded in so much secrecy.* Whole secret cities, like Oak Ridge in Tennessee, Hanford in Washington State, and Los Alamos in New Mexico, sprung up from nowhere in a matter of months. If the Deep State is an evolved structure, nuclear weapons were the genetic mutation that gave it the key characteristics it possesses today: a penchant for secrecy, extravagant cost, and a lack of democratic accountability.

By 1945, what *Time* magazine publisher Henry Luce called the American Century was at hand. The American people and their leaders had reason to be proud of their collective accomplishments. But that pride transmuted into a hubris that gave us the mistaken belief that we could remake the world in our own image. The history of the next two generations is replete with examples of where this hubris would lead: Korea, Vietnam, Central America, and our more recent series of misadventures in the Middle East. In a more subtle fashion, the tremendous victory in the

---

* Actually, more money was spent to develop and produce the B-29 bomber than on the atomic bomb. But since the B-29 was necessary to deliver the bomb over long distances, the two projects should be considered related efforts. Together, the bomb and its delivery vehicle dwarfed all other projects in cost.

Second World War and the responsibilities of world leadership that came with it intellectually corrupted the American political class.

The first indication came in 1947, when President Harry S. Truman struggled with how to sell Congress on the idea of committing large sums of financial assistance to Greece and Turkey, then perceived to be under threat of takeover by Soviet-backed insurgencies. Arthur Vandenberg, the Republican chairman of the Senate Foreign Relations Committee, told Truman that if he wanted Congress to support his policy, the president would have to "scare the hell out of the American people."[1] Thus did the seed of one of the Deep State's prime tactics germinate: fear became the tool of choice for America's postwar political class, as exemplified by the president's salesmanship of what became known as the Truman Doctrine. In line with Senator Vandenberg's advice, Truman darkly described the "totalitarian regimes" that threatened to extinguish freedom all over the globe. He got the money he asked for: $400 million, equal to at least $4 billion in today's prices.

The concept of a permanent, peacetime national security apparatus became gradually institutionalized with the National Security Act of 1947, which established the Department of Defense, the CIA, and the president's National Security Council. NSC-68, a 1950 White House policy document, sketched out a grand strategy for containing communism by means of a permanent peacetime military buildup. The year 1952 saw the statutory creation of the National Security Agency. These policy measures represented the congealing of an idea unprecedented in American history: that the United States should, and would, maintain a large, capable military and a comprehensive intelligence establishment regardless of whether it was in a formal state of war.

Relations with the Soviet Union over the next four decades varied between tolerable and awful, but there were at least no major direct armed conflicts between the two powers, regardless of the involvement of one or both countries in proxy wars in the third world, as well as numerous small incidents between U.S. and Soviet forces. Nevertheless, the universal use of the term "cold war" implied that the United States and the USSR were at war in all senses save for shots being fired; this way of thinking fed periodic national panics such as the McCarthyite hysteria over internal subversion and the frenzy over *Sputnik*. Present-day Democrats who are tired of being perpetually accused by Republicans of being weak on defense would do well to remember that the shoe was sometimes on the other foot during the 1950s. Some Democrats charged the Eisenhower administration with allowing a "bomber gap" with the Soviet Union, and in 1960, presidential candidate John F. Kennedy accused Eisenhower of presiding over a "missile gap."* Both gaps were wholly imaginary, since the United States was well ahead both in numbers and quality of both types of weapons. It is one of those conveniently disremembered ironies of American history that Kennedy, the darling of American liberalism, should have accused the chief organizer of American victory in Europe during World War II of being weak on defense.

President Eisenhower already recognized the danger of the permanent war mentality, and in his January 1961 farewell address he presciently warned about the "disastrous rise of misplaced power" of a new "military-industrial complex" on American soil. By the middle of the 1960s, the twin neuroses of paranoia and hubris that exemplified the mentality of the national security state led us into the mud of Vietnam. The Deep State, with the military-industrial complex at its core, was well on its way to crystallization by the 1960s, but Vietnam and the attendant domestic tumult showed that such an outcome was neither inevitable nor irreversible. Popular protests compelled even hawks like Richard Nixon to campaign on the pretext that they could end the war, forced an end to the draft, exposed and limited the extensive domestic spying on U.S. citizens opposed to the war (code-named COINTELPRO), and fueled the

---

* The "bomber gap" arose because during the 1955 May Day parade, the Kremlin leadership ordered its entire inventory of ten jet bombers to fly over Red Square several times in a large aerial circle. Western military attachés in attendance were deceived by this elementary trick into believing they saw a large fleet of bombers— possibly because they wanted to believe it. On the strength of this ruse, U.S. intelligence projected an eventual eight hundred Soviet jet bombers.

revelation (in the Pentagon Papers) of the heretofore secret and mysterious world of national security policy. Nixon's criminal overreaction to the leak of the Pentagon Papers led inexorably to the first-ever resignation of an American president.

The political changes of the 1970s—reform of the CIA as a result of the Church Committee hearings, reining in the FBI after J. Edgar Hoover's four decades of autocratic directorship, and the Foreign Intelligence Surveillance Act (FISA) placing domestic national security surveillance under supervision of a court—appeared to blunt the advance of the national security state and in some cases to reverse it. In retrospect, however, the 1970s were a temporary detour from the upward trajectory of the Deep State. The same social currents that caused massive popular rejection of the Vietnam War also led to the rise of a far more powerful and longer-lasting domestic countermovement.

This countermovement considered itself the bedrock of American patriotism and American values—the core of what Sarah Palin took to calling "real America." It perceived itself to be under siege by the same groups of suspect Americans who attacked the Vietnam War and the national security state: dissidents, malcontents, flag-burners, antipatriots. This countermovement, which composed much of corporate America that had nothing to do with the military, had been contained and tamed since the New Deal. It was now feeling beleaguered by the wave of health, safety, environmental, and proconsumer legislation that was a legacy of the 1960s and early 1970s. It is worth recalling that Richard Nixon, the arch-ogre of Watergate, was behind the creation of the Environmental Protection Agency and other domestic initiatives that would be unthinkable for a Republican president of today.

This business-led countermovement was something of a departure from the prevailing postwar corporate consensus. During the 1930s and 1940s, democratic parliamentarianism narrowly overcame a profound global crisis that had in part been brought on by the failure or refusal of democratic countries to rein in the worst excesses of their capitalist economies. These unreformed excesses led directly to the greatest economic collapse in modern history and a mortal challenge from the totalitarian systems that exploited the crisis. The democratic systems that emerged after a cataclysmic war claiming 60 million lives dedicated themselves to broader and deeper citizen participation in government and the creation of social remedies that would buffer against the threat of mass destitution. The National Health Service in Britain, Medicare in the United States, codetermination (worker participation in management) in Germany, and lifetime employment in Japan were all examples of postwar social policy in democratic governments. These innovations helped achieve unprecedented levels of broadly shared prosperity and drove economic growth throughout the industrialized world at a rapid pace.

Corporate America was largely on board with the prevailing postwar consensus. After all, the terrors of the Crash of 1929 had been banished, profits were rising, and a high-wage policy meant that workers were avid consumers of industry's output. But the twin shocks of persistent inflation beginning in the late 1960s and the oil shock of 1973 undermined business confidence just at the time neoliberal economic theories were arising out of academic obscurity to challenge that consensus. That said, this shift in attitude was only partly about concern over business conditions or the regulatory regime in Washington. The tenor of the times— the antiwar Left, the beginning of the Weather Underground's bombing campaign, the atmosphere of cultural permissiveness—got the attention of business leaders because it suggested an anticapitalist climate taking hold in the country.

The Powell Memo and the Laissez-Faire Philosophers

In 1971, a corporate lawyer representing the tobacco lobby wrote a memo titled "Attack on the American Free Enterprise System."[2] This memo advocated aggressive action by the business community against a perceived left-wing assault on business. The author advocated "constant surveillance" of textbook and television content, as well as a "purge" of left-wing elements in important institutions like universities, the press, and churches. He also proposed institution building among business interests in the furtherance of influencing government policy. Nixon would soon appoint the memo's author, Lewis Powell, to the Supreme Court, where he served until 1987.

The Powell Memorandum became the manifesto and battle plan for a rollback of the New Deal and the enthronement of corporations as persons. Powell, like the probusiness conservatives he wrote for, considered himself a practical, pragmatic problem solver in contrast to the woolly-headed theorizers of contemporary liberalism. Jude Wanniski, another savant of the probusiness movement, published a book in 1978, and its title, *The Way the World Works,* emphasized the purportedly commonsensical and practical nature of the economic ideas he was peddling. But as Keynes famously said, "Practical men, who believe themselves to be quite exempt from any intellectual influences, are usually slaves of some defunct economist." Just as twentieth-century socialism rested on German thought from the nineteenth century, the theoretical structure of Powell's business conservatism rested on a German intellectual foundation.

Friedrich Hayek, Ludwig von Mises, and Wilhelm Röpke are generally considered to be the founders of the radical free-market doctrine that is now confusingly called neoliberal economics.* Hayek, the most famous of the three, described himself as a radical pragmatist and empiricist, but, as is usual in the German philosophical tradition, his followers systematized and dogmatized his theory to the point where it became a materialist religion, a mirror image of Marxism. According to the current neoliberal catechism that is Hayek's legacy, the market is a deity which must be worshiped with elaborate rituals, while the government is Satan; Wall Street is heaven, and Washington is hell. These days, Hayek's ghost is the reigning Supreme Being of the *Wall Street Journal*'s editorial page, and there is a Ludwig von Mises Institute in Alabama, of all places.

---

* The seeming contradiction of conservative politicians embracing something called neoliberal economics is explained by the fact that "liberal" and "conservative" have vastly different definitions in Europe and America.

Throughout America's history, corporate and military interests have hardly been strangers, but the American historical tradition—at least until the permanent mobilization of the cold war—of rapid and complete military demobilization after the wars meant that boom would quickly turn to bust. Apart from inconsistent profitability, there were manufacturers, mostly in the Midwest, who on pacifist or other principles wanted to avoid military contracts. In 1940, British plans to have Ford Motor Company manufacture under license the Rolls-Royce Merlin engine for the Spitfire fighter aircraft went awry when the isolationist Henry Ford, Sr., personally vetoed the project.[3]

By the time of the Powell Memo, twenty-five years of permanent cold war mobilization had mellowed a lot of attitudes. A significant slice of corporate America was by now partially or wholly dependent on defense contracts. That sector of the economy was not enamored of the deep military drawdown advocated by 1972 presidential candidate George McGovern. Neither were the defense sector's executive suites—so many of them occupied by former military officers—in sync with the cultural values implicit in McGovern's candidacy. The military sector's complaint about the political and social changes during the 1960s broadly corresponded with those of Lewis Powell: they believed they just couldn't make a living anymore because of the leftist, regulatory state.

The business community responded to Powell's call to arms. In 1972, brewer Joseph Coors founded the Heritage Foundation, and in 1974, energy magnate Charles Koch endowed the Cato Institute. Many others followed. The great majority of foundations were and are politically innocuous (although the designated charitable status of some may give one pause); but the overtly political among them have set the tone in Washington, a city where politics never sleeps. The policy think tanks have provided a vast reserve army of partisan policy experts, reams of tendentious studies, and mountains of prefabricated legislative ideas for members of Congress who are too busy raising money to think about governing. The policy think tanks even came to provide jobs for political operatives when their party was voted out of power—in fact, the habit of these ostensibly charitable organizations of providing an income, a megaphone, and the veneer of a respectable job for out-of-work political operatives may be their most important function in assuring a continuity of personnel for the Deep State.

The Wall Street–Pentagon Nexus

A robust military-industrial complex implied heavy government spending and a significant portion of the American industrial base being dependent on government contracts—the very antithesis of the low-spending, low-tax, noninterfering state that Powell and his academic forebears demanded for the sake of free enterprise. Another contradiction was that all earlier periods of war in our history were accompanied by tax hikes, increases in government intervention, and even, during World War I, temporary nationalization of the railroads. But corporate-funded think tanks such as the American Enterprise Institute and the Heritage Foundation have thrown intellectual consistency to the winds by habitually proposing higher military budgets and knee-jerk overseas intervention within a smaller federal budget embodying fewer business regulations.

The embrace of militarism even by those corporate interests that have no vested material interest in militarism has been a remarkable development in the world history of economics. The continental European founders of neoliberal economic theory had always claimed that their championing of individual enterprise was the sovereign remedy for the wars abroad and the state oppression at home that plagued contemporary Europe. But even Hayek, who said his economic writings were influenced by his personal experience in World War I and the oppressiveness of the European dictatorships that followed, appears to have changed course in this matter.

In the 1970s and 1980s, Hayek was feted by Chile's dictatorial regime headed by General Augusto Pinochet, and in the course of several visits there he claimed he had "not been able to find a single person even in much maligned Chile who did not agree that personal freedom was much greater under Pinochet than it had been under [his overthrown predecessor] Allende."[4] It is possible that he never met such a person because the Centro de Estudios Públicos, a Chilean free-market economic think tank whose honorary chairman he was, did not receive many visits from the relatives of the three thousand people known to have been killed or "disappeared" by the Pinochet regime.

The Reagan administration's 1980 campaign platform skillfully espoused this paradoxical philosophy of free-market capitalism and heavy state spending on the military. It carried out the largest peacetime military buildup in the nation's history while cutting taxes; curtailed health, safety, and environmental regulations; and began the long unwinding of the legal structures designed to prevent institutions from engaging in reckless speculation, creating financial bubbles, and endangering the financial security of depositors and pensioners. The first of these measures was the Garn–St. Germain Depository Institutions Act of 1982, which loosened restrictions on savings and loan associations and allowed banks to issue adjustable-rate mortgages. This contributed to the savings and loan crisis of the late 1980s, the first major U.S. financial disaster since the creation of the New Deal regulatory regime more than fifty years before. The unleashing of Wall Street also began the process by which financial services displaced manufacturing as the primary source of American wealth. In 1979, U.S. employment in manufacturing peaked.[5] Beginning with the Reagan administration, manufacturing began its long, thirty-year slide, as did real incomes of the middle class. Wall Street was firmly in the saddle for the first time since 1929, and it has never relinquished the reins.

It might have been expected that Democrats, the nominal opponents of Reagan and all his works, would have labored to stop the deregulation of Wall Street. But during Bill Clinton's two terms in office, he signed the repeal of the Glass-Steagall Act—the linchpin of New Deal banking regulation—and in 2000, he approved the near-total deregulation of derivatives with his signing of the Commodities Futures Modernization Act. It only remained for his Republican successor, George W. Bush, to push through further tax cuts and anesthetize the Securities and Exchange Commission by appointing as chairman a useful idiot, former Republican congressman Chris Cox, for the completion of the deregulation process. In the words of former International Monetary Fund economist Simon Johnson, Wall Street had captured Washington.[6]

The military-industrial complex saw a similar elevation to unchallengeable status over the same period. By the late 1980s, the cold war had gone on for so long that it became practically impossible to radically pare down the national security state. When the Soviet Union, America's only serious military competitor, collapsed, the military drawdown that did take place was far less severe than those undertaken after America's previous major wars, and a pretext was soon found for yet another expansion.

The Cold War as a Restraint on Laissez-Faire Doctrine

For many years I have had the nagging feeling that the end of the cold war and the triumph of vulture capitalism were deeply entangled issues. This belief came not just from the obvious connection made by Francis Fukuyama and others that the demise of the Soviet Union would open additional markets and usher in global consumerism. There was another, darker symbiosis between the cold war's conclusion, the rise of supercharged laissez-faire economics, and the dismantling of the New Deal consensus. In the early post–World War II years, U.S. policy makers were quite clear that the nation-states of shattered Western Europe should never again be subject to the same kind of social polarization, rampant inequality, and economic misery that gave rise to Hitler and the other dictators. If postwar Europe were to repeat the follies of the 1920s and 1930s, the Soviet Union could benefit by supporting extremist parties and, when the time was right, coming in and picking up the pieces.

Accordingly, U.S. administrators implemented aid and development policies, such as the Marshall Plan, which coordinated well with the building of social market economies in Europe that granted broad economic opportunity to their citizens. It was no coincidence that John Maynard Keynes, the most articulate opponent of laissez-faire economics of the era, warned the Western Allies not to repeat the mistakes they had made after World War I in dealing with Germany. Capitalism was universally understood to be in competition with communism, and it was necessary, as a matter of national security, to soften its sharper edges so as to create a positive example. America was thenceforth on (relatively) good behavior. This applied to social policies at home as well: America preferred to set a good example and practice what it preached, although this was frequently honored more in the breach than in the observance.

I recall my grandparents' return from a visit to Sweden, the country of their birth, in 1962. It was the depth of the cold war: the Berlin Wall had been erected the year before, the Cuban missile crisis was brewing, and Soviet premier Nikita Khrushchev blustered nonstop. But what did my grandfather say was the lead story in the European papers at that time? It was the activities of the Freedom Riders in the American South and the other civil rights struggles in our country. Washington was very conscious of the fact that the European public was paying attention.

Lyndon Johnson no doubt pushed his civil rights legislation for all kinds of noble reasons, but America's international image in competition with communism was a significant consideration. The more socially conservative Dwight Eisenhower had sent the 101st Airborne Division into Little Rock, Arkansas, several years before, with the same motivation. When trying to inveigle the North Vietnamese into peace negotiations during the mid-1960s, LBJ offered as bait a U.S.-funded "TVA plan" to harness the rivers of Southeast Asia and generate hydroelectric power. (After the collapse of communism, offering a Tennessee Valley Authority to your adversary would be unthinkable: these days, we would be more likely to offer an International Monetary Fund austerity plan to cut wages and benefits while privatizing public utilities. To sweeten the deal, we might push a flat tax.)*

---

* In 2003, the U.S. Coalition Provisional Authority in fact decreed a 15 percent flat tax for occupied Iraq.

By the time of the Plaza Accord between the United States, Japan, and the major European governments in 1985, the neoliberal Washington consensus had been cemented into the DNA of the leading noncommunist powers (the Plaza Accord was an international central bankers' adjustment of currency exchange rates intended to fine-tune the global terms of trade and correct the growing U.S. trade deficit, although it did nothing to fix the creeping structural rot of U.S. manufacturing). From this point on, a Washington-led economic consensus ruled, and political parties in the mature industrial powers adjusted accordingly; social democratic parties (and, in the United States, the Democrats), became "me too, but less" followers of the prevailing orthodoxy. After the USSR's collapse, there was no longer any global ideological competition, so the commanding heights of corporate America were free to say "no more Mr. Nice Guy."

Clinton and Post–Cold War Hubris

It was at the apogee of cold war triumphalism that Bill Clinton came into the presidency. Hoping to cast aside the antimilitary reputation of the Democratic Party, Clinton refashioned the military into a force in readiness for rapid intervention in places like Haiti, the Balkans, the Horn of Africa, and the Middle East. Even that was not enough for his secretary of state, Madeleine Albright, who groused to the chairman of the Joint Chiefs of Staff, General Colin Powell, "What's the point of having this superb military that you're always talking about if we can't use it?"[7]

During the prelude to the U.S.-NATO bombing campaign against Serbia in 1999, a U.S. Army colonel who was a friend of mine had been posted to NATO Headquarters in Brussels. From his new vantage point, he passed along unclassified information about Clinton administration and interallied decision making not normally available on Capitol Hill (all administration presentations on the Hill are predicated on the notion that whichever administration is running the show is infallible). According to my friend, Albright was continually pressuring the CIA to find whatever evidence of Serbian perfidy was necessary to justify NATO military intervention. His reports had the ring of truth as they dovetailed not only with Albright's previously expressed itch to deploy U.S. troops in combat, but also with her near megalomaniacal representation of U.S. virtue and clairvoyance ("If we have to use force, it is because we are America; we are the indispensable nation. We stand tall and we see further than other countries into the future, and we see the danger here to all of us").[8] The colonel's reports also confirmed a disturbing pattern of saber-rattling officials pressuring the intelligence agencies to find pretexts for military action. The trumped-up evidence of Saddam Hussein's purported weapons of mass destruction was not the first instance of cooked intelligence, nor is it likely to be the last.

9/11

The September 11, 2001, attacks sent the political system into overdrive: the United States began waging endless war and vastly expanding the national security apparatus (even creating a large new agency, the Department of Homeland Security). The USA PATRIOT Act legitimated heavy domestic surveillance, but even that was not enough for the Deep State, which proceeded to violate the law and the Fourth Amendment of the Constitution. Congress obligingly gave the perpetrators absolution in 2008 by retroactively legalizing the activity. Even torture crawled out of the unlit recesses of the national id.

All of these dark doings unrolled even as fortunes piled up on Wall Street, the Dow Jones average ascended to new heights, and no-document mortgages were extended to anyone with a pulse. The contradictory, even schizoid, nature of the Deep State is implied by the two most vivid cultural markers of the first decade of the twenty-first century. Less than a week after the September 11 attacks, Vice President Cheney, appearing on *Meet the Press,* hinted at what he called the "dark side" of the war on terrorism—meaning kidnapping, rendition, torture, and assassination. In so doing, he supplied a shorthand description of the dark and fearful mental atmosphere of the ensuing decade. But this was equally the decade of $5 million birthday parties and three-hundred-foot yachts, paid for by synthetic collateralized debt obligations (CDOs) made up of bundled sucker loans.

The decade's creeping militarized authoritarianism coexisted with an extreme libertarian individualism that bordered on anarchy. While the two cultures superficially appeared far apart in their internal dynamics and values, the seemingly clueless George W. Bush intuitively grasped their symbiotic nature as he unleashed the war on terrorism at the same time he told Americans to go shopping.

Far from being an exceptional country that lives outside the history of the rest of world, the United States has for the last thirty years been merely the *primus inter pares* of a community of nations which has little by little forgotten the lessons of a wrenching depression and a cataclysmic war. Ronald Reagan was not really the trailblazer that many believe him to be—Margaret Thatcher preceded him by two years. For their parts, Thatcher, Reagan, and their successors completed the foundation that had been dug by a handful of practically unknown European intellectuals, as modified by free-market academics from the University of Chicago and a few generously endowed think tanks. *Ideas Have Consequences* is an abiding truth as well as the title of a book by conservative political philosopher Richard M. Weaver, published in 1948 by the University of Chicago Press. It is an even more profound statement than it appears on first sight.

4

DO ELECTIONS MATTER?

I think I can say, and say with pride, that we have some legislatures
that bring higher prices than any in the world.
—Samuel L. Clemens, *Sketches, New and Old*
(vol. 19 of the *Writings of Mark Twain*, 1875)

Increasingly I found myself spending time with people of means—
law firm partners and investment bankers, hedge fund managers
and venture capitalists. . . . I found myself avoiding certain topics
during conversations with them, papering over possible differences, anticipating their expectations. . . . I know that as a consequence of my fund-raising I became more like the wealthy donors I
met, in the very particular sense that I spent more and more of my
time above the fray, outside the world of immediate hunger, disappointment, fear, irrationality, and frequent hardship of the other
99 percent of the population—that is, the people that I'd entered
public life to serve.
—President Barack Obama, *The Audacity of Hope*, 2006

Politics, from West Virginia to Afghanistan

In January 2014, toxic chemicals spilled into the Elk River in West Virginia, contaminating the drinking water of a nine-county area surround-
ing the state capital and forcing residents to drink bottled water for two
months. It was found that the leaking storage tanks had not been inspected
by a government agency for fifteen years, and, as it turned out, the law did
not require them to be inspected, even though they lay near the river, up-
stream of the intakes of a drinking water filtration plant.[1]

Do the citizens of the world's oldest constitutional republic consciously decide with their votes that the safety of their drinking water is a lesser priority than delivering suitcases of off-the-books cash, reportedly totaling tens of millions of dollars, to a corrupt satrap running Afghanistan named Hamid Karzai—an extraordinary act of philanthropy that failed to make him any easier to work with?[2] More to the point, do their representatives and senators in Washington deliberately prioritize the stated requirements of the Pentagon and CIA above the most basic needs of their constituents? Yes, if those legislators have developed the unfortunate tendency to go into a trance every time someone utters the magic phrase "national security." In truth, it happens often enough, and many times over the course of my career I saw Congress respond to that occult incantation like iron filings drawn to a magnet. But the problem is not quite so simple.

Congress has abdicated a lot of control over foreign policy to the executive branch, but it still retains the constitutional power of the purse. So why do congressmen keep funding extravagances like a $7 billion sewer system in Baghdad and not take care of matters closer to home? And what does the public at large think of this behavior?

Public trust in government has with temporary fluctuation steadily declined from a high of around 75 percent in the mid-1960s to a level of distrust near 80 percent in 2010.[3] One 2013 survey result from Public Policy Polling ranked Congress below head lice or cockroaches in public esteem, although it did manage to pull in ahead of the Kardashians and North Korea.[4] The American people clearly believe that something is wrong, and something plainly is. Adjusted for inflation, median household income peaked in 1973, and has been stagnant or falling ever since. The 2008 financial crash merely exacerbated already existing long-term trends and resulted in a further drop in the American standard of living.[5] The public knows from its own material condition that governmental decision making is defective, yet the same decision makers keep getting elected. Why?

"Ordinary Citizens Have No Influence Over Their Government"

In practice, the American political system allows only two political parties, which are wholly dependent on corporations and wealthy individuals to fund the most expensive campaigns in the world. Political campaign spending totaled $6 billion in 2012, which works out to $18 per voter. In a well-established democracy like the United Kingdom, spending, by contrast, comes to only about 80 cents per voter.[6] The operatives of these two American parties engineer state electoral laws and gerrymander voting districts so that third-party alternatives are in practice impossible. It is a system that would have felt comfortably familiar to the Whig oligarchs of eighteenth-century England, who ensured that popular participation was a purely formal process.

Martin Gilens of Princeton University and Benjamin Page of Northwestern University examined almost two thousand surveys of American opinion on public policy matters between 1981 and 2002, and discovered how those preferences correlated with policy outcomes. "[T]he preferences of economic elites," Gilens concludes, "have far more independent impact upon policy change than the preferences of average citizens do. . . . I'd say that contrary to what decades of political science research might lead you to believe, *ordinary citizens have virtually no influence over what their government does in the United States.* And economic elites and interest groups, especially those representing business, have a substantial degree of influence. Government policy-making over the last few decades reflects the preferences of those groups—of economic elites and of organized interests."[7] Our president concurs: during the 2012 election campaign, Obama informed a group of wealthy donors that included Microsoft moguls Bill Gates and Steve Ballmer, "You now have the potential of two hundred people deciding who ends up being elected president every single time."[8]

Let's look at an example of how the preferences of economic elites prevail over the wishes of constituents. The Trans-Pacific Partnership is a trade agreement that is wildly popular among the corporate classes and wildly unpopular in the rest of the country. The progressive Left and unions hate it like poison, as might be expected, but so does the conservative base, believing it cedes national sovereignty. Representative Alan Grayson (D-FL) claimed that a Republican colleague "confided in me that his calls and emails were running 100-to-1 against" a vote to fast-track, or expedite, consideration of the trade agreement.[9] Yet the vast majority of Republicans (190 out of 246), along with just enough Democrats, ended up voting for fast track and ensured the bill's passage, much to the delight of the U.S. Chamber of Commerce. H. L. Mencken once said that a campaigning politician would cheerfully pronounce himself in favor of cannibalism if he thought it would gain votes. With all due respect to the Sage of Baltimore, his aphorism is now in need of revision. Today, the only way cannibalism could gain support would be if the cannibals hired a lobbyist, formed a political action committee, and began writing checks.

While today's politicians engage in sonorous generalities about jobs, faith, family, and so forth, once the issues move from the ethereal realm of sloganeering into specific policies, they do *not* seek to identify with the desires of the majority, except insofar as those desires happen to overlap with the preferences of those who are footing the bill. Single-payer health care, tax breaks for hedge fund managers, minimum wage policy—on these and a host of other issues, the American public lines up on one side and wealthy elites on the other. And every time, the position favored by those elites prevails. Most of the art and science of politics these days consist of camouflaging a politician's real stance on an issue.

The Dumbing Down of Congress

Over the course of the nearly three decades I spent in Congress, the institution dumbed itself down, reducing the size and professional qualifications of analytical staff and downsizing essential support agencies like the Congressional Budget Office.[10] The chief instigator of this process was Newt Gingrich, who was Speaker of the House from 1995 to 1999. His intent was to centralize control of legislation in the Speaker's office, but the effect has been a self-administered lobotomy that has made Congress less effective. Since 2011, the House of Representatives under the influence of the Tea Party has reduced the number of committee staff members by almost 20 percent; at the same time, press office personnel within those same House committees has grown by about 15 percent.[11] Why bother to have legislative experts on staff when bills can be written by lobbyists, or the Heritage Foundation, or the American Legislative Exchange Council, the legislative drafting arm of corporate America?

The press office is now the focus of the whole congressional operation in order to pump out a smokescreen of misleading propaganda claiming that Congressman X really cares about you. Accompanying this deliberate dumbing down is the circumstantial dumbing down resulting from the need for constant fund-raising, which requires members of Congress to spend up to 40 percent of their work week going on bended knee to their contributors, either in person or by telephone (both parties maintain offices just beyond the perimeter of the Capitol grounds where members can go to "dial for dollars" and avoid violating the law against fund-raising in a government building). Committee chairmen are rarely chosen for their seniority or subject matter expertise anymore. These days, the congressional leadership selects chairmen on the basis of their willingness and ability to use their chairmanship as a platform to raise funds for the party.

The Cash Nexus

One of the staples of American political science research has been a curious inability to demonstrate that money buys votes. At most, the studies will find that money buys physical access to politicians, a conclusion that elected officials concede is true, possibly because "access" isn't against the law.[12] Even if a politician's votes on issues can be found to correlate strongly with contributions from donors with financial interests, he will say his votes align because he agrees with them on the issues. And yet a prevalence of corrupting influences is likely to lead to corrupt elected officials.

When Las Vegas megadonor Sheldon Adelson began throwing

around tens of millions of dollars to push legislation to ban Internet gambling in order to protect his billion-dollar casino interests, it wasn't long before Senator Lindsey Graham of South Carolina introduced a bill to ban Internet gambling. When asked about the curious coincidence of timing, Graham said his Southern Baptist constituents in South Carolina shared Adelson's aversion to Internet gambling, so there was no quid pro quo. That may be so, but Graham has held federal elective office since 1995, and yet he felt no driving urge to introduce such legislation until 2014, precisely when Adelson began showering him with money. Graham's transaction with his sugar daddy apparently does not meet Supreme Court chief justice John Roberts's narrow definition of an illegal quid pro quo as expressed in the court's 2010 *Citizens United* decision.

These financial arrangements between donor and legislator do not affect only our domestic politics. Their impact on the conduct of national security policy occasionally belies the normal assessment that Congress is a doormat for the executive branch. U.S. policy toward Iran is a prime example of this. It is long past time for us to wind down the decades-long hostility between our country and Iran, and Obama took the opportunity not only to improve relations, but to try to prevent Iran from obtaining nuclear weapons through negotiations rather than war.

Obama ran headlong into a Republican-controlled Congress that invited Israeli prime minister Benjamin Netanyahu to make an address explicitly designed to derail the U.S.-led effort by six major nations to curtail Iran's nuclear capabilities. This incident, in breach of diplomatic protocol, was followed by forty-seven Republican senators sending the Iranian government a letter informing it that any agreement it signs with the United States could be nullified by the legislative branch (ironically, Israel's own general staff and intelligence services have concluded that the six-power nuclear agreement with Iran may lessen, not increase, Iran's threat to Israel).[13]

Some of this behavior can be explained by the sheer rancorousness of political polarization in Washington. Had the agreement with Iran somehow been negotiated by a Republican president, GOP lawmakers would have lined up to hail it as a "Nixon goes to China" diplomatic master-stroke. As it was, Obama was president, so the deal had to be fought tooth and nail. It must be understood, though, that this dynamic does not oper-ate all the time, and especially not in regard to national security policy. When the policy is assassination by drone, intervention in Libya, military strikes inside Iraq and Syria, or arming Ukraine, Republican opposition to executive initiatives is usually quite muted. Or rather, objection from Republicans arises only in the claim that Obama is not militarily aggres-sive enough. It is mainly when the president avoids military confronta-tion, as with Iran, that he faces flat rejection. So it has been with the Iranian nuclear deal: when, for once, Obama sought a negotiated solution to a problem in the Middle East rather than unilaterally employing force, Republicans presented a nearly united wall of opposition that even in-cluded Rand Paul, perhaps eager to placate his donor base now that he was himself eyeing the presidency.

The other factor is that domestic political considerations involving money increasingly determine foreign policy. A visitor from outer space would find it peculiar that Netanyahu, a foreign head of government, has been called the leader of the Republican Party—the same party that habit-ually flaunts its xenophobic "America First" patriotism.[14] Senator Graham has gone so far as to say he would follow whatever policies the Israeli prime minister might propose, an arresting statement in light of the senator's oath to the Constitution and the voters he represents.[15] It is all the more strange if one considers that well within living memory the Israeli prime minister and his coreligionists would have been barred from entering many of the social establishments run by the people who were once called "country-club Republicans." What caused this sea change in the GOP?

For the answer, follow the money. While the American Israel Public Affairs Committee has long been a highly influential political force,* the

---

* When Tom DeLay was House majority leader, I found out that any legislative pro-vision having anything to do with the Middle East had to be vetted and approved by AIPAC before the bill could move forward.

Citizens United decision greatly magnified the effect of individual donors. In 2012, Adelson's cash infusions kept Newt Gingrich alive as a Republican candidate far longer than would otherwise have been the case, and for 2016, Adelson has vowed to double the $150 million he spent in the previous election cycle.[16] The transaction cost of getting $300 million from one donor is of course far less than collecting the same sum from a myriad of small contributors, so it is easy to understand why Republican candidates should react as they do when Adelson issues a request. The fact that his sole political interests are his casinos and the Likud Party gives his recipients a short and easy-to-remember checklist.

Adelson, who has advocated attacking Iran with nuclear weapons, has been accompanied in this endeavor by Paul Singer, a hedge fund CEO who specializes in deliberately buying distressed or defaulted bonds at a steep discount and then successfully suing for full repayment in a friendly court, and who has lately advised his clients to short U.S. Treasuries.[17] Singer has been a heavy funder of the Republican Jewish Coalition, the Jewish Institute for National Security Affairs, the Israel Project, and was the biggest single donor to Mitt Romney's super PAC Restore Our Future in 2012. After Netanyahu's speech to Congress, the *New York Times* found that heavy contributions to Republicans by rich, hawkish donors like Adelson and Singer have fueled a trend toward stronger support for Israel in the GOP.[18]

At least one lawmaker has been less pusillanimous than Graham in discussing the cash nexus between donors and politicians. Representative Vance McAllister, a Louisiana Republican, openly told an audience at the University of Louisiana's Monroe campus that members of Congress expect to receive campaign contributions for voting the right way on bills. "Money controls Washington," he told the group. McAllister claimed that fellow members often see their job as a "steady cycle of voting for fundraising and money instead of voting for what is right." Referring to a pending bill, he said a colleague, whom he didn't name, told him in the House Chamber that if he voted no on the bill, he would receive a contribution from the Heritage Foundation (the freshman McAllister apparently confused the organization with Heritage Action, which can legally make donations; Heritage Foundation, its parent organization, is barred from making contributions).[19] McAllister was defeated in his party's 2014 primary; his kind of candor is seldom rewarded.

Graham and McAllister are Republicans, but this kind of behavior is found on both sides of the aisle. Steve, a lobbyist of my acquaintance, told me that during the writing of the Senate bill to repair the damage on the East Coast from the October 2012 superstorm Sandy, lobbyists were vying to insert their special projects into the legislation. He said it was a virtual auction: if you contributed to Democratic senator Charles Schumer of New York, a member of the Senate leadership, it would greatly improve the odds of getting your provision accepted.

There are other methods for wealthy interests to purchase the obedience of public officials than just giving money to their campaigns. As the controversy over Hillary Clinton's well-compensated orations has made clear, speechmaking by former officeholders is a major racket and a significant growth industry. In the year prior to Clinton's declaring her candidacy, companies like Fidelity, KKR, and Goldman Sachs were putting money directly in her pocket at an average of $200,000 per speech.[20]

Hillary's husband, Bill, has been a trailblazer in making public office pay off during retirement, rendering the image of Harry Truman pottering around his house at Independence, or of Ike sitting in his rocker at Gettysburg, as obsolete as the Paleolithic Age. The *Washington Post* reported that since leaving the presidency, Clinton has made $105 million in speaking fees, or "honoraria," as the industry chastely calls them. The bulk has come from corporate interests and particularly the financial services industry, suggesting that it might be considered a form of deferred compensation for services rendered in enacting legislation like the North American Free Trade Agreement (NAFTA) and repealing noisome impediments like the Glass-Steagall Act, which separated commercial and investment banking.

Former Federal Reserve Board chairman Ben Bernanke, who deluged banks with money at near-zero interest rates (with which they built up cash reserves or purchased higher-yield securities abroad rather than lending to consumers or businesses), has been the recipient of considerable corporate gratitude during his retirement. Like Hillary, he commands around $200,000 per speech. In a normal world, one might have thought that the views of these people would have been more interesting, or at least more significant, when they were actually holding public office and their actions directly affected national policy. At that time their golden words would have been free to the listener. It is difficult to imagine Goldman Sachs investing so much simply for the privilege of listening to Hillary's shopworn platitudes about hard choices.

A lot of money is changing hands, both in campaign fund-raising and honoraria to government personnel whose "distinguished" careers set them up for a payday beyond imagining for most Americans. But that still leaves questions: is that money always synonymous with power, and where does the real power lie? We know that in many respects, particularly in national security affairs, Congress's constitutional powers are moribund, if only because it chooses not to act. Where did those powers go? In 1973, as the Watergate crisis gathered into a storm cloud and President Nixon's crimes and misdemeanors became all too evident, Arthur Schlesinger, Jr., wrote a critique of executive overreach called *The Imperial Presidency.*

Schlesinger argued that since the beginning of the Republic, and with increasing speed and intensity during the cold war, presidents have seized constitutionally unsanctioned power unto themselves, particularly in national security matters. His argument was persuasive, as far as it went: there is no question that the notion of checks and balances envisioned by the founders is all but dead in national security matters, and that on the surface the president appears to be decisively dominant in these fields. From a twenty-first-century perspective, however, there are problems with Schlesinger's thesis.

The first is the author's partisanship. Schlesinger had been a fixture of Democratic salons and kitchen cabinets back to the time of Harry Truman. Somehow, at the time of the events about which he wrote later, he never summoned the outrage to critique in such scathing fashion Truman's decision on war in Korea without a congressional declaration, Kennedy's Bay of Pigs fiasco, or Johnson's obsession with Vietnam. It was Nixon who moved him to write his searing condemnation of presidential overreach; and when another Democratic president, Bill Clinton, in the face of a rare rejection of an authorization for the use of force by the House of Representatives in 1999 during the president's bombing campaign against Serbia, nevertheless continued with the military action, Schlesinger did not make a sound.

But an objection more fundamental than that of partisan bias remains. If most of the American government's power flows to the presidency, creating a regime Schlesinger called a plebiscitary presidency (one in which the supreme leader is popularly elected but has all or virtually all the power while in office), why do Americans in season and out keep electing presidents who behave imperially, authorizing unconstitutional surveillance and embroiling the nation in one foreign conflict after another? Have we become so blind or masochistic as to believe that these are desirable policies, or are there perhaps institutional pressures that impel a president, any president, to act in certain ways, ways often directly opposed to the platform that he campaigned on in order to convince voters to elect him? A look at the last several presidencies shows a pattern that suggests the presidency may not be so imperial after all.

What I Saw at the Reagan Revolution

When I began working in government, Ronald Reagan was in his first term as president. He was not yet the sainted dream figure of the GOP—witness the successful movement during the 1990s to name airports and buildings after him, and even Grover Norquist's goofy campaign to get Reagan's likeness on the dime and carved into Mount Rushmore. He was, by many accounts, fast becoming the archetype of the successful modern presidency.

This assessment was bipartisan. When campaigning in 2008, which former president did Barack Obama identify as one he was keen to emulate? Would he pick any of the traditional standard-bearers in the Democratic pantheon: FDR, Truman, or Kennedy? Not at all: "Ronald Reagan changed the trajectory of America in a way that Richard Nixon did not, and a way that Bill Clinton did not." And how did he do this? According to Obama, Reagan appealed to a popular demand for sunny days, satisfying voters who insisted: "We want clarity, we want optimism, we want a return to that sense of dynamism and entrepreneurship that had been missing."[21]

This attitude was in evidence during my days on the House Budget Committee. In the mid-1990s, the standard narrative for justifying ever-increasing defense spending in the annual budget resolution would invariably invoke the nostrum that "Ronald Reagan won the cold war." No one has ever suggested that Lincoln won the Civil War in the single-handed manner of Muhammad Ali knocking out George Foreman, but by then the sanctification of Reagan was well under way. In GOP circles these days there is a cult of Reagan, and his presidential library is now a kind of Lourdes for true believers.

But was he really so remarkable? This was not the universal assessment of the fortieth president when he was in office, even from his own inner circle. Thanks to the memoirs of insiders such as Larry Speakes, his presidential press secretary, and Donald Regan, his treasury secretary and chief of staff, we know that his was a remarkably stage-managed presidency. Speakes told us he made up quotes to make his boss sound more incisive and in charge, and Donald Regan boggled at the president's passive acceptance of his subordinates' maneuvers. "I did not know what to make of his passivity," he wrote in his memoir after one notable personnel shake-up. "He seemed to be absorbing a fait accompli rather than making a decision. One might have thought that the matter had already been settled by some absent party."

Even Republicans would from time to time consider whether Reagan was fully in charge of his own administration. In the mid-1980s, at the height of the debate over procurement scandals and defense reform, Congressman John Kasich, my boss, was one of several members of Congress invited to the White House to hear the president's views. I never did learn exactly what transpired, but Kasich returned to his office in a bad mood, heatedly said, "Reagan is senile," and disappeared into his office.

Reagan's defense in the defining scandal of his presidency, the Iran-Contra affair, hinged on the public's willingness to believe that his underlings could have concocted and executed an egregious crime right under his nose without his having an inkling of it. The public bought it without a blink: it fit a character assessment that was widely accepted. A colleague told me Speaker Tip O'Neill described congressional meetings with Reagan as encounters with an actor on a set reading his lines and hitting his mark. "He came into the room, read from note cards, and tuned out," Tip said. No doubt Reagan's publicists would have described this behavior as focusing on the Big Picture, or choosing to remain above the fray. Some have retrospectively come to see Reagan's presidency as transformational in a more ominous sense: "Reagan was the Trojan horse in which a regiment of eager strategists hid, peering through its eye-holes as they wheeled it surreptitiously into the White House," wrote Meagan Day. "The people at the helm had their sights set on a total overhaul of the relationship between state, government and capital. They were activists, people with a vision, steeped in emergent neoliberal economic theory and intent on revising the agenda."[22]

Secret agencies, clandestine programs, and hidden agendas have been a fact of life since the Manhattan Project. What was new in the Reagan administration was the rise of the expertly choreographed presidency that eased the chief executive out of the messy business of formulating policy and into the realm of the ceremonial. During Watergate, there was no question where culpability and accountability lay. No one was in doubt that Nixon was in charge—that is why his denials rang so hollow. Iran-Contra was far more ambiguous. Who was really running the show? Was it Reagan or a rogue colonel in the West Wing? The Keystone Cops aspect of the affair (we remember National Security Adviser

Bud McFarlane flying to Tehran with a cake and a Bible) may have obscured the larger truth that Iran-Contra was a conspiracy to subvert the Constitution.

Reagan may not have been much on policy, but when it came to the ceremonial presidency, he set the gold standard. His time in office coincided with the final triumph of presidential campaign packaging, where an artfully staged and likable persona is deemed more electable than a candidate who has mastered policy issues but does not possess a relatable backstory. It was in the 1980s that the focus group—an opinion survey that began during World War II as a way to gauge the effectiveness of propaganda films—came into its own in political campaigns. A new emphasis was put on subliminal and emotional reactions to candidates at the expense of any rational evaluation of their policy positions.

Most succeeding presidents have been more hands-on than Reagan (we trust their schedules were not set by astrologers), but the template has remained: in every instance their campaign was less about policy or competence (presidential candidate Michael Dukakis ran on a platform of "competence" in 1988 and got walloped at the polls) than a character narrative voters could identify with. All the messy stuff about which government programs would have to be cut to achieve deficit reduction and what, beyond a few sonorous slogans, our Middle East policy ought to be, would be left to the scriptwriters and the set dressers.

Where all this stage management has evolved to in the present sometimes reads like a vignette from the political satire *Thank You for Smoking*. In February 2015, the *Washington Post* reported that a horde of advertising executives had descended upon Hillary Clinton's (as of then yet-to-be-announced) campaign in order to "rebrand" a woman who had been on the national stage for more than twenty years. Their advertising patter sounded like a parody of Madison Avenue advertising talk: "It's exactly the same as selling an iPhone or a soft drink or a cereal," gushed Peter Sealey, a longtime corporate marketing strategist. "She needs to use everything a brand has: a dominant color, a logo, a symbol. . . . The symbol of a Mercedes is a three-pointed star. The symbol of Coca-Cola is the contour bottle. The symbol of McDonald's is the golden arches. What is Clinton's symbol?"[23]

Bill Clinton, Triangulator of Deep State Interests

When Bill Clinton was elected president in 1992, he had an ambitious agenda, even if it was overshadowed in the campaign by the frequent need to tamp down what his staff called "bimbo eruptions" (it was on the strength of his ability to talk his way out of these scandals that he proudly wore the moniker "the Comeback Kid"). He found, on taking office, that his agenda would be trimmed down, whether he liked it or not.

His top priority was to grow the economy through an ambitious program of federal spending. But his advisers quickly told him that his scheme would have to be significantly scaled back as adverse reaction from the bond market would raise interest rates, choke off growth, and nullify any stimulative effects of the spending. His response: "You mean to tell me that the success of the economic program and my re-election hinges on the Federal Reserve and a bunch of f*cking bond traders?"[24]

Clinton took the hint and surrounded himself with money men. Within a year he had replaced his treasury secretary, Lloyd Bentsen, who had previously been a senator, with banker Robert Rubin, who had been running Goldman Sachs. When Rubin left to cash in on the repeal of Glass-Steagall, Clinton nominated Lawrence Summers to fill the post and reappointed Ayn Rand fanboy Alan Greenspan as chairman of the Federal Reserve Board. When Brooksley Born, Clinton's chairman of the Commodity Futures Trading Commission, proposed to regulate the derivatives market, she was crushed by the troika of Greenspan, Rubin, and Summers. On his way out the White House door in December 2000, Clinton signed into law a bill prohibiting the regulation of derivatives. Later, Clinton claimed he could not buck a veto-proof majority in Congress on this issue, but a documentary filmmaker who interviewed him about this said that it was one of "the most amazing lies I've heard in quite a while," as Clinton's operatives had actually been lobbying for the bill.[25]

Clinton was a quick learner. He understood early in his first term that the presidency is not always imperial and that if he did not accommodate unelected power he would become a one-term president. He accordingly adjusted his goals to the expectations of Wall Street and loaded his administration with the Street's fixers. As for his original policy goals, his "bridge to the twenty-first century" led straight to 2008 and the financial meltdown. Wall Street did not forget to show its gratitude for services rendered: the financial industry has paid him $23 million in speaking fees since he left office.[26]

Bush the Decider

On the surface, Clinton's successor, George W. Bush, bulldozing his way into office after the Florida recount travesty, could hardly have been more different. He knew what he wanted and brooked no opposition—not that there was any to speak of. There can be little doubt that the disastrous policies of his administration were *his* policies (even if the invasion of Iraq had been sketched out by a cabal of neoconservatives long before he became president). His subordinates, chosen for their loyalty, eagerly carried out his plans, and those who harbored doubts, like Treasury Secretary Paul O'Neill, soon found themselves looking for work. Bush was, in his own words, "the decider."

Or was he? It is a commonplace observation that Vice President Cheney was a virtual co-president—the kind of relationship GOP operatives nearly imposed on Reagan in the 1980 Republican Convention, when party grandees were convinced that they needed a co-presidential number two on the ticket like Gerald Ford to do the actual governing. Throughout Bush's presidency, the most dogged proponent of presidential authority was Cheney, who knew that the vice president's powers had been fuzzily defined both in the Constitution and by custom. By increasing the president's powers, he would increase his own. He even claimed executive privilege extended to him just as it covered the president.

Bush was new to Washington; Cheney had been a top-level inside operator for thirty years and he knew what made the wheels go around. He had been Ford's chief of staff; when offered the possibility of a cabinet appointment, he turned it down because he knew the real power often lay in positions that are less impressive on paper.

Throughout the 1980s, as ranking Republican on the House Intelligence Committee, Cheney participated with his friend Don Rumsfeld (then out of office) in secret "continuity of government" exercises. The premise of the drills was that in the event of a nuclear attack, three teams would go to separate locations around the United States to prepare to take leadership of the country. The participants became familiar with the emergency powers available to them in the event of a crisis, and, according to one participant, took the unconstitutional position that in an extreme situation it would be better to operate without Congress altogether.[27] "Over three decades, from the Ford administration onward, even when they were out of the executive branch of government, they were never too far away," wrote James Mann, a Bush biographer and the author of *The Rise of the Vulcans*. "They stayed in touch with its defense, military, and intelligence officials and were regularly called upon by those officials. Cheney and Rumsfeld were, in a sense, a part of the permanent, though hidden, national security apparatus of the United States."[28]

Cheney's selection as vice president was fishy. Although the Bush campaign went through the motions of interviewing candidates for a running mate (with Cheney, of course, in charge of that operation), he had already decided to join Bush on the ticket, and the Republican hopefuls lining up for a chance at the vice presidential slot were wasting their time. Kasich, who toyed with running for president and dropped out early in the 2000 campaign, immediately threw his support to Bush and was one of those invited to participate in the charade of the candidate interviews. Afterward, commiserating with him about how Cheney, looking for the most qualified candidate, had by sheer happenstance stumbled upon himself, I asked Kasich, half-jokingly, whether he thought Bush had chosen Cheney or Cheney had actually chosen Bush. "That's a really interesting question," was his only response.

While the war on terrorism bears the indelible stamp of the Bush presidency, it is an open question whether he or his operatives set policy in some of the most contentious areas. Bush has much to answer for, but evidence from the Senate Intelligence Committee's report on the CIA's conduct of torture suggests that he was not entirely in control of his own administration, and that policy was being made with the president deliberately kept "out of the loop."* We read that White House counsel Alberto Gonzales deleted any mention of waterboarding from the talking points used to brief the president. Elsewhere, the report cryptically quotes an unnamed official saying that "there would be no briefing of the President on this matter."[29]

Deniability is everything in Washington, and these evasions may have been concocted with a nod and a wink. But it is in the nature of institutions that such arrangements become habitual. The tail ends up wagging the dog, and the president, by insensible degrees, transforms into the dupe of his own subordinates. Americans do not consciously elect co-presidents, and they certainly do not expect that his underlings will serve him best by keeping information from him. But if Bush was clueless and never one to read briefing memos of any length, his successor was a far more disciplined student—a constitutional scholar, no less, and a man capable of penning his own rhetorical flourishes. So what would happen when Barack Obama entered the White House? Many waited with hope and anticipation.

Barack Obama, Reluctant Chairman of the Deep State

In 2008, Barack Obama the change agent ran against the legacy of George W. Bush. But when he assumed office, his policies in the areas of national security and financial regulation were strikingly similar. Even the Afford-

---

* It is possible that Cheney, who wrote the dissenting views to the Iran-Contra committee's report, learned from that affair that it is vital to keep a president "out of the loop" when illegal policies must be implemented.

able Care Act, which Republicans vilify with uncontrollable rage, is hardly different in outline from Bush's Medicare Prescription Drug, Improvement, and Modernization Act (both expand medical coverage by subsidizing corporate interests). Still, Obama remains misapprehended by friend and foe alike.

According to his opponents, Obama is an un-American Muslim socialist worthy of every term of abuse in the Republicans' voluminous lexicon. His defenders counter that while he has not achieved what they had hoped, this was principally due to the GOP's relentless obstruction. They forget that during his first two years in office, he had a Democratic majority in Congress: Lyndon Johnson did not waste this opportunity in similar circumstances.

Why has Obama generated such polarizing opinions despite an actual record that corresponds neither to the fears of his enemies nor the hopes of his friends? His motivations are difficult to understand because of his diffident and aloof manner. Silly-clever gossip columnists like Maureen Dowd have reduced this critique to the lowest common denominator by complaining that he should not play golf when anything is happening in the world.[30]

More substantively, something about his style does not please the national security establishment, despite the fact that his administration undertook the surge in Afghanistan, quietly expanded a rigorous internal security apparatus within the federal government, significantly widened his predecessor's drone campaign in Pakistan, and has either supported or acquiesced in the NSA's surveillance policies.

In his campaign for the presidency, Obama promised to close the prison at the Guantánamo Bay Naval Base because its operation made a mockery of due process and served only as a recruitment tool for Islamic extremists. He was on firm ground—the American judicial system had a much better record of prosecuting and convicting terrorists, like Zacarias Moussaoui, a 9/11 conspirator, than did Guantánamo Bay's legally questionable process. On the day he took office, Obama even signed an executive order to wind down and close the facility. Yet nothing came of it.

When panicked members of Congress stampeded themselves into supporting a ban on closing Guantánamo, Obama did nothing but talk in
vague generalities. He could have wielded his veto pen and forced some
serious horse trading in the tradition of Harry Truman, a tough little
banty rooster who thirsted for a scrap with Congress. Obama's veto pen
lay unused. In his presidency to date, Obama has issued fewer vetoes than
any other president since James Garfield, who was assassinated six
months into his administration.

The Deep State's disappointment in Obama for only reluctantly doing what they wanted is mirrored by the disillusion of many of his former
supporters for doing those things at all. After more than a dozen long
years, the American people have grown tired of an endless succession of
wars that have brought no tangible benefit at enormous cost in lives and
treasure, just as they are spooked by the implications of a surveillance
state. At the same time, Americans are constantly bombarded with new
threats—ISIS, Russia, even Somali terrorist groups threatening to attack
American shopping malls. The public is less antiwar than simply shell-
shocked into a state of apathy and resignation.

When Obama took office in 2009, he was immediately confronted
with what to do in Afghanistan. While he had campaigned on the premise
that Iraq was the "dumb" war and Afghanistan the "good" one, he still
wanted to end the latter conflict as quickly as prudently possible. In a series of White House strategy meetings, Obama debated the options in
Afghanistan with his senior national security team, and, according to
Bob Gates's memoir, Obama and Biden both aggressively pushed back at
the military's off-the-shelf plan for an increase of 40,000 U.S. troops.

Gates chose to regard it as discourtesy toward professional military
officers that Obama and his vice president should poke holes in the ratio-
nales of Generals David Petraeus and Stanley McChrystal, the main proponents of the surge in Iraq. Both generals claimed that if the Taliban were
not defeated, the group would invite al-Qaeda back into Afghanistan,
though it later turned out there was no intelligence to support the asser-

tion.[31] Gates also said Obama accused the military of "gaming" him by forcing a strategy on him with no alternatives.

The military reacted in its accustomed fashion. Leaks sprang in the press, linked to anonymous sources at the Pentagon, CIA, and State Department, suggesting that Obama's reticence about the surge and preference for focusing on al-Qaeda rather than the Taliban was endangering the mission.[32] Obama soon acceded to the pressure and compromised on 30,000 additional troops and set a date for withdrawal. But it did not end there: determined to lengthen the time allotted for the mission, Gates and Clinton undercut the agreed-to policy in congressional testimony, arguing that the withdrawal date was not firm.

It was a textbook case of how the permanent state boxes in and bypasses its own elected leaders by spreading false intelligence, leaking to the press, and stirring up opposition on the Hill. The Gates-Clinton-Petraeus squeeze play raises serious questions about civilian control of the military and whether an elected president can control his own bureaucracy.

The national security state's project to maintain an overseas military empire, however it may disguise or rebrand itself, has been discredited, but that has not dulled its ambitions. Although it has temporarily cut its losses in Iraq, and is still attempting to do so in Afghanistan, the Pentagon has continued to roll out ambitious new military policies to force the president's hand.

The so-called Pivot to Asia, which calls for a buildup of military forces on the periphery of China, is the Pentagon's attempt to reverse any perceived contraction of empire. The strategy was publicly previewed in an article in *Foreign Policy* by then–secretary of state Clinton in October 2011, titled "America's Pacific Century," but the driving force behind it was Dr. Andrew Marshall, director of the Pentagon's Office of Net Assessment.* The DOD was looking for a successor strategy to the war on

---

* Marshall embodies the permanent government: he was appointed as director of the office in 1973, serving continuously in that post until January 2015.

terrorism, which after a dozen years of futility had become tedious to all concerned. The Pivot to Asia was a slightly more ambiguous version of the old cold war strategy of militarily containing the Soviet Union by encircling it with a chain of U.S. allies who provided basing rights for our troops at great expense.

The Pivot was supposed to provide "reassurance" to America's East Asian allies, although what threat they are supposed to be reassured about is left somewhat vague, because it is diplomatically awkward for the United States to refer to China, its biggest sovereign creditor, as a military threat. The actual meat of the Pivot was what Marshall's Net Assessment Office calls Air-Sea Battle, a military doctrine that requires buying more expensive combat ships and long-range aircraft, which are of minimal use in the war on terrorism but maximize the money flow to defense contractors.[33]

What did Obama do when this new strategy bubbled up from the bureaucracy? Did he force an extended debate on its advisability and demand alternative strategies? No, he dutifully trekked to East and Southeast Asia with draft agreements for the opening of U.S. bases in the region. After his trip, the military-industrial complex gradually began soft-pedaling the Pivot to Asia, possibly because overt hostility to China would endanger too many American investments, and maybe also because Vladimir Putin makes a more pleasing bad guy than Xi Jinping. Nevertheless, Obama formally committed himself to Containment 2.0—and the future spending it entails—without satisfying either the war hawks of the permanent state or his disillusioned voting base.

A similar example of the Pentagon engineering a fait accompli in contravention of Obama's previously stated positions can be found in U.S. strategic nuclear policy toward Europe. Throughout the quarter century after the dissolution of the NATO–Warsaw Pact rivalry, the United States and its NATO clients foresaw the possibility of using nuclear weapons in a European war. Until the 2014 annexation of Crimea, such a contingency would have been so remote as to seem absurd, but after the crisis in Ukraine it is at least conceivable as the result of a gradual escalation leading to a fatal miscalculation.

The Obama administration could have officially jettisoned the old cold war doctrine of Flexible Response (a euphemism meaning the potential first use of nuclear weapons) in the 2010 Nuclear Posture Review, a quadrennial policy statement on the role of nuclear weapons in U.S. strategy. Obama's 2009 speech in Prague, where the president held out the idealistic hope of a nuclear-weapon-free world, raised expectations of sweeping changes in nuclear policy. Instead, a largely Pentagon-driven interagency process dictated that the nuclear policy review recommend the retention of forward-deployed nuclear weapons in Europe. Pouring old wine into new bottles, the bureaucrats christened the doctrine (which was basically the same as Flexible Response) Extended Deterrence.

As always, there was big money in play: concocting a rationale for the operational use of nuclear weapons would necessarily require the hardware to carry out the doctrine. That, in turn, meant that America's aging arsenal of nuclear warheads would have to be modernized. The thirty-year cost of modernizing the weapons and the systems to deliver them— missiles, bombers, and submarines—comes to approximately $1 trillion.[34] Once again, Obama agreed to this policy, an express repudiation of the principles of his Prague speech. Yet the Wise Men of the Pentagon are still unconvinced that he is tough enough to deal with Putin.

The puzzle of the Obama presidency is that he keeps going through the motions of conducting military interventions and covert operations, as well as signing off on ambitious strategy reviews, while not appearing to have his heart in it. There is a small degree of validity to the Republican criticism that Obama doesn't have the will to win foreign conflicts—he would have been much better off politically had he never given anyone the impression that the United States would militarily intervene in Syria in 2013. Likewise, the scalding rhetoric that came out of the White House over Russia's annexations in Ukraine: the president conveyed the immanent likelihood of draconian actions, which were never actually on the table. His ambivalence has alienated his progressive voting base, who thought they were electing a peace candidate (although they were insufficiently attentive to his carefully constructed campaign rhetoric), while at the same time failing to satisfy Robert Gates, the *Washington Post* editorial board, and all the serious grown-ups at the Council on Foreign Relations that he has the stuff to "show leadership."

Puzzling ambivalence has also been evident in his domestic policy. For six years running, Obama sought bipartisan compromise with the deluded persistence of Captain Ahab, despite abundant evidence that the GOP was in no mood for it. If we are to believe Bob Woodward's ticktock account of the 2011 negotiations over the debt limit, Obama surrounded himself with people like Tim Geithner who advised him to cave to most of the Republican demands in order to get the debt-limit extension. So much time was wasted on the assumption that the GOP could be bought off with reasonable concessions that the clock almost ran out (Standard & Poor's still issued a debt downgrade, despite the fact that default was averted). He finally pacified the Republicans with sequestration (meaning across-the-board cuts) of all government accounts. It is almost certain he did not have to do that, as in manufactured crises like government shutdowns and debt-limit breaches, the side initiating the crisis always loses politically and must eventually fold its hand.

After frittering away those six years when he had at least one house of Congress in Democratic hands, Obama emerged from the 2014 midterm debacle with an epiphany: now was the time to display the populist president that his supporters thought they had elected in 2008. He proposed increases in the minimum wage, paid worker's leave, infrastructure spending, and free tuition for community college. There was only one problem: how was a lame duck president going to get this agenda through the most numerically dominant Republican Congress since 1929?[35] That absurd dilemma sums up the reality of his presidency.

Obama's personality is more impenetrable than that of any other president in recent history. Yet he may be, like Napoleon III, a sphinx without a riddle: merely an ambitious politician who tested well with focus groups, and who arrived at the right moment, promising hope and change as a pretext to administer an entrenched system without any conviction. Throughout his presidency, he has been whipsawed by bureaucratic interests that have reduced his stated agenda to mush. His behavior has unleashed predictable rage on the Right, but also despondency among many on the Left.

It is surprising how much fear his timid policies have generated among the big-money boys. There are no rational grounds for the hyperthyroid reactions of hedge fund bosses like Steven Schwarzman when Obama is largely a champion of the status quo who raises much of his money among Schwarzman's colleagues. Nevertheless, the neoliberal mandarins at the venerable *Economist* say Obama has an image as one "who is hostile to business."[36]

It is one thing to shake our heads at the behavior of gun nuts who fear Obama will take away their firearms and send them to a FEMA concentration camp in Montana and quite another to consider that many canny Wall Street operatives, whose business model is based on a reptilian calculation of their own material interests, have succumbed to the irrational idea that totalitarian socialism is just around the corner and that Obama is going to usher it in, when he is only a more hesitant version of his predecessor.

That such a weak reed, who has acceded time and again to the entrenched interests of the permanent state, should incite so much negative passion among so many in the billionaire class suggests they are displacing their fears of the simmering discontent among the 99 percent onto a convenient political symbol. Their touchy defensiveness reveals the contradictions within the political system they dominate. President Obama, who appears to administer that system without enthusiasm or belief, has dissatisfied key constituencies of the Deep State even as he has alarmed the traditionalists who defend the remnants of the constitutional state.

Perhaps the most telling example of the relationship between President Obama and the Deep State comes from a March 2015 interview of John Brennan, his frequently embattled CIA director. Obama has shown Brennan great loyalty through two presidential terms. How did Brennan repay that loyalty—with a humble demonstration of gratitude and respect, perhaps? Obama, he said, did "not have an appreciation" of national security when he came into office, but with tutelage by himself and other experts "he has gone to school and understands the complexities." The tone of headmasterly condescension is unmistakable, giving the listener ample grounds to wonder who is really in charge, the president or his national security complex. It is the inner workings of that national security complex that we shall turn to next.

5

DOES OUR DEFENSE ACTUALLY DEFEND AMERICA?

Of all the enemies to public liberty, war is, perhaps, the most to be dreaded, because it comprises and develops the germ of every other. War is the parent of armies; from these proceed debts and taxes; and armies, and debts, and taxes are the known instruments for bringing the many under the domination of the few. . . . No nation could reserve its freedom in the midst of continual warfare.

—James Madison, in "Political Observations," 1795
(*Letters and Other Writings of James Madison*, 1865, vol. IV)

The whole aim of practical politics is to keep the populace alarmed (and hence clamorous to be led to safety) by menacing it with an endless series of hobgoblins, all of them imaginary.

—H. L. Mencken, *In Defense of Women*, 1918

Meet Comrade Frolov

From time to time in the course of my career in government, the FBI or Congress's own security offices would warn congressional staff members with security clearances that foreign intelligence agencies were targeting Capitol Hill. In 2000, when I was working at the House Budget Committee, I had a chance to experience this firsthand. I was invited to attend a downtown conference on the Balkans, then an important topic because the United States had intervened militarily in Serbia the previous year and the region was still unstable. Once the conference was over, a member of the audience accosted me, presumably because I had asked a question during the session and had identified my place of business, a formality required at such meetings. He introduced himself and gave me his business card—Vladimir Frolov of the press section of the Russian embassy. After some perfunctory small talk ending with his invocation of stock Washington etiquette ("We should have lunch sometime"), I pocketed his card and headed back to the Hill.

Patriotism, logic, and self-preservation all dictated that the first thing I did when I got back to my desk was phone my friend Rob Walsh, a recently retired FBI agent. He set the wheels in motion, and soon I was invited to meet with Bureau representatives in the office of the House sergeant at arms. I handed over Frolov's card, and the agents proceeded to tell me that he was already on their radar screen. He might attempt to cultivate me, they explained; how far was I willing to string him along? I wasn't much inclined, as method acting was not my forte, and in any case I had more than enough of my own professional business to attend to. I told them, though, that I'd keep them apprised of any further contacts.

A couple of months later, he called. It was obvious he was speaking from a cell phone, and quite surprisingly the number was not blocked when I looked at my caller ID. The bureau was duly appreciative of the phone number I retrieved, and that was the last I heard from Frolov, as he evidently had bigger fish to fry.

How big I only found out several months later, in March 2001, when the Bush administration expelled fifty-one Russian embassy personnel as "persona non grata," diplomatic-speak for "spies." Frolov was not among them, as he had abruptly bolted for Russia just prior to the expulsion order. If the U.S. government intelligence sources who leaked additional details to the press were correct, Frolov was the handler of Robert Hanssen, an FBI agent who had spied first for the Soviets and then for the Russian Federation for twenty-two years. The Justice Department described the Hanssen case as "possibly the worst intelligence disaster in U.S. history."[1]

I still don't know whether my infinitesimal contribution to the FBI added another tile to the intelligence mosaic or not, but the conclusion of this tale shows just how the worm can turn: back in Mother Russia, Frolov became a legitimate journalist, and he has lately been quite critical of Russian president Vladimir Putin.

These days, I suspect that cloak-and-dagger activity in the manner of a Robert Ludlum novel, while still practiced, is receding in importance compared to cyberespionage. In my last few years on the Hill, Capitol security personnel emphasized that all electronic communications were under regular assault from foreign sources, China most prominent among them.

For many years, the Pentagon, the State Department, Homeland Security, and U.S. businesses have been subject to a perpetual torrent of cyberintrusions and cyberattacks from foreign countries. This is an advanced method of waging war that is both covert and stays beneath the traditional legal threshold of state-to-state warfare. No longer does a country need to take the trouble to invade another country militarily in order to plunder its resources (and no longer does the main source of wealth reside in mineral deposits or agricultural bounty or even factories, but in intellectual property and research know-how). Nor does a country need to conduct bombing campaigns in order to disrupt business operations or normal life in the territory it targets.

The hacking of Target in late 2013, when 40 million customer credit cards were compromised, gave us a small taste of the potential economic disruption that we may face in the future. The NSA, whose self-aggrandizing and totalitarian description of its so-called collection posture is to "collect it all, exploit it all, partner it all, sniff it all, know it all," and which scours Facebook posts both for biographical data and photographs for its facial-recognition data banks, neither averted the Target hack nor shut it down as it continued for several weeks. In January 2015, we learned that as early as 2010 the NSA had covertly inserted spyware into the computers of North Korean government-sponsored hackers, allowing the agency to know what the North Koreans were targeting. How, then, did the North Korean regime succeed in hacking Sony? Likewise, the inexcusable breach of the personnel files of the Office of Personnel Management, which exposed detailed records of 22 million current and former employees. Why are American government, businesses, and individuals so vulnerable if the NSA possesses such comprehensive investigative tools?

These basic deficiencies plague the other intelligence agencies as well. Has the CIA's analysis of foreign events improved since the weapons-of-mass-destruction debacle in Iraq, when the CIA's director declared the presence of WMDs there to be such a certainty as to constitute a "slam dunk"? Did the CIA's analysts provide the White House with an accurate assessment of Vladimir Putin's likely moves as the United States attempted in early 2014 to edge Ukraine toward association with the European Union and possible membership in NATO? Putin had clearly telegraphed his intentions back in 2008, when he struck out at Georgia under nearly identical circumstances. While the bulk of responsibility for the unfolding tragedy in Ukraine lies with the Kremlin, Washington bears considerable blame for its accessory role in stoking the unrest in Kiev that led to the coup. Later in the book, I shall describe some of the professional operatives involved in that project. That the CIA was either professionally incapable of seeing where their caper could lead, or suspected but did not tell the White House, is shocking. These glaring deficiencies in the basic functioning of the NSA and the CIA urgently need to be rectified.

The Pentagon: Sparing No Expense Not to Defend Us

The United States needs a defense establishment and an intelligence apparatus; only a hopeless idealist or an ostrich would deny that. In some ways, however, our huge national security establishment has been lagging in its role of defending the country from the newer forms of espionage and warfare. That said, providing for a military and intelligence establishment that protects the country and keeps our leaders adequately informed about world developments is not to be confused with maintaining, at crushing expense, a globe-girdling military colossus. Figures vary according to how one defines a military base, but, according to the *Department of Defense Base Structure Report for Fiscal Year 2013*, the Pentagon has

598 overseas bases in forty foreign countries. There were 193,111 U.S. military personnel deployed overseas, exclusive of those in Afghanistan. During 2014, U.S. Special Operations Forces deployed to 133 countries for a variety of liaison, training, and covert missions.[2] Paying for these and related military activities together constitutes by some estimates the largest single category of the federal budget. For 2014, Congress enacted a defense budget of $587 billion. While this sum is smaller than annual spending for Social Security, there is much more to the national security state than the Pentagon's far-from-modest budget.

Winslow T. Wheeler, a former national security analyst with Congress and the Government Accountability Office, is of the view that the Department of Defense budget leaves out significant related costs and legacy financing: DOD's military retirement costs are carried elsewhere in the federal budget; nuclear weapons are in the Department of Energy's budget; and the cost of caring for veterans is borne by an independent agency. Wheeler believes the State Department's budget should be included as well: since the end of the cold war, State has emphasized so-called coercive diplomacy, and several secretaries of state have been far more eager for military intervention than DOD's military and civilian leaders. Finally, he includes the Department of Homeland Security (DHS).

Some may argue with this choice, as Homeland Security fulfills a domestic function, but I believe Wheeler is right: DHS was created as a direct result of 9/11, when a blowback resulted from repeated U.S. interventions in the Middle East and the arming and training of questionable insurgent groups. The Department of Defense, for all its hundreds of billions of annual spending, was incapable of defending our national territory, or even its own headquarters, the Pentagon. Ironically, the heraldic symbol of the U.S. Army's Military District of Washington is an image of the Washington Monument with a sword placed diagonally across it in a protective manner. The motto is "This we'll defend." But not anymore—it's now a job for DHS. A former Hill colleague who went on to work at DHS recalled a meeting with personnel from the DOD's Northern Command, which is tasked with giving military support to civilian authorities in case of a domestic emergency. He said Northern Command was hard-pressed to think of *any* circumstance in which it would employ the DOD's assets. Given the Pentagon's virtual nonstop involvement in foreign interventions and unpreparedness to defend U.S. territory, perhaps it should change its name to the Department of Offense.

Wheeler calculates that all of this national security spending by the various agencies totals around $1 trillion a year.[3] To put that in perspective, during the first dozen years of the twenty-first century, the Pentagon alone spent money at an average rate of more than a billion dollars a day—every single day. For twelve years, the United States was spending more on its military than the next ten countries combined.[4] Only such staggering largesse could permit the military to incur costs of anywhere from $100 to $600 per *gallon* to deliver motor fuel to the scene of combat in Afghanistan.[5] A country that indulges in that kind of extravagance risks imposing severe constraints on the resources available to improve the health, safety, and economic productivity of its citizens.

Throughout 2013 and 2014, press attention focused on budget cuts to the Pentagon arising from the Budget Control Act of 2011. What the media almost always neglected to point out was that military spending, even after reductions mandated by the act, remained well above the average defense budget during the cold war—a time when the United States faced the combined militaries of the Warsaw Pact.

Since the removal of U.S. combat troops from Iraq on December 31, 2011, the American people have been under the impression that the United States has been withdrawing forces and cutting military budgets. Republicans, in particular, have kept up a constant oratory about defense cuts as part of their perennial campaign to make any Democrat occupying the Oval Office look weak on defense. They are clearly intent on depicting the 2014 withdrawal from Afghanistan, which was both an Obama campaign promise and a move a majority of Americans approved of, look like some sort of strategic calamity in the making. In the end, the president compromised, maintaining a floor of 9,800 U.S. troops in Afghanistan after 2014 with no time limit mandating their withdrawal.

But all of the talk about cuts and retreat creates a misleading impression of what the military is actually doing and, more important, its plans for the future. Military spending is down only slightly from its peak in 2010, and then mostly because of the decline of the exorbitantly expensive combat activity in Iraq and Afghanistan, as well the mandatory budget sequestration that Republicans themselves insisted upon. Once the drawdowns in Iraq and Afghanistan were completed—although, as recent events have shown, any sigh of relief at being done with Iraq has been premature—the military-industrial complex immediately set its gaze on new horizons.

The Pentagon Seeks New Theaters of Conflict

Few Americans have heard of AFRICOM, or the U.S. African Command. It did not officially exist before 2008, although planning for it began in 2004. Incongruously, its headquarters are in Stuttgart, Germany, where it will remain for the foreseeable future. It has only one permanent, acknowledged military base in Africa, but it maintains a shadowy and secretive temporary presence in most of the continent's fifty-five nations—including, for example, a surveillance drone operation at a facility called Base Aérienne 101 at the international airport in Niamey, the capital of Niger.

The only base that the Pentagon openly acknowledges is Camp Lemonnier, a former French Foreign Legion facility in Djibouti, in the horn of Africa. It is host to approximately 4,000 military personnel and contractors, and the military has big plans for it. On May 5, 2014, President Obama announced that he had reached an agreement with the president of Djibouti, Ismaïl Omar Guelleh, to lease Camp Lemonnier for the next ten years for the substantial sum of $630 million. The annual lease fee is nearly double the $38 million per year that the United States had been paying to that point. In 2024, the United States has the option to renew the lease for a further ten years at a renegotiated rate.[6]

President Guelleah commented afterward: "The fact that we welcome the U.S. forces in our country shows our support for international peace and for peace in our region as well. We do that all for peace in the world and for peace in Africa." Left unmentioned was the issue of why, if all this was done for the sake of peace, it was necessary for the policeman to bribe the protected party for the privilege of protecting him. The comments of Djibouti's president were all the more ironic in light of the later revelation that local air controllers have expressed hostility to their American guests, have slept on the job (miraculously, there have so far been no aviation catastrophes at the base), and U.S. personnel have been threatened.[7]

Setting aside the question of cost to the taxpayer, the base will certainly be a boon to military infrastructure contractors. In 2013, five contracts worth more than $322 million were awarded for Camp Lemonnier. These included a $25.5 million fitness center and a $41 million joint headquarters facility. All of this suggests the U.S. taxpayer, knowingly or not, is deeply invested in the global war on terrorism business for at least two decades to come. It also suggests that those in the Pentagon who are seeking to emulate Lawrence of Arabia's warrior spirit clearly did not inherit his asceticism. Twenty-five million dollars for a fitness center? How much can a few sets of barbells and workout machines cost? Congress, which investigated the General Services Administration's junkets to Las Vegas with the thoroughness of Inspector Javert, might wish to cast a jaundiced eye on the more than half a trillion dollars the Pentagon spends every year.

The common narrative about AFRICOM, when it is discussed at all, is that this new organization represents our national security policy for dealing with an ever-evolving Islamic extremism: it would appear our military and intelligence services' eternal whack-a-mole game with al-Qaeda and its affiliates, franchises, and wannabe clones has merely shifted from the mountains of the Hindu Kush to the sands of the Sahara and the Sahel belt farther to the south. There are, however, alternative or at least supplementary explanations.

One of these is that the United States receives about one-quarter of its imported oil from Africa, while China, our principal sovereign creditor, now gets roughly a third of its oil from the continent. The fact that China is investing much of its huge capital surplus—derived in large part from its trade with the United States—in Africa has attracted notice in Washington: there are now more than two thousand Chinese companies and well over a million Chinese citizens on the continent.[8] They can be found wherever there are mines, oil fields, container ports, or manufacturing facilities. The dollar volume of China's trade with Africa is double that of U.S.-African trade, and the disparity will only become greater in the future.[9]

When confronted with the suspicion of ulterior motives for America's sudden interest in Africa, official Washington demurs. The U.S. Army War College has produced a publication about AFRICOM that, among other things, "debunks" the "myths" that the activities of AFRICOM are about access to African petroleum or countering Chinese moves there.[10] But in testimony before Congress supporting the creation of AFRICOM in 2007, Dr. J. Peter Pham, who has been an adviser to the DOD and the State Department, openly stated that oil and China were precisely what AFRICOM was about: "This natural wealth makes Africa an inviting target for the attentions of the People's Republic of China, whose dynamic economy, averaging nine percent growth per annum over the last two decades, has an almost insatiable thirst for oil as well as a need for other natural resources to sustain it. . . . Intentionally or not, many analysts expect that Africa—especially the states along its oil-rich western coastline—will increasingly become a theatre for strategic competition between the United States and its only real near-peer competitor on the global stage, China, as both countries seek to expand their influence and secure access to resources."

My own hunch, based on three decades of professional observation, is that there is something to the charges of critics that this is about oil and global strategic rivalry. But what do a few score, or a few hundred, special forces operators and their supporting contractors running around the acacia savannas of the African Sahel on "training missions" have to do with the much larger narrative of the Deep State: the financialization of the American economy, income stagnation, rotting infrastructure, the comprehensive surveillance of citizens, and the erosion of popular democracy? The answer has a lot to do with how you define the concept of national security.

War in Perpetuity?

Overwhelmingly, our government and media choose to categorize national security as the identification of foreign (and occasionally internal) threats and the selection and employment of violent, coercive, or covert means to neutralize those threats. The 2014 Quadrennial Defense Review (QDR), the Pentagon's primary summary of strategic goals, identifies the following regions as arenas for potential national security concern: the homeland (a tiresome post-9/11 buzzword meaning the landmass of the United States), Europe, Russia, the Middle East, South Asia, China, Northeast Asia, Southeast Asia, Oceania, the Indian Ocean, Latin America, Africa, the Arctic, and Cyberspace. Other than Antarctica and the nonpolar regions of Canada, that pretty much covers the planet. It is a pretty expansive definition of national security, one that requires a heavy monetary commitment to back it up.

The QDR's definition of vital interests also implies that the United States will be in a condition of war, cold war, or near war in perpetuity. This state of affairs has already had profound effects on politics, behavioral patterns (as anyone who has passed through an airport in the last dozen years will have discovered), and even psychology. Just as a state of perpetual war has lodged the Teutonic-sounding and creepy term "homeland security" in the national vocabulary, so has our military virtually ceased to consist of citizen-soldiers in popular speech.

Traditional slang terms for a soldier—GI, dogface, ground-pounder, grunt—used to be humorous and mildly self-deprecating designations connoting a citizen who happened to be in uniform performing an onerous task. Now the preferred term is "warrior," a term not often heard before in American history in reference to our soldiers. In tribal societies, warriors are members of a caste, like priests and aristocrats, and the term does not seem fitting in a constitutional republic. I am still unsure whether "warrior" is a popular coinage that emerged on its own or whether Pentagon public relations operatives inserted it into the national demotic speech by means of constant repetition. But it is one small semantic clue as to how our governing classes define national security and the citizen's role in it. The all-volunteer force has evolved from GIs into warriors.

Courtiers in Uniform

Parallel to the transformation of the citizen-soldier to a professional warrior, there has been an alarming evolution among senior officers. The military writer Thomas Ricks recently devoted a book to the thesis that the U.S. military's general officer class has become distinguished by its mediocrity.[11] To get ahead, one must go along and get along, and the officer evaluation system rewards play-it-safe behavior and avoidance of mistakes rather than creativity and risk taking. This syndrome has fostered a culture of conformity that serves to weed out unconventional problem solvers. Unlike during World War II, when the Army's chief of staff, General George C. Marshall, routinely sacked generals who failed to perform, the tradition during the last fifty years, beginning with General William C. Westmoreland in Vietnam, has been to "stay the course" with the same failed plans implemented by the same commanders.

The postretirement careers of the senior officer corps also encourage a don't-rock-the-boat attitude. According to Bloomberg News, "The top 10 U.S. defense contractors have 30 retired senior officers or former national security officials serving on their boards. Press releases issued by those companies since 2008 announced the hiring of almost two dozen prominent flag officers or senior officials as high-ranking executives." The article also states that senior executives at the largest U.S. defense contractors are paid from $1 million to $11 million a year. Could this explain the enthusiasm in the general officer ranks for overpriced weapon systems?

To what Ricks has written, I would add that that our dysfunctional politics have exacerbated the military's inability to reform its personnel system. The knee-jerk reflex to "support the troops" in any and all circumstances tacitly means "support the generals." While civilian administration officials testifying before congressmen of the opposite party can usually be assured a rough time, congressional interrogators always want to make sure that their patriotism and love of the military are on public display, so they make an exception when questioning uniformed officials. Generals who appear as witnesses get markedly politer treatment, and the incisiveness of the questioning declines in proportion.

I was struck by how senior senators like Lindsey Graham, John McCain, or Joseph Lieberman fawned over General David Petraeus like fans of a pop star. Their technique of questioning the general did not always increase the sum total of knowledge about military problems in the Middle East. These generals, in turn, do the American people a disservice when they routinely sloganeer about how the U.S. military is the finest fighting force in history: its record since Korea has been decidedly mixed.

That said, one should not blame the generals overmuch, and the troops not at all—to a considerable extent, they and the institution they represent have been betrayed by a civilian leadership that has frequently used the armed forces as a first, rather than last, resort, and in circumstances of dubious national interest. There are certainly exceptions to Ricks's critique: the most sensible statements by a senior official at the onset of the Ukraine crisis came from General Martin Dempsey, the chairman of the Joint Chiefs of Staff. His noninflammatory comments were a refreshing change from the usual calls to escalate the situation, and Dempsey emphasized that he kept in daily contact with his Russian counterpart: a wise move when two nuclear powers are at loggerheads.

Weapon Systems as Wedgwood China

During the early 1990s, the president and CEO of Lockheed Martin, Norman Augustine, joked that combat systems were becoming so expensive that eventually the U.S. military would have only one supremely expensive, supremely capable airplane that the separate services would take turns sharing. Augustine's jest about diminishing numbers of aircraft is becoming a reality, although many experts do not believe the newest generation of combat fighters is supremely capable. According to the International Institute for Strategic Studies, the combined U.S. Air Force, Navy, and Marine Corps tactical fighter strength of 5,783 in 1992, at the end of the cold war, dropped to 3,985 in 2000, and continued to fall to 3,542 in 2008, despite many years of record budgets. The Congressional Budget Office projects combined inventories could fall to around 2,500 after the year 2020, despite the services' having mortgaged virtually their entire aviation budgets to buy the F-35.[12]

The planes such as the F-22 and the F-35 that are replacing the previous generation of aircraft are extravagantly expensive to purchase and require an exorbitant number of maintenance hours per flight hour; their stealth coating is so delicate that the military brass seems loath to risk them in conflicts. In addition, they gulp fuel at a rate that limits their tactical flexibility and stretches the availability of aerial refueling aircraft. The F-22, at a shocking total acquisition cost of $412 million per aircraft, was introduced into squadron service in 2007, but finally saw action against ISIS targets in Syria only in late 2014.

One would think an air-superiority fighter like the F-22 would have been ideal for enforcing the no-fly zone over Libya, but instead it was a no-show. Likewise, in 2014, when the Air Force deployed combat aircraft to Eastern Europe to deter the purportedly fearsome Russian bear, it sent the workhorse F-16, which had been in service for thirty-four years. The F-22 is like the good china that stays in the dining room buffet rather than running the risk of being chipped. As for the $135-million-a-copy F-35, the "cheap" fighter for our future inventory, two RAND Corporation analysts war-gamed its performance in a hypothetical matchup against Chinese fighter aircraft. The F-35s, overweight and ponderous because of their complexity, were bested by their adversary. RAND, dependent on government contracts, backed away from the study after being pressured.[13] The Pentagon has many such examples of gold-plated weapon systems that are too expensive to use in any but benign and controlled environments and with lavish support.

Contracting Out Morality

Much of that support will come from contractors at a premium price. In 1992, at the initiative of then–secretary of defense Dick Cheney, the military began contracting out many of its logistical and support functions. Cheney's scheme has succeeded so well that, in contradiction to Napoleon's dictum, today's Army cannot travel on its stomach. Having Halliburton or Sodexo as its caterer may have improved the taste of the food, but that arrangement wouldn't work if the military were ever again to get into a really desperate slugging match like the Battle of the Bulge. The Pentagon and the State Department have even contracted out combat to soldiers for hire. The lack of training, discipline, and accountability of mercenary organizations is notorious, as it became evident with Blackwater's shooting of seventeen innocent civilians in Nisour Square, Baghdad, in 2007.

While it was clear after the bloodletting that Blackwater's trigger-happy actions had further jeopardized the U.S. position in Iraq and made our soldiers' jobs even more difficult, the real story did not come out for another seven years. Even before the massacre, State Department investigators were probing the company's operation in Iraq, calling the firm's culture "an environment full of liability and negligence." But the probe ended when a top Blackwater manager threatened to kill a State Department investigator, saying that "no one could or would do anything about it as we were in Iraq."[14] The American embassy in Baghdad, which had been all but taken over by intelligence operatives and contract personnel of various kinds, sided with Blackwater against the State Department, its own nominal superior.

Contractors, the offspring of the Deep State, now have such impunity that they can threaten and intimidate their own paymaster, the very government that created them. And they get away with it! If a crude and gangsterish upstart like Blackwater is able to back down the senior cabinet agency in the government with criminal threats of violence, it does not require much imagination to theorize why the Justice Department felt unable to bring criminal indictments against the executives of a half-dozen megabanks whose assets make up more than 50 percent of the country's GDP. To sum up, there is literally nothing that the Deep State does not contract out to the corporations that provide campaign donations to the political figureheads nominally in charge of the whole enterprise: the Arlington, Virginia–based contracting firm CACI is facing a federal lawsuit for its alleged involvement in torture at Abu Ghraib prison. Privatization has been great for contractors, not so good for taxpayers or winning wars.

The Military-Industrial Complex: Seeing Crisis as Opportunity

The military-industrial complex is, alongside the financial industry, one of the largest and most powerful of the special interests that keep our politicians well provisioned with cash. The fact that national security spending reached a post–World War II high in 2008, precisely at the time when American living standards were under the severest stress since the Great Depression, is no coincidence.* Already during the early 1980s, economist Seymour Melman documented that high levels of military spending depressed overall economic productivity, and that heavy involvement of a specific industrial sector (such as the machine tool industry) in defense contracting rendered its commercial activities less competitive internationally.[15]

---

* Even after adjusting for inflation, the Pentagon spent more in the crash year of 2008 than during the peak of involvement in Korea and Vietnam. Both of those earlier conflicts were much larger wars than the current war on terrorism, and both wars occurred while the United States was simultaneously containing a peer competitor, the Soviet Union. Not only are we seeing unprecedented military spending, we are getting less for our money.

The "cost plus" mentality that inevitably arises from dependence on DOD contracts turns a business enterprise into a hothouse plant that cannot withstand the cold winds of the marketplace, where efficient production is imperative. Even defense industry executives have conceded the truth of Melman's thesis. In 1991, William Anders, CEO of General Dynamics, told a group of industry executives that "most weapons manufacturers don't bring a competitive advantage to non-defense business. . . . Frankly, sword makers don't make good and affordable plowshares."[16]

Former Pentagon insider Franklin C. "Chuck" Spinney has picked up where Melman left off, arguing that the mutually dependent interaction between contractors and the DOD has evolved into a system in which the primary objective is cash flow rather than military effectiveness. More ominously, he goes on to say, "Continuing small wars (or the threat thereof) are essential for the corporate component of the MICC [military-industrial-congressional complex]; these companies have no alternative means to survive."[17]

Perhaps that total dependence explains why in March 2014, during the week that the Russian government announced the annexation of Crimea, I learned that at a fund-raiser for Representative Mike Rogers (R-MI), the chairman of the House Intelligence Committee, the atmosphere among contractors in the room was "borderline euphoric." By coincidence (or not), the following Sunday, Congressman Rogers, appearing on *Meet the Press,* became one of the first major political figures to advocate arming Ukraine.

Six months after this incident, members of Congress had just returned from its August recess to confront the calamity over ISIS. A close friend who previously worked in Congress and at the Pentagon told me he was accosted at a fund-raiser he attended at that time by defense industry lobbyists urgently inquiring as to whether the new blowup in the Middle East would force Congress to exempt the DOD from the spending caps of the Budget Control Act. Following the old Chinese proverb, every crisis is a lucrative opportunity.

Fear Feeds the Beast

Nearly a decade and a half after the September 11, 2001, attacks, the Deep State's operatives continue to exploit them. On July 23, 2014, the members of the original 9/11 Commission released a review assessing the government's progress in implementing the findings of the panel's original 2004 report. The commissioners—permanent Washington fixtures like Lee Hamilton, Thomas Kean, and the other 9/11 panel members never really go away—predictably interviewed current and former high officials in the national security establishment, and just as predictably discovered from them that the government was doing a pretty darn good job in combating terrorism. "The government's record in counterterrorism is good," the report states, and "our capabilities are much improved." Is it time to breathe a sigh of relief? No, or this wouldn't be a Washington report.

Despite all this good work, the threat from terrorism is, in the words of one of those interviewed, FBI director James Comey, "an order of magnitude worse." A 2011 study by Brown University's Watson Institute for International and Public Affairs found that, counting all agency costs across the government, the war on terror cost up to that point about $4.4 trillion, and deficit financing costs for that expense could add another $1 trillion by the year 2020.[18] Is Comey suggesting we need to spend an order of magnitude more money than that to meet the threat? During my tenure in government, the solution to any agency's problem was always a bigger budget. The commissioners agreed with his hyperbole, writing darkly about the American public's ostrich-like ignorance: "On issue after issue ... public awareness lags behind official Washington's." To counter the "creeping tide of complacency" that has overcome the American people, the report, reading like a televangelist's sermon, urges the government to make clear "the evil that was stalking us."

While the report makes heavy weather of the breakdown of security in Iraq during 2014 as the Next Big Threat, it says not a word about how persons in our government, having used fear and exaggeration to exploit public emotions after 9/11 and hijack the war on terror by invading Iraq for the sake of their own agenda, created the very circumstances that led to that breakdown. Nor, when decrying the terrorist breeding ground of the Syrian civil war, do the commissioners acknowledge the decades-long role of U.S. allies like Saudi Arabia in fomenting and subsidizing jihadist movements.

Finally, the panel does not ask the most fundamental question: has America's distinctive style of fighting the war on terror, with its full-dress military invasions, drone strikes, secret prisons, torture, and special renditions, created more terrorists than it is capable of killing or incarcerating? As an inquiry into the complex subject of international terrorism, the 9/11 Commission's tenth-anniversary reprise was a slipshod farrago of circular argumentation, faulty reasoning, and naïve gullibility. But as an example of how the Deep State and its operatives exploit a witches' brew of fear, selective amnesia, and agency agenda setting to entrench the interests of both the governmental and corporate segments of the Deep State, the report was a standout.

6

ECONOMIC WARFARE: BIG BANKS AND THE NATIONAL SECURITY STATE

The blockade had become by that time a very perfect instrument. It had taken four years to create and was Whitehall's finest achievement; it had evoked the qualities of the English at their subtlest. Its authors had grown to love it for its own sake; it included some recent improvements which would be wasted if it came to an end; it was very complicated, and a vast organization had established a vested interest. The experts reported, therefore, that it was our one instrument for imposing our peace terms on Germany, and that once suspended it could hardly be re-imposed.

    —John Maynard Keynes, on the 1919 post-armistice economic blockade of Germany, in his book *Two Memoirs—Dr. Melchior: A Defeated Enemy; and My Early Beliefs*, 1949

"We have heard that a half million children have died. I mean, that's more children than died in Hiroshima. And, you know, is the price worth it?"

"I think this is a very hard choice, but the price—we think the price is worth it."

    —Leslie Stahl interviewing Secretary of State Madeleine Albright on the subject of economic sanctions on Iraq, *60 Minutes*, May 12, 1996

The Crony Capitalist Warfare State

When it was not unleashing the restless spirit of capitalism, the Reagan revolution called for an unprecedented peacetime military buildup. The genius of the architects of Reagan's policies was to recognize that the superficially disparate interests of Wall Street and the Pentagon could in fact be harmonized. For public relations purposes, the Reagan team claimed that the expensive military buildup and tax-cutting deregulation were both natural, patriotic impulses desired by the real America. The evident contradiction between a budget-busting military policy and the small-government, balanced-budget sloganeering of business conservatism could be smoothed over by constantly pounding on the theme that both were expressions of old-fashioned American freedom.

For the next thirty years, tax law, trade treaties, and national security policies were to be coordinated in such a way as to prioritize the varied needs of Wall Street and the military-industrial complex. With the collapse of the Soviet Union, the United States most likely did not need to maintain its military spending at a level greater than the next ten countries combined; but this hypertrophied military machine, together with a forward-deployment strategy that stationed U.S. troops in some 150 countries, became the ultimate backstop for what the Pentagon described as "maintaining global stability" and "shaping" the international environment. Ever since the dissolution of the Warsaw Pact, a series of Pentagon strategic reviews has emphasized the military's global role in a nebulous and coded fashion. During the days of U.S.-Soviet rivalry, the rationale for America's then-unprecedented global buildup was straightforward: to resist the advance of a purportedly monolithic and expansionist global communism. However much this was an oversimplification of the geopolitical situation, it was at least plausible in view of the Soviet Union's rough nuclear parity with the United States, its huge conventional military forces, and the existence of several Soviet client states.

Beginning in the early 1990s, our military strategy became more ambiguous, more oriented toward hazily defined global economic objectives, and ultimately much more ambitious than the cold war strategy. Early in the Clinton administration, defense committees on the Hill would frequently ask the chairman of the Joint Chiefs of Staff, Colin Powell, who the new enemy was supposed to be. "The enemy is instability," was his gnomic answer. This formulation met with very little controversy at the time because it was so vague, but it implied a vast expansion in the Pentagon's assignment of strategic threats. Subsequent strategy reviews have given more specificity to Powell's statement. In a strategy document released at the end of President George H. W. Bush's administration, the Pentagon declared that it was now fighting for an "open economic system"—that is, a global economic model suitable for U.S. investment and financial penetration.[1]

This policy was further refined in the 2002 edition of the *National Security Strategy of the United States of America:* "The great struggles of the twentieth century between liberty and totalitarianism ended with a decisive victory for the forces of freedom—a single sustainable model for national success: freedom, democracy, and free enterprise."[2] Apart from the uncomfortable fact that feudal monarchies like Saudi Arabia and dictatorships like Egypt were linchpins of the U.S. national security strategy, it appeared that evangelizing on behalf of a particular economic model had become a key component of America's national strategy. The military had become the coercive instrument of a U.S.-led global economic order whose aim is to maintain unfettered access to raw materials and buttress a favorable climate for U.S. investment.

The free enterprise system—or, more accurately, its doctrinaire neoliberal interpretation—is not just a throwaway talking point in a national security strategy document that no one bothers to read. The United States uses its military muscle to sustain its economic model and dissuade other countries from deviating from its orthodoxies. For decades, a popular criticism of U.S. foreign policy has been that it is all about oil. But oil is just one component (albeit a major one) of a larger objective: the maintenance of the U.S. dollar as the world reserve currency.

Dollar Recycling as National Security Strategy

The United States emerged from World War II with the world's largest economy and a powerhouse industrial base, so it is unsurprising that the dollar soon became a near-universal medium of international exchange. But why, in view of the last forty-five years of economic history, was it not displaced by a basket of leading currencies at the very least for international transactions like commodities purchases? Beginning in the mid-1960s, the United States experienced persistent and ever-worsening trade deficits, exacerbated by the heavy expenditures of the Vietnam War. Since the country was still on the gold exchange standard, it suffered a relentless "gold drain," which threatened the basis of the world system of fixed exchange rates.*

In 1971, President Nixon suddenly took the country off the gold exchange standard: the dollar became a fiat currency whose value could now float. In actual fact it sank: over the course of the 1970s the U.S. dollar steadily dropped in value relative to most major currencies like the Swiss franc, the yen, or the deutschmark. It did not seem promising over the long term as a global store of value, particularly after the "oil shock" of 1973 further added to the U.S. trade deficit.

Normally, under such circumstances, a country will attempt to increase its exports and improve its balance of trade if it wants to have a viable currency. This was not the U.S. strategy. The bankers and financial engineers who were beginning to displace industrialists at the helm of our economy didn't particularly care about exports; they focused instead on manipulating the value of the currency. If commodities, especially oil, were no longer priced in dollars, the American system could no longer crank out cash and maintain some semblance of stable exchange rates. In fact, the dollar could maintain its status as the world's reserve currency *only* if the countries we paid in dollars were obliged to find a use for them, such as buying commodities or engaging in the types of financial transactions that are officially denominated in dollars.

This peculiar loop explains why the United States has been able to run up large trade deficits year after year and still maintain the dollar as the world reserve currency. It also allows the government to operate a fis-

---

* President Roosevelt had prohibited private ownership of gold in 1933, but the United States still maintained a "gold exchange standard" until 1971: current account imbalances between the United States and other countries were settled in gold.

cal policy based on imprudent tax cuts and budget-busting military spending without having to worry about an eventual day of reckoning. Finally, it allows policy makers to neglect domestic manufacturing and ignore the consequent steady erosion of wages for hourly workers. After all, Americans can still maintain more or less the same level of personal consumption thanks to the availability of cheap imported products. The "Walmart effect," whereby employees are paid such low wages that they can only afford to shop at places like Walmart that stock cut-price imported goods, is one result.

As for exporting countries like China, the dollar recycling system gives them a strong incentive to run a trade surplus with the United States, so that they can accumulate the dollars they will need to pay their oil bills. Thus the whole international system of recycling overseas U.S. dollars has become a giant perpetual motion machine. But aside from creating huge domestic economic distortions, it is a precarious system and it will only work if all the major players are obliged to play the game.

America's Double Standard in Foreign Policy

This dollar recycling system is one reason why even if U.S. dependence on foreign oil continues to decline, the Deep State will feel compelled to maintain military forces ready to intervene in the Middle East. An interruption of supplies will not only cause industrial slowdowns in affected countries, it will render untenable the jerry-rigged financial system on which U.S. fiscal and monetary policy is dependent.

The George W. Bush administration trotted out all manner of excuses for its invasion of Iraq, but it was clearly mindful of the fact that Saddam Hussein's decision in 2000 to denominate the country's oil sales in euros rather than dollars could hardly set a good precedent.[3] Former treasury secretary Paul O'Neill revealed in his "as told to" memoir that finding a way to forcibly get rid of Saddam was Topic A at the Bush administration's very first National Security Council meeting, a mere ten days after Bush's inauguration.[4] That urgency may have been increased by the fact that the euro gained 17 percent in value against the dollar between 2000 and 2003, the year the United States invaded Iraq. Once Iraq was under U.S. control, the medium for oil sales switched back to the dollar.

Prior to the 2011 U.S.-backed intervention in Libya that toppled Muammar Gaddafi and killed him, the Libyan strongman had developed a plan to quit selling Libyan oil in U.S. dollars, demanding payment instead in dinars (a then-notional African regional currency based on gold). Gaddafi's regime, sitting on a mountain of gold, estimated at nearly 150 tons, was urging other African and Middle Eastern governments to follow his lead.[5] This scheme could not have made Gaddafi popular in Washington. His regime was one of the world's few governments with a 100 percent state-owned central bank unconnected to other major central banks. Curiously, the ragtag band of U.S-backed Libyan rebels created their own Western-style central bank and appointed its director months before they even formed a government, while the fighting was still continuing. In hindsight, the alleged humanitarian rationale for Gaddafi's overthrow has begun to look awfully thin, especially in light of the subsequent behavior of the thugs who replaced him.

So Gaddafi was brought down, but countries with the most appalling human rights records get a pass. Saudi Arabia, which still beheads people after kangaroo trials for adultery, apostasy, and sorcery, and whose subsidization of foreign jihadists has caused no end of lethal mischief, remains unmolested by any threat of sanctions from Washington.* In the days after 9/11, several dozen Saudis, including relatives of Osama bin Laden, were whisked out of this country on charter flights arranged by the U.S. government. They received FBI escorts, but the Bureau did not even interview them.[6] One reason why the 9/11 Commission's report reads like a cover-up disguised as an exposé may be that twenty-eight pages from the draft report about the Saudi relationship with al-Qaeda were excised on

---

* Beheadings have become such a growth industry in Saudi Arabia that in spring 2015 the kingdom began advertising for executioners.

order of the Bush administration. President Obama promised to declassify them, but so far he has not.[7]

Saudi Arabia's deep complicity in terrorism gets a "never mind" from the Deep State's leadership. The kingdom's role as a leading producer of fossil fuels is not the only thing that gives it immunity from official censure. It is worth considering what the kingdom does with all those dollars (estimated at $405 billion during 2014) that it accumulates from its oil sales.[8] Under the aegis of the United States–Saudi Arabian Joint Commission on Economic Cooperation, the kingdom dutifully recycles its huge petrodollar overhang back into U.S. investments, buys U.S. Treasuries, and stocks up every few years with multibillion-dollar weapons purchases. In short, the feudal tyrants of the Arabian Peninsula are one of the bevel gears that make the whole global money machine function.

In January 2015, we got a glimpse at just how important the U.S.-Saudi relationship was. That month, Obama could not be bothered to attend the mass gathering of international leaders in Paris in a rally for solidarity against terrorism—an assistant secretary was the highest-ranking American present. Yet two weeks later, when Saudi king Abdullah died, the president broke off an official visit to India, where he had lectured an audience on women's rights and religious tolerance, in order to make a beeline to Riyadh. Obama was hardly alone: his secretary of state, national security adviser, and CIA director joined him. Senator John McCain and House Minority Leader Nancy Pelosi, who hardly agree on anything, agreed this time that they had to go to Riyadh, and even former U.S. government officials like James Baker and Condoleezza Rice felt compelled to attend. This pilgrimage of American luminaries occurred just as the Saudis were sentencing Raif Badawi, a Saudi blogger, to ten years in prison and one thousand lashes for criticizing the regime. The reaction of the U.S. delegation, many of whom have long been sanctimonious champions of human rights, was muted to the point of dead silence.

The same indulgence applies to other Persian Gulf countries. Qatar has an abysmal human rights record: its *kafala* migrant worker system is comparable to slavery, and it has financed violent insurgent groups in

Syria, making a mockery of the U.S. government's alleged puzzlement at the explosive growth of ISIS. Yet Qatar is considered to be a member in good standing of the U.S.-dominated "international community"; its capital, Doha, has even been host to the most recent multiyear round of World Trade Organization negotiations on trade and tariffs.

For all of its indignant huffing and puffing about "violent Islamic extremism," it is our government's fatal dependence on the monarchies in the Arabian Peninsula for their role in keeping our currency system afloat that makes our leaders pull their punches whenever the subject of ISIS or other Sunni Muslim terrorist groups comes up.

War Is Good for Business

French economist Thomas Piketty's *Capital in the Twenty-first Century* posits that over time, individual wealth obtained from the growth of capital will outpace personal wealth gained from labor, except under unusual circumstances that reduce the accumulated capital of the wealthy. One of those circumstances is war. As he notes, none of the belligerent powers could have secured the financial resources necessary to fight World Wars I and II without extremely heavy taxes on the wealthy and on corporate profits. While Piketty concentrates on Europe, and particularly France, his observation that war is a destroyer of accumulated personal capital is largely true of America's experience in World Wars I and II. Income inequality in America dropped sharply during both world wars, not only as a result of income taxes and luxury taxes, but because the conscription of so many men into the armed forces placed a premium on scarce labor.

Piketty's finding holds less true when applied to the kinds of wars the United States has been fighting since 1945. Both the Korean and Vietnam wars saw some surtaxes and scattered labor shortages, but these were minor compared to the world wars, and the two conflicts did not see income distribution change appreciably. The Iraq war of 2003 was a milestone.

From an economic point of view, it was a major war: in inflation-adjusted dollars, it exceeded the costs of both Korea and Vietnam, and even World War I. Yet throughout the conflict, income inequality in the United States increased at an accelerating rate.

There are several reasons why the new American way of war does not conform to the experience of most industrial countries in the twentieth century. First, Iraq was the only large war in modern history fought by a major industrial power that was accompanied not by tax increases, but by a tax cut—not only on incomes, but also on capital. As a result, the war was conducted by deficit financing coupled with a low-interest-rate policy designed to reduce the interest costs of the ballooning debt. These fiscal and monetary policies eventually fed an asset bubble that allowed speculators to make billions on Wall Street even as the second-most-expensive war in American history was being fought. Second, the Pentagon's new wars were fought with a smaller, all-volunteer force that did not draw civilians out of the workforce in large numbers as in previous wars. (Iraq made no change whatever to American labor markets.) Finally, the war was privatized to an unprecedented degree. Almost all of the U.S. military's logistical tasks were undertaken by stock-issuing corporations like Halliburton. War, rather than destroying capital, would beget even more capital, at least for those at the top of the income pyramid. The trajectory for wage earners, meanwhile, has been more uneven.

The succession of major "free trade" deals has been highly favorable for Citigroup's position in Mexico, Goldman Sachs's ability to operate in Europe, and Apple's production platforms in China; but they look far less favorable from the point of view of an assembly-line worker in Detroit or Toledo. The stagnation of middle-class incomes (and thus their ability to pay commensurate taxes), the offshoring of American investments (putting them out of reach of the IRS), and the high cost of maintaining the security apparatus of the Deep State have together ensured an almost unbroken series of large federal deficits for three decades. But Wall Street, however phobic it claims to be about government deficits, rarely, if ever, calls for trimming military spending.* Instead, the cry is always for "entitlement reform": cutting the Social Security and medical benefits that a beleaguered middle class needs in order to maintain its footing at a time of skyrocketing home prices, medical costs, and school tuitions.

From Blockade to Sanctions: A Century of Economic Warfare

If it seems that America is always at war or on the verge of war, there is good reason. Since 1980, the United States has deployed military forces to roughly two dozen "hot" armed conflicts. The Congressional Research Service, using a more expansive definition of operational deployment to include rescues, evacuations of American citizens from war zones, and deterrence missions, counts dozens more instances.[9] As for CIA covert and paramilitary operations, they are a closely held secret and will continue to be until most of us are long dead.†

One might be tempted to imagine that the Department of Defense and the intelligence agencies charged with carrying out these overt and covert operations represent the sum total of America's political engagement with the outside world, since old-fashioned state-to-state diplomacy has receded into public relations symbolism. But the Deep State's commitment to international coercion is too ambitious to be limited to military action exclusively. While not as flashy as an F-22 flyby, or as ruthless as a drone kill, economic warfare has in many respects become Washing-

---

* The editorial page of the *Wall Street Journal,* the advocate of the investor class, has tirelessly campaigned since the 1970s for increases in military spending, even as it has championed cutting social safety net programs.

† During the early years of the Clinton administration, when the collapse of the Warsaw Pact temporarily led to a more relaxed security atmosphere, the White House ordered the declassification of old government documents to be stepped up. The action resulted in, among other things, the declassification of a 1917 document describing U.S. troop movements against the kaiser's Germany. But given the mania for increased classification since 9/11, declassifying information after a mere seventy-five years is no sure thing in the future.

ton's weapon of choice. Just as weapons and logistics contractors are a necessary component of military conflict, America's big banks are an indispensable partner in the U.S. government's economic conflicts around the world.

Economic sanctions go back historically to the naval blockade, in which a fleet would physically seal off the harbors of an opposing state and prevent it from trading with third parties. The blockade was an act of war and was governed by the laws of war at sea. Its most famous instance in the twentieth century was the British blockade of Germany during World War I. It caused real privation among civilians (including starvation and malnourishment of children), but did not prevent the Germans from launching a huge offensive during the last year of the war that almost drove the British army off the Continent. The blockade was continued for seven months after the armistice as a means of diplomatic coercion that would force Germany to sign a peace treaty on the terms demanded by the Allies. This "peacetime" blockade killed about 250,000 people, mostly from diseases caused by malnutrition. Thus was born a preferred instrument for conducting our modern wars.

Four of the most notable cases in the modern era of American sanctions policy are the imposition of economic sanctions on North Korea in 1950, the Cuban embargo in 1960, sanctions against Iran after the takeover of the U.S. embassy in Tehran in 1979, and Iraq beginning in 1990. None of these economic blockades, one of which is in its seventh decade, has had the desired effect of forcing the target state to align its policies with U.S. desires (the collapse of the apartheid regime in South Africa was a special case unlikely to be encountered elsewhere: the vast majority of South Africans were black and strongly supported economic measures against the white-controlled regime that ruled them). Sanctions policy has, however, been successful according to the standard Washington metric of foreign policy achievement: it projects an image that the president is "tough" and "doing something." In effect, sanctions take another country's civilian population hostage in order to get its leaders to acquiesce. Madeleine Albright perfectly expressed the Washington consensus when she told *60 Minutes* that, yes, the deaths of half a million Iraqi children were worth it in the complex calculus of sanctions.

With the fall of the Soviet Union and the corresponding decline in Washington's need to offer carrots rather than sticks to nonaligned countries with questionable political systems, economic sanctions became the go-to policy for dealing with countries that chose to flout the will of the Washington-run international community. It is no accident that at about the same time, the theory of rogue states became popular within the Beltway: it allowed us to suggest that some countries do not possess enough legitimacy to give them a legal and moral right to complain about economic coercion or military invasion. There are now twenty-six countries, from Russia and Burma to Zimbabwe, under various forms of U.S. economic sanctions.

After 9/11, sanctions took another turn. Since more and more terrorist groups were nonstate actors, economic sanctions against countries would not directly affect them. The Treasury's Office of Foreign Assets Control began devising new sanctions targeted against individual people and businesses. In addition, the Treasury and intelligence agencies gained more access to financial transactions around the world. The Society for Worldwide Interbank Financial Telecommunication (SWIFT), based in Brussels, is the global messaging service for thousands of banks all over the world: if a bank in the United States wants to send money to Italy or vice versa, SWIFT facilitates it. SWIFT's governing board consists of the world's biggest banks. The Treasury did not previously have access to the huge stream of financial data the system generates, but after the September 11 attacks, SWIFT acceded to U.S. demands and began providing information.[10]

The loosening of regulations on interstate banking in the United States and the repeal of the act prohibiting institutions from being both commercial and investment banks has had the fortuitous consequence of giving a few American megabanks, Citigroup and JPMorgan Chase among them, membership on the SWIFT board. In their current role, these banks are a critical point of entry for any international flow of money in violation of sanctions. The American banks do not touch those transactions, and will avoid doing business with foreign banks that do. This has the effect of cutting off those foreign banks from doing business in the United States, or even being able to clear dollar-denominated transactions in the New York market. At the same time, the Treasury has an easier management task in having to deal only with a handful of megabanks with worldwide reach. As journalist Andrew Cockburn, who has written extensively about the American sanctions regime, told me, getting the big American banks to enforce sanctions is "the key to the system." He believes that in view of the heavy legal penalties for violating sanctions, the banks "do it out of fear."[11]

That fear may be softened, however, by a degree of recognition on both parts that the banks are now an essential cog in Washington's economic warfare machinery. While some foreign institutions with banking operations in America like HSBC and BNP Paribas have been hit with billion-dollar fines for money laundering and sanctions evasion, the American-based megabanks have avoided this fate. Moreover, they have evaded criminal prosecution for recent questionable domestic activities like mortgage fraud, robosignings, and selling securities designed to fail, a far different outcome from the aftermath of the savings and loan crisis of the late 1980s, when numerous executives were convicted of crimes.

Economic sanctions are now an integral part of the Deep State's array of tools for coercing adversaries. But do they work? Sixty years of experience suggests that they do not. Sanctions on North Korea since the early 1950s have not prevented the ruling clique in that country from obtaining nuclear weapons and maintaining a huge military. Sanctions on Cuba were a colossal failure and only succeeded in impoverishing ordinary Cubans. Sanctions on Zimbabwe have not resulted in President Robert Mugabe's departure. President Putin seems singularly unimpressed by American-led Western sanctions against his country. Former Treasury official Juan Zarate has written in his book *Treasury's War* that the Iranian sanctions are effective, but more than thirty years of ever-tightening economic strictures have not made the Iranian government bow to the U.S. will, let alone succeeded in creating a popular Iranian movement to overthrow that government. Did the sanctions bring Iran to the table for nuclear talks? William Miller, a former foreign service officer and onetime diplomat in Iran, doesn't think so: "Sanctions only made them more defiant," and they have always had ways of evading them.[12] Zarate also wrote about the growing effectiveness of using American control of key nodes of the international banking system to cut off financing to terrorist organizations. His book was published in 2013, before the cancerous spread of ISIS, which is an extremely well funded terrorist organization. Apparently, our efforts to prevail upon our "friends" in the Arabian Peninsula to cease funding radical Sunni jihadists have been less than completely successful.

Given the growing list of countries that have had economic sanctions imposed on them—in 2015, when Venezuela was added to the list, White House spokesman Josh Earnest had a hard time keeping a straight face while insisting that the country was a "national security threat" to the United States—it was heartening to see some semblance of common sense in the improvement of our relations with Cuba. But why did it take such a ridiculously long time to lift our sanctions?

Other nations such as Canada long believed America's policy toward Cuba was idiotic as well as cruel, since it only hurt innocent citizens and made little impression on their leadership. Our Cuba policy was a fascinating variation on Gilens and Page's thesis that powerful interest-group goals almost always trump the desires of the broader public when it comes to getting the attention of Congress.

Gilens and Page were referring to moneyed, elite interest groups; the Cuba lobby certainly did not have the financial clout of Wall Street or Silicon Valley, but organized money counts for something, particularly when the opposing view is not nearly so well mobilized. The fact that the lobby was demographically concentrated in a key swing state, and possessed the obsessive single-mindedness of a terrier staring down a rat hole, gave it an outsized role in the formulation of America's policy toward the Caribbean. Since 1983, the United States broadcast radio and television programming to Cuba to foment discontent with the Castro regime. When the signals were not jammed, fewer than 2 percent of Cubans tuned in, according to a 2010 report by the Senate Foreign Relations Committee. But funding, at $27 million per year, still continued. Why? Because for over fifty years the lobby in favor of that policy could outmuscle those who thought it was a waste of money, and neither party wanted to lose Florida's twenty-nine electoral votes. None of this had anything to do with rational statecraft or advancing America's diplomatic, humanitarian, or commercial interests.

Obama's move in late 2014 to improve relations with Cuba was a policy conspicuous by virtue of its rarity. Predictably, he was lambasted by Senator Marco Rubio, the self-appointed champion of a maximalist line against Cuba, but he also came in for heavy editorial criticism from the *Washington Post,* the bulletin board of Beltway interests, according to the curious rationale that fifty years of sanctions were not enough time for them to work.[13] The president was able to lift a portion of the Cuban economic sanctions by executive order, but removing the rest will require congressional action that is by no means guaranteed. Some observers believed that the March 2015 imposition of sanctions against Venezuela was linked to the thaw in U.S.-Cuban relations, and that America needed another enemy to avert a deficit of bogeymen and placate South Florida's political concerns.[14]

And so Washington's sanctions policy grinds on. Cockburn sees a parallel between America's use of sanctions and our country's longtime love affair with the military doctrine of precision bombing, which began with the strategic bombing campaigns of World War II, became more firmly embedded in our thinking during the Vietnam War, and has now (post-Bosnia and -Iraq) been technologically refreshed by resort to cruise missiles and drones. Both sanctions and bombing give the illusion of precision, calibration, and the capacity to ratchet up coercion in a gradual escalation. And both have the capacity to cause tremendous suffering among innocent third parties while having far less strategic effect than their advocates claim. "Sanctions are economic drone warfare," Cockburn says.

Economics, as we have seen, is one of the principal weapons in America's arsenal for waging virtual wars abroad, despite its dismal record. Meanwhile, the three-decades-long war at home—the class war—has also been waged with economic weapons. It has been much more successful.

7

THE COMMANDING
HEIGHTS

People of the same trade seldom meet together, even for merriment
and diversion, but the conversation ends in a conspiracy against the
public, or in some contrivance to raise prices.
　　—Adam Smith, *The Wealth of Nations*

This is an impressive crowd, the haves and the have-mores. Some
people call you the elite. I call you my base.
　　—George W. Bush at the Al Smith Memorial Dinner in New York,
　　October 19, 2000

Have the Superrich Seceded from America?

At some point in 1993 during congressional debate over the North American Free Trade Agreement, I had a memorable lunch in the cafeteria of
the Longworth House Office Building with a staffer for one of the rare
Republicans who opposed the policy of so-called free trade. To this day I
remember something she said because it was the first time I'd heard someone identify a growing trend that most people as yet had not given much
thought to: "The elites of this country have far more in common with their
rich friends in London, Paris, and Tokyo," she said, "than with their fellow
American citizens." This was only the beginning of the period when the
consequences of outsourced manufacturing, a financialized economy,
and growing income disparity seeped into the public consciousness, so at
the time it seemed like a striking statement.

　　My dawning recognition of the real significance of free trade coincided with the end of the cold war. At that time several writers predicted

the decline of the traditional nation-state. Some looked at the demise of the Soviet Union and foresaw that other states would break up into state-lets of different ethnic, religious, or economic compositions. This has happened in the Balkans, Czechoslovakia, and Sudan, and appears to be happening in Iraq and the Congo, but remarkably few state boundaries have been redrawn in the last twenty-five years. Others predicted a weak-ening of the state due to the rise of irregular armies and the inability of national armies to adapt to the new threat. The trajectories of Iraq and Afghanistan, Yemen, Somalia, and even Pakistan lend credence to that theory. There have been numerous books about globalization and how it would eliminate borders, but I am unaware of a well-developed theory from that time suggesting that the superrich and the corporations they ran would effectively secede from public life even as they tightened their control over the government of their respective nation-states.*

By secession, I do not mean physical withdrawal from the territory of the state, although that does happen from time to time. Erik Prince, who was born into a fortune, is related by marriage to the even bigger Amway fortune, and made yet another fortune as CEO of the mercenary-for-hire firm Blackwater, moved to the United Arab Emirates in 2011; and some Republicans, who are so quick to say "America, love it or leave it," showed a remarkable sense of latitude when Eduardo Saverin, a Facebook co-founder, renounced his citizenship. When Democrats introduced a bill to make expatriate tax dodgers pay a 30 percent tax rate on all future U.S. investments and ban them from the country, Republican operative Gro-ver Norquist likened the bill to the actions of Nazi Germany against Jews.[1]

These examples apart, what I mean by secession is a withdrawal into enclaves, an internal immigration whereby the rich disconnect them-

---

* Possibly the only writing that approached such a theory was a novel: *Snow Crash*, written by Neal Stephenson in 1992, which foresaw a future United States in which the federal government had ceded most powers to private corporations and high-tech entrepreneurs. Stephenson was genuinely inspired and frightfully accurate when he predicted that mercenary armies would be competing for defense contracts.

selves from the civic life of the nation and from concern about its well-being. Our plutocracy, whether the hedge fund managers in Greenwich, Connecticut, or the Internet moguls in Palo Alto, now lives like the British did in colonial India: ruling the place but not of it. If one can afford private security, public safety is of no concern; to the person fortunate enough to own a Gulfstream jet, crumbling bridges cause less apprehension, and viable public transportation doesn't even compute. With private doctors on call and a chartered plane to get to the Mayo Clinic, why worry about Medicare?

Being in the country but not of it is what gives many contemporary American superrich their quality of cluelessness. Perhaps this helps explain why, during the 2012 presidential campaign, Mitt Romney's regular-guy anecdotes always seemed a bit strained, even if he did follow his handlers' advice and wear jeans and an open collar on the hustings. His idea of connecting with the common man was to say that his wife drove "a couple of Cadillacs."

I once discussed this syndrome with a radio host who recounted a story about Robert Rubin, the former treasury secretary. He recalled that Rubin was being chauffeured through Manhattan to reach some event whose attendees consisted of the Great and the Good such as himself. Along the way his limousine encountered a traffic jam, and on arriving late to the event, he complained to a city functionary with the power to look into it. "Where was the jam?" asked the functionary. Rubin, who had lived most of his life in Manhattan, a place predominantly of east-west numbered streets and north-south avenues, couldn't tell him.

To some degree the rich have always secluded themselves from the gaze of the common herd; their habit for centuries has been to send their offspring to private schools, but lately this custom has been exacerbated by the plutocracy's animosity toward public education and public educators.[2] Public education reform is popular among right-wing billionaires such as the DeVos family, the Waltons, Netflix CEO Reed Hastings, and their tax-exempt foundations like the American Federation for Children, many of which hope to divert some of the more than one-half trillion dollars in annual federal, state, and local education funding into private hands. What Halliburton did for U.S. Army logistics, school privatizers may end up doing for public education. A century ago, at least we got some attractive public libraries out of Andrew Carnegie, but the spirit of noblesse oblige is sorely lacking among most of our new plutocrats.

If You're Not Rich, It's Your Fault

In both world wars, even a Harvard man or a New York socialite might know the weight of an army pack. Now the military is for suckers from the laboring classes whose subprime mortgages you just sliced into collateralized debt obligations and sold to gullible investors in order to buy your second Bentley or rustle up the cash to employ Rod Stewart to perform at your birthday party. The sentiment among the superrich toward the rest of America is often one of contempt. To quote Bernard Marcus, cofounder of Home Depot, "Who gives a crap about some imbecile?"[3] One recovering former hedge fund trader acknowledged the syndrome: in his last year on Wall Street he made a bonus of $3.6 million and was angry that he hadn't made more until he slowly began to recognize that he and many of his colleagues were suffering from a money addiction that had warped their moral judgment.[4]

Stephen Schwarzman, the billionaire CEO of the Blackstone Group who famously threw himself a $5 million birthday party, believes it is the riffraff that is socially irresponsible. Speaking about low-income citizens who pay no income tax, he says: "You have to have skin in the game. I'm not saying how much people should do. But we should all be part of the system."[5] And yet this often-voiced view ignores the fact that millions of Americans who do not pay federal income taxes *do* pay federal payroll taxes. These taxes are regressive, and the dirty little secret is that over the last several decades they have made up a greater and greater share of federal revenues. In 1950, payroll and other federal retirement contributions constituted 10.9 percent of all federal revenues; by 2007, the last "normal" economic year before federal revenues began falling, they made up

33.9 percent. By contrast, corporate income taxes, which were 26.4 percent of federal revenues in 1950, had fallen to 14.4 percent by 2007, and since then they have fallen further, to barely 10 percent.[6] Who has skin in the game now?

Trends in personal income show the same picture. As University of California economics professor Emmanuel Saez has demonstrated, from 2002 until the last precrash year of 2007, 60 percent of all income growth went to the wealthiest 1 percent of Americans. Since the recovery began in 2009, that figure increased to 95 percent.[7] As stark as those statistics sound, even that level of income inequality may be understated, as some of the richest Americans keep a portion of their assets in foreign tax havens. Gabriel Zucman, an assistant professor of economics at the London School of Economics and a visiting scholar at the University of California, believes that government statistics understate the large amount of offshore wealth belonging to U.S. citizens, which he pegs at roughly $1.2 trillion.[8]

The Historical Roots of Wealth Worship

That wealth worship and a consequent special status for the wealthy should have arisen in the United States is unsurprising in view of the peculiar sort of Protestantism transplanted here from the British Isles: a Christianity that regarded wealth in a different way from older Christian traditions. Starting with the Puritanism of New England, there has been a long and intimate connection between the sanctification of wealth and America's political structure.

A crucial political debate of the young republic was what to do about the rising financial power in the country. Andrew Jackson defined the populist nature of his presidency by his relentless opposition to the wealthy elites who controlled the Second Bank of the United States. But in the long run Jackson's efforts did not succeed. At the beginning of the Civil War, financier Jay Cooke wangled the franchise to sell war bonds for the U.S. Treasury and made a fortune on the commissions, vindicating Cicero's quip that the sinews of war are infinite money.

Wall Street's first period of real ascendancy began just after the Civil War. Most present-day Americans, if they think about the historical roots of our wealth worship at all, will say something about free markets, rugged individualism, and the Horatio Alger myth—a literary construct of the post–Civil War era. But perhaps the most notable nineteenth-century exponent of wealth as virtue and poverty as the mark of Cain was Russell Herman Conwell, a canny Baptist minister, founder of the first tabernacle large enough that it could be called a megachurch, and author of the immensely famous "acres of diamonds" speech of 1890 that would make him a rich man. This is what he said:

> I say that you ought to get rich, and it is your duty to get rich. . . . The men who get rich may be the most honest men you find in the community. Let me say here clearly . . . ninety-eight out of one hundred of the rich men of America are honest. That is why they are rich. That is why they are trusted with money. . . . I sympathize with the poor, but the number of poor who are to be sympathized with is very small. To sympathize with a man whom God has punished for his sins . . . is to do wrong . . . let us remember there is not a poor person in the United States who was not made poor by his own shortcomings.[9]

Spoken like a real Fox News commentator! Evidently, Conwell knew better than to engage in the sob-sister moralizing that we read in the Sermon on the Mount. Somewhat discordantly, he had been drummed out of the military during the Civil War for deserting his post: for Conwell, just as for the modern tax-avoiding expat billionaire, the dollar sign tended to trump Old Glory. Back then our great-grandparents referred to Wall Street as "the money power" or "the money trust." Successive panics, as financial crashes were then called, occurred in 1873, 1884, 1893, and 1907. They always led to mass unemployment and bankrupted farmers, but somehow, the bankers on Wall Street dusted themselves off each time and soon began engineering the next financial time bomb.

The money power's influence on government policy began to be felt internationally just before the beginning of the twentieth century. Grover Cleveland's 1895 "Venezuela message" served notice that henceforth, the United States would invoke the Monroe Doctrine to keep the European great powers out of the Western Hemisphere—meaning that Latin America was to become America's playground for lucrative investment. The United States abandoned its traditional policy of isolationism and nonintervention and embarked on a string of military interventions in Latin America: the Spanish-American War (1898), the forcible separation of Panama from Columbia (1903), the occupation of Nicaragua (1912–1933), intervention in Mexico (1914–1917), and the occupations of Haiti (1915–1934) and of the Dominican Republic (1916–1924). In every case, banks and the protection of U.S. private investments were at the heart of the decisions to act. As General Smedley Butler, a participant in many of these interventions and two-time winner of the Congressional Medal of Honor, later admitted, he was protecting big business interests, not the U.S. national interest:

> I spent 33 years and four months in active military service and during that period I spent most of my time as a high class muscle man for Big Business, for Wall Street and the bankers. In short, I was a racketeer, a gangster for capitalism. I helped make Mexico and especially Tampico safe for American oil interests in 1914. I helped make Haiti and Cuba a decent place for the National City Bank boys to collect revenues in. I helped in the raping of half a dozen Central American republics for the benefit of Wall Street. I helped purify Nicaragua for the International Banking House of Brown Brothers in 1902–1912. I brought light to the Dominican Republic for the American sugar interests in 1916. I helped make Honduras right for the American fruit companies in 1903. In China in 1927 I helped see to it that Standard Oil went on its way unmolested. Looking back on it, I might have given Al Capone a few hints. The best he could do was to operate his racket in three districts. I operated on three continents.[10]

At the beginning of World War I, Woodrow Wilson adopted a policy of neutrality, but it was not to last. Several factors impelled the United States into the war in 1917, but the fact that the Morgan Bank, which was then the most powerful financial institution in the country, participated in underwriting three-quarters of the external financing of the Allies had something to do with Wilson's decision to save the world for democracy. Once it had extended the loans, Morgan had a compelling interest in seeking an Allied victory: defeat and potential occupation of France by Germany would have meant the repudiation of those loans. At the end of the conflict, Thomas W. Lamont, a Morgan partner and private citizen, accompanied Wilson to Versailles, where he (rather than a government official such as the secretary of the treasury) represented the U.S. position in negotiations over German reparations. During the 1920s, Lamont described himself as "something like a missionary" for Italian Fascism and expressed his admiration for Benito Mussolini, "a very upstanding chap."[11] Later, in the mid-1930s, a congressional investigating committee chaired by Senator Gerald Nye (R-ND) found that bankers, along with the munitions industry, had pressured Wilson to intervene in the war.

The identification of Wall Street's interests with the national interest reached an apotheosis of sorts in the 1920s, when, as Calvin Coolidge said, "The business of America is business," the stock market reached unheard-of heights, and the fabulously wealthy financier Andrew W. Mellon became secretary of the treasury so that he could rewrite the nation's tax laws to the benefit of himself and his friends. This was also a time when the pseudoreligious wealth gospel was at its most popular. The long American tradition of conjoining wealth, Christian morality, and the American way of life reached a crescendo in Bruce Barton's 1925 book *The Man Nobody Knows*. The son of a Congregationalist minister, Barton, an advertising executive, depicted Jesus as a successful salesman, publicist, and the very role model of the modern businessman.

The Crash of 1929 and the New Deal

This peculiarly American creed took a severe hit after the Crash of 1929, when wealth ceased to be equated with godliness. While the number of Wall Street suicides has been exaggerated in national memory, Jesse Livermore, perhaps the most famous of the Wall Street speculators, shot himself, and so did several others of his profession. There existed then a lingering old-fashioned sense of shame now generally absent. While many of the elites hated Franklin Roosevelt—in a famous *New Yorker* cartoon of the era, a rich socialite tells her companions, "Come along. We're going to the Trans-Lux to hiss Roosevelt"—most had the wit to make a calculated bet that they would have to give a little of their wealth, power, and prestige to retain the rest. Even a bootlegging brigand like Joe Kennedy reconciled himself to the New Deal and became FDR's man on the Securities and Exchange Commission to police Wall Street. (The president must have been operating on the theory that it takes a thief to catch one.)

The New Deal was the first comprehensive attempt to tame Wall Street in the nation's history. The Banking Act, the Glass-Steagall Act, and the establishment of new regulatory agencies such as the Securities and Exchange Commission, the Federal Energy Regulatory Commission, and the National Labor Relations Board were just some of the measures designed to claw back Wall Street's power that went into effect. While the titans of Wall Street may have grumbled about Roosevelt's "socialist experimentation," most were chastened by a popular mood that was borderline revolutionary. There was a real question as to the survivability of democratic institutions. Communism and fascism were then viable alternatives—even in capitalist America. Besides, anything was better than the horrible period between November 1932 and March 1933, the interregnum between Presidents Hoover and Roosevelt, when the circulation of cash nearly ceased in some areas of the country. Dangerous as the New Deal was to the entrenched interests, at least it offered lucrative construction contracts for work on projects like the Tennessee Valley Authority and the Grand Coulee Dam.

For the next several decades, until the 1970s, Wall Street became the servant of the American economy rather than its master. While fortunes could still be made on the Street, the restless animal spirits of capitalism were contained by a skein of laws and regulations. The share of national wealth possessed by the superelite—the top one-tenth of the wealthiest 1 percent—fell steadily until the post–World War II years, leveled off, and did not rise significantly until 1978. Those decades also saw some of the most impressive economic growth rates in our history and the making of the American middle class.

Fabulous fortunes were made in World War II (we need only think of Henry J. Kaiser, the shipbuilding king who turned out Liberty ships like sausages), but they were subject to a windfall profits tax. Tycoons like Kaiser constructed ships, planes, and the critical infrastructure, such as the "Big Inch" oil pipeline and the Alaska Highway, that were necessary to win the war (and incidentally put in place the infrastructure required for the postwar boom), rather than concocting synthetic CDOs and other fantastic instruments of the type that precipitated our latest economic collapse.

During the 1950s, many Republicans pressed President Eisenhower to lower the prevailing 91 percent top marginal income tax rate, but, citing his concerns about the deficit, he refused. In view of our present $17 trillion gross federal debt, perhaps Ike was right. Characteristic of the era was the widely misquoted and misunderstood statement of General Motors CEO and later secretary of defense Charles E. "Engine Charlie" Wilson that "what was good for the country was good for General Motors, and vice versa." He was expressing, however clumsily, the view that the fates of corporations and citizens were conjoined. His view was a world away from the present regime of downsizing, offshoring, and profits without production. The now-prevailing economic dogma first evangelized by Milton Friedman, an acolyte of Friedrich Hayek, holds that a corporation that acts responsibly toward the community in which it does its business is shirking its only duty: to maximize its short-term stock val-

uation.* Yet during the 1950s the country managed to achieve higher average GDP growth rates than Americans have experienced in the last
dozen years.

Back to the Gilded Age

The median level of inflation-adjusted household income peaked in the
United States in 1973. Around the time that the Powell Memo called on
big business to liberate itself from the suffocating embrace of government, an extraordinary ferment of pro–Wall Street pamphleteering com-
menced: from Louis Rukeyser at the popular level to George Gilder's
ideological tracts to Friedman and his colleagues in the Chicago school of
economics, the propagandists of neoliberal ideology skillfully advocated
free markets, which is to say, fewer restraints on Wall Street and privatization of key government activities. Across-the-board deregulation, ten-
tatively nurtured under Carter, would become one of the two core beliefs
of the Reagan revolution (the other was its faith in a large military buildup,
and the deficit be damned).

By the first decade of the twenty-first century, the Gilded Age had
returned. As in the days of John D. Rockefeller, Sr., legislatures could be
bought, even our national legislature. Only it was now camouflaged as
campaign contributions, rather than arriving in black bags full of cash.
On those occasions when money wasn't quite enough, and things had to
move fast, Wall Street and its emissaries could rely, just like the
military-industrial complex, on a healthy dose of fear.

During the late afternoon of September 18, 2008, the Senate had

---

* Friedman became the Lenin to Friedrich Hayek's Marx in making his chosen ideology more extreme. Like Hayek, he was a fan of the Chilean dictator Augusto Pinochet. Friedman once declared that pure food and drug laws were cumbersome and
unnecessary since producers out of their own enlightened self-interest would ensure
that their products were safe. One wonders whether Friedman was really that naïve,
or whether there was some calculated bad faith involved.

wrapped up its work for the week. It was a Thursday, so senators were "smell-ing the jet fumes," as the saying goes. They were eager to leave the Capitol complex and fly back to their home states (much of the time, Friday's sched-ule in the Senate consists of a pro forma session with only a handful of mem-bers in attendance). But on this Thursday evening, the secretary of the treasury, Henry (Hank) Paulson, asked the congressional leadership and senior figures on the key committees of both houses for an emergency meeting in the Speaker's office with him and Federal Reserve Board chair-man Ben Bernanke. Although there had been bad economic news all spring and summer, apparently it hadn't registered with some in Congress.

In the hastily called meeting, Paulson and Bernanke depicted a finan-cial system on the verge of collapse, predicting 25 percent unemployment if something wasn't done immediately. I was detained on Capitol Hill that evening, and although I was not in the room, and participants were not supposed to talk about specifics, the Hill's grapevine telegraph instantly transmitted the gist. I sensed a crisis atmosphere, much as there had been after the news of the airliners striking the World Trade Center and the Pentagon.

When Paulson said that he needed action immediately, he didn't mean after hearings and committee reporting of legislation. Bernanke suppos-edly said, "If we don't do this tomorrow, we won't have an economy on Monday." What "this" turned out to be was a Treasury draft of legislation that arrived at the Hill the next day. Congress was supposed to pass it at once and without amendment. It was barely three pages long, and it was the greatest grant of power to the executive that I had ever seen: $700 billion—the largest single-purpose request for money in history up to that time—would be handed to the Treasury Department with no strings attached to bail out the banks as Paulson saw fit (Paulson's subor-dinate Neel Kashkari was to be the administrator of the money; he later told an economist friend of mine that the $700 billion figure was "a num-ber plucked out of the air").[12]

Congress actually took a bit more time than the executive branch de-manded. The bill, officially named the Emergency Economic Stabilization Act, but often called the TARP bill, for the Troubled Asset Relief Program that it authorized, was not enacted until October 3, after the House had rejected the bill on a previous vote. Congress put in some safeguards, like an inspector general to oversee the disbursements, as well as a few other window-dressing items, but Paulson and company got pretty much what they wanted. There had been rumblings from consumer groups and some Democrats that the bailout plan should help keep mortgage holders in their homes, that courts should be given the power to write down mortgages, and that the bill should set compensation limits on executives of the bailed-out banks, but all those proposals somehow fell by the wayside.* It is remarkable what you can get out of a legislature when you cultivate an atmosphere of panic.

"We Didn't Want to Do It, but We Had To"

Retrospectively, proponents have justified the bailout as preventing another Great Depression. That debatable counterfactual is the leitmotif of Bernanke's memoirs, and of Timothy Geithner, Paulson's successor as treasury secretary, as well as Paulson himself. They and other Washington operators insisted that as personally distasteful as overseeing the bailout supposedly was to them, it was imperative to save the financial sector in order to rescue the broader economy: in short, saving Wall Street saved Main Street. Besides, the bailed-out banks repaid the money with interest, so what was the problem?

First, the interest on TARP loans to the banks was far below prevailing market interest rates, giving the banks a subsidy. Second, in the initial round of TARP payouts, the Treasury paid $254 billion for bank assets worth only $176 billion, giving the banks a $78 billion taxpayer-funded windfall.[13] Third, bailing out Wall Street did not bail out Main Street: the

---

* Only *after* the bailout was the full extent known of many of these banks' mortgage fraud, deliberate promotion of financial instruments intended to fail, and robosignings of counterfeit foreclosure documents.

banks not only took money from the Treasury, they also borrowed billions at a near-zero interest rate from the Federal Reserve System. But these funds did not translate into consumer or business loans as intended. Instead, the banks used the money to buy higher-yield foreign financial instruments and pocketed the arbitrage. In addition, an obscure provision in the bailout bill authorized the Fed, contrary to all sound banking practices, to pay banks a higher interest rate on deposits from banks than the banks had to pay to get loans from the Fed: banks could then borrow money from the Fed and turn right around and park their excess reserves back at the Fed. Instead of stimulating the economy, the money became a risk-free arbitrage mechanism for our biggest banks.

Finally, credit ratings agencies from then on have priced in the likelihood that the bailed-out institutions would always get rescued in the future; that assumption means those banks have a built-in competitive advantage over smaller banks and are able to borrow funds at lower cost. What TARP and the other bailout programs accomplished, then, was to recapitalize the banks, further concentrate them (the five largest American banks had assets equal to 43 percent of U.S. gross domestic product before the crash; by 2012 they made up 56 percent), and send them mostly unreformed on their merry way to the next asset bubble.[14]

Why this entire process was preferable to operating the failing big banks that had commercial depositors under the conservatorship of the Federal Deposit Insurance Corporation so as to protect those depositors, and concentrating Treasury and Federal Reserve resources directly on boosting consumer demand, illuminates how Wall Street has captured and assimilated the decision-making process at the upper levels of government. There is no question that the economy was in a grave state in September 2008, but Paulson's comments were still hyperbolic and, by panicking investors, likely helped create a self-fulfilling prophecy.

It is not clear to me whether the 778-point drop in the Dow Jones Industrial Average after the House's initial rejection of the TARP package was a rational market response or whether the groundwork for a panic sell-off had not already been laid by Paulson's pronouncement that the sky would fall if the bill were not passed. The treasury secretary's handling of the crisis appeared intended to foreclose options other than those he wanted. Seeing bank CEOs among the ranks of the unemployed was apparently such an intolerable outcome that it was necessary to use fear of an economic Armageddon to stampede Congress into approving a virtual no-strings-attached package.

Proponents of the bailout attribute the recovery from the 2008 crash to Paulson's, Bernanke's, and Geithner's actions. But an examination of income and wealth statistics shows that the recovery, if that's the name it merits, was different from that of the recovery from the Great Depression in one key respect. After the earlier crash, inequality of wealth was narrowed for the next forty years. But TARP, the Fed's lending programs, and the other measures that supposedly saved us from an economic abyss set the stage for a rapid wealth rebuilding by those at the top income levels, while people in the bottom 90 percent have seen their personal holdings stagnate or decline.

Although I had worked on the House Budget Committee since 1995 and the Senate Budget Committee since 2005, the financial crisis of September 2008 was my first full immersion into the world of Wall Street. My usual portfolio had been national defense, but from September 18, 2008, onward it was "all hands on deck" for anyone with a pulse to gather information and try to make sense of the catastrophe. To be sure, some people on the Hill stood around numbly, watching the stock ticker on CNBC as their 401(k) accounts melted down like a snow cone in a blast furnace. But the whole affair seemed oddly familiar to me. Although the financial jargon, such as TARP, TALF, and repo, was new, the modus operandi of those in charge bore an eerie resemblance to national security crises of times past. There is a striking similarity between Wall Street and "War Street," the national security state, when they really need to get things done in a hurry.

Bernanke's prediction of Armageddon if Congress did not give him and Paulson immediate carte blanche bears comparison with statements by national security officials in the aftermath of the September 11, 2001, terrorist attacks. In order for policy makers to accomplish their goals, the initial targets in both cases were American public opinion and the legislators who represented them. In the wake of 9/11, the national security state did its best to instill in the public the fear that a stateless group of terrorist criminals represented an existential threat to the United States, and that they were in league with a foreign government whose leader conveniently happened to be the hereditary enemy of the Bush clan.

When fear is great enough, it justifies preemptive measures against anyone claimed to be a threat, even when the evidence of their wrongdoing is thin. Bush's national security adviser, Condoleezza Rice, insisted: "The problem here is that there will always be some uncertainty about how quickly Saddam can acquire nuclear weapons. But we don't want the smoking gun to be a mushroom cloud." In both cases, rather than letting Congress fully deliberate the issues and examine alternative courses of action, the executive branch presented Congress with blank-check draft legislation and a deadline to pass it. The House and Senate did make a few changes to the draft bills, but the Deep State achieved what it wanted in both cases: the big banks got recapitalized amid a horrible financial crisis without having to fundamentally restructure, just as the military-industrial complex got the war it was hankering for.

Virtually all of the grotesque features of Wall Street that contributed to the 2008 crash—too big to fail, overcompensated executives responsible to nobody, exotic financial instruments designed to implode, impunity from criminal prosecution—remain to this day, sometimes in disguised form.* Other than increasing capital requirements for banks,

---

* Collateralized debt obligations, or CDOs, were a weapon of mass financial destruction that helped blow up the residential mortgage market in 2008. Since then, financial engineers have launched a strikingly similar instrument, the collateralized loan obligation, or CLO. With Wall Street having already wrecked the housing market and thrown millions of properties into foreclosure, private equity groups are now snapping up those houses and renting them. The rental streams are then bundled into financial instruments and sold in an unregulated market—paralleling the financial industry's behavior with CDOs a few years before, merely substituting rents for mortgage payments.

Obama and his economic team have done little with the 2010 Dodd-Frank financial reform bill to remedy the defects of Wall Street's turbocharged financial operations.

Ever since the first ziggurats rose in ancient Babylonia, the so-called forces of order, stability, and tradition have feared a revolt from below. Beginning with Edmund Burke and Joseph de Maistre after the French Revolution, a whole library of political literature, some classical liberal, some conservative, some reactionary, has emphasized this theme. The title of Ortega y Gasset's most famous work, *The Revolt of the Masses,* tells us something about its mental atmosphere, a Freudian fear of defilement by the great unwashed.

But in our globalized postmodern America, what if this whole vision of order, stability, and who threatens those values is inverted? The idea of a revolution from below, still conceivable in 1933, is almost preposterously unthinkable now. What if Christopher Lasch came closer to the truth in his book *The Revolt of the Elites,* in which he said, "In our time, the chief threat seems to come from those at the top of the social hierarchy, not the masses." Lasch held that the elites, by which he meant not just the superwealthy but also their managerial coat holders and professional apologists, were undermining the country's promise as a constitutional republic with their prehensile greed, their asocial cultural values, and their absence of civic responsibility. Lasch wrote this in 1995. Now, two decades later, the superrich have at last achieved escape velocity from the gravitational pull of the society they control. They have been able to do this in part because laws were bent or reinterpreted in their favor.

8

THE DEEP STATE, THE LAW, AND THE CONSTITUTION

The abuse of buying and selling votes crept in and money began to play an important part in determining elections. Later on, this process of corruption spread in the law courts and to the army, and finally, when even the sword became enslaved by the power of gold, the republic was subjected to the rule of emperors.
—Plutarch, *Gaius Marcius (Coriolanus)* 14.2

There is something wrong in this country; the judicial nets are so adjusted as to catch the minnows and let the whales slip through.
—Eugene V. Debs, speaking at Terre Haute, Indiana, November 23, 1895

Equal Justice Under Law?

The motto inscribed on the frieze of the United States Supreme Court Building says, "Equal Justice Under Law." A stickler for semantics would say that the modifiers "equal" and "under law" are redundant, since justice by definition is equal treatment under a system of written and publicly accessible rules. It is a noble sentiment in any case. The United States has undeniably made progress in fulfilling that ideal with respect to racial and gender equality over the course of the past century, but the rise of institutions with the power to seize government at its source and operate it for their own benefit is raising questions as to whether the United States is gradually slipping back into a condition that would have been recognizable in antiquity, when the Greek historian Thucydides remarked, "The strong do what they will, the weak suffer what they must."

The financial meltdown of September 2008 has provided plenty of raw material for the belief that there is one law for the rich and another for the common clay. Practical as opposed to explicit inequality before the law is common in societies all over the world; it usually boils down to how legal procedures are applied as opposed to the letter of the law. Officials who pledged to uphold the law will always protest that they are neutral and unimpeachable executors of justice, and that it is insulting to suggest otherwise. But sometimes the truth slips out.

On March 6, 2013, testifying before the Senate Judiciary Committee about the state of banks in the aftermath of the financial crisis, Attorney General Eric Holder stated the following: "I am concerned that the size of some of these institutions becomes so large that it does become difficult for us to prosecute them when we are hit with indications that if you do prosecute, if you do bring a criminal charge, it will have a negative impact on the national economy, perhaps even the world economy." When banks hold a gun to the head of the economy, the relationship between regulator and regulated becomes a hostage relationship, made more complex in this instance by the fact that the hostage taker indirectly has political influence over the regulator by means of campaign contributions.

Holder made this statement shortly after his agency concluded a settlement with HSBC: the bank would pay $1.9 billion in fines and restitution for laundering $850 million in funds used by narcoterrorists. The penalty sounds huge, but it is almost derisory in view of the bank's $21.9 billion in global profits in the year the settlement was reached.[1] The key fact is that no senior executive was prosecuted for money laundering, a serious crime. If anyone was going to suffer from the small subtraction from the bank's revenues, it would be shareholders and depositors who had nothing to do with the crime, rather than the managers who committed it. HSBC's executives purchased a get-out-of-jail-free card with their shareholders' money. And so we see another baleful example of what the doctrine of corporate personhood means in practice: blame is shifted to a conveniently nonliving entity while the executives who break the law continue in their jobs unpunished.

Despite Holder's contention that criminal prosecution could have negative consequences for the economy, what would actually happen if a bank's management committed a crime and the government prosecuted them? At its most extreme, Federal regulators could seize the bank and operate it as a conservator in the same way that the FDIC has done in hundreds of instances over many decades. Innocent stakeholders, whether low-level employees, shareholders, or depositors, would be protected. Holder's fearmongering about the risk of endangering the world economy has no basis. He seems not to have considered that *not* prosecuting financial institutions might have the more negative consequence of inviting banks to factor in fines as a cost of doing business as they continued the same reckless (or illegal) practices. He also ignored the corrosive effect that "too big to jail" has on the public's faith in the law.*

It is easy to conclude that it is not the size, complexity, or fragility of the financial system that stays the hand of criminal prosecution, but rather the status of those who committed the wrongdoing. Apparently, robbing a bank is only a criminal activity depending on which side of the teller's window you stand, and whether you are upper management or a $12-an-hour cashier. Congress appears not to be overly concerned by the impunity of Wall Street executives. Shortly after Holder's astonishing admission, the Senate Banking Committee favorably recommended Mary Jo White, who spent years as a corporate lawyer defending Wall Street interests, to the full Senate for confirmation as chairman of the Securities and Exchange Commission. She was duly confirmed. Republicans, who often obstruct nominees purely out of habit, did not raise a peep.

---

* On leaving the government in 2015, Holder returned to a lucrative position at Covington and Burling, a law firm whose clients have included Bank of America, JPMorgan Chase, Citigroup, and Wells Fargo. The law firm also represented MERS Corp, the electronic mortgage registry responsible for many falsely registered mortgage documents discovered after the 2008 financial crash. These clients were among the institutions Holder said he was reluctant to prosecute because of their alleged systemic importance.

White, like Holder, is not a fan of prosecuting the executives of big banks, as her confirmation testimony made clear. Since her confirmation, she has relentlessly fought against provisions in the Dodd-Frank financial reform legislation that would permit the Federal Reserve to subject asset management funds (for instance, mutual funds) to more stringent standards, such as higher capital requirements, standards that banks must adhere to. This would be prudent policy, as asset management firms collectively hold $53 trillion in funds, and if the 2008 meltdown taught us anything, it is that no segment of the financial services industry is immune from a panic-induced run. But White not only does not see a problem, she publicly lobbied against the measure at a forum sponsored by the financial services industry.[2]

Justice for the Rest of Us

Perhaps the big shots really are above the law. This does not mean, however, that the mighty wheel of justice does not turn in this country. Somebody must be getting prosecuted, given that the United States has more people in prison than any other country, including China, which has four times our population. Our incarceration rate is no accident: we have embraced a vast number of harsh punishments for essentially victimless crimes like drug possession, and "three strikes" provisions in many states virtually guarantee the highest rate of imprisonment since the days of Stalin's gulags. Thousands of juveniles—legally, they are children—are locked up every year for minor nonviolent "status offenses" such as school truancy or curfew violation.[3]

As ever in world history, increasingly unequal justice has been accompanied by an increasing militarization of the legal system. According to *The Economist,* SWAT teams were used about 3,000 times in 1980 but are now used around 50,000 times a year: "Baltimore and Dallas have used them to break up poker games. In 2010, New Haven, Connecticut, sent a SWAT team to a bar suspected of serving underage drinkers."[4] Now that the military's withdrawals from Iraq and Afghanistan have left the Department of Defense with excess equipment, much of it is going to domestic police forces. Local constabularies across the country have obtained more than four hundred of the army's surplus MRAP (Mine Resistant Ambush Protected) vehicles, a fourteen-ton behemoth that is ludicrously impractical for typical police work and hideously expensive to operate, but whose appearance intimidates "civilians," as police officers are now wont to call their fellow citizens.* Police in thirty-eight states have obtained military surplus firearm silencers, which have no tactical use except for conducting covert assassinations.[5] It makes you wonder just what the cops have in mind for us. It is not surprising that 2015 saw an outbreak of urban protest against harsh, militarized policing. Meanwhile, America waits in vain for the criminal prosecution (let alone SWAT-style bust) of the perpetrators of liar loans, investments deliberately designed to fail, and other swindles.

State legislatures have kept pace with Congress in creating unequal justice. One might think that the exposure of unsanitary conditions and animal cruelty in the corporate farming and food-processing industries would provoke lawmakers to punish the perpetrators and tighten laws protecting the safety of our food supply. But no, in several states they have instead directed their fury against the citizen-activists who exposed the wrongdoing by levying heavy penalties against the surreptitious photographing of inhumane outrages.[6] Republican legislators in North Carolina introduced a bill to make it a felony to disclose the chemicals (some of which are toxic to humans and animals) employed in fracking for natural gas. The bill also authorized drilling companies to oblige emergency responders cleaning up chemical spills to sign a confidentiality agreement

---

* Police in one Indianapolis suburb said they required an MRAP against a potential attack by berserker military veterans returning from the wars. This is an example of the Deep State creating a negative feedback loop: it must now up-arm police against military veterans it had trained and sent on multiple deployments into wars of choice. Pentagon insiders of my acquaintance refer to this behavioral pattern as a "self-licking ice cream cone": a business model that perpetuates and amplifies the very problem it purports to solve—one that is, needless to say, very lucrative for contractors.

promising not to disclose the names of the chemicals in their proprietary stew to the public—or their toxicity. So it is that even duly authorized state authorities may soon be unable to carry out their public health and safety duties if it inconveniences corporations.[7]

This bifurcation of law, with a few flamboyant transgressors virtually immune while the many are subject to the full force of the law, has been accompanied by some of the severest criminal sentencing guidelines in the developed world. With draconian prison terms looming over defendants, it is no wonder that most criminal processes end in plea bargains rather than jury trials: even an accused person believing himself innocent may plead guilty to lesser charges (charges that will still land him in prison, albeit for a shorter term) rather than face bankrupting legal fees or risk the possibility that an incompetent appointed counsel will secure him a sentence lasting decades. Human Rights Watch believes that the American justice system has practically abolished the constitutional right to trial for poorer defendants charged with certain crimes.[8]

Even the constitutional right to counsel (competent or not) is not always provided, as Holder admitted in a speech he gave in 2013.[9] The big banks, with their extensive in-house legal departments and reserves of cash, have no such concerns. Their attorneys are skillful enough, and have sufficient resources, to file change-of-venue motions so as to escape the wrath of unfriendly judges or demagogic district attorneys itching for higher office and lusting for juries to inflame.

As a practical matter, ordinary citizens have no such recourse. The expense of purchasing adequate representation is only part of the problem. Local police departments have been aggressively applying civil asset forfeiture laws in order to deprive citizens of their property without any legal proceeding or presentation of evidence whatsoever. According to a *Washington Post* investigative series, police have seized $2.5 billion from citizens in tens of thousands of such actions since 2001. Many of these are no better than armed shakedowns of innocent motorists amounting to third-world–style police banditry, with corrupt law enforcement agencies pocketing the loot just as they would in Mexico or Guatemala.[10]

Some officials concede that it is inadvisable to lock up more and more people, perhaps less out of ethical concern than worry about the financial drain from incarcerating so many live bodies that have to be fed (mass incarceration is even a minor political theme these days, with officials as diverse as Barack Obama and Rand Paul having broached the subject). Traditionally a function of the state, prisons represent a large input of taxpayer dollars whose only output, other than license plates, is a social sense of safety and security, an intangible value. But corporate America has come up with an answer to that as well: the private prison industry. The growing private prison lobby can offer a much more tangible benefit to politicians than the promise of security: campaign donations. We can be sure that lobbyists and consultants will invent more and more ingenious felony statutes for state legislatures to pass into law so as to keep their prisons full and profits flowing, as we have already seen happen in Arizona, where lobbyists induced lawmakers to take up a bill to vastly expand the grounds for incarcerating undocumented persons.[11]

Justice for the Unpersons

Thus far we have dealt with the law: hatched with malign intent, corruptly enforced, and unequally applied, perhaps, but a law that can be found in the United States Code or the state statutes. But justice for foreigners and those American citizens who have been declared outlaws enters the realm of the Wild West, where there is neither law nor redress. International treaties such as the Geneva Convention or treaties against torture are assumed to be null and void for the purposes of U.S. government conduct.

Should a group like Amnesty International wish to argue on behalf of an injured party before a United States court and to take up a case involving unjust incarceration and torture, the plaintiff will be deemed to lack standing to sue because he is not the injured party. Should the injured party himself seek redress, he will be told that he lacks standing because of his status as an "illegal enemy combatant." Should all else fail and the court wish to avail itself of some other excuse not to hear the case, it can always turn to the state secrets privilege, a made-up doctrine derived from a case in which the executive branch committed perjury.

Let me explain. The Supreme Court first formulated the state secrets privilege in its 1953 ruling for *United States v. Reynolds*. When three civilian engineers died in an Air Force B-29 crash, their widows sought the accident reports and claimed damages for wrongful death. The government refused to hand them over, claiming that the mission was national security–related and that to do so would reveal secrets that could harm national security. The Supreme Court, which took the government at its word, dismissed the plaintiffs' claim. The justices explained their rationale with Catch-22 logic: "The court itself must determine whether the circumstances are appropriate for the claim of privilege, and yet do so without forcing a disclosure of the very thing the privilege is designed to protect."[12]

Fifty years after the ruling, a daughter of one of the men killed in crash, Judy Loether, discovered on the Internet that the government had declassified the accident report, without ever informing her. She bought a copy and discovered that no classified matter had been mentioned in the report. It was all a ruse to shield the aircraft maker from charges of defective manufacture.[13] And so the precedent was deliberately deceptive, but the judicial automatons of the federal bench have pretended for the past sixty years that despite the government's having brazenly lied about the existence of classified information, this case should establish the precedent that, thenceforth and forever, all government assertions about classified information must be taken as true, definitive, and legally binding.

One suspects a similar morass of dishonesty lies behind the Obama administration's drone policy. In deciding to use drones to carry out assassinations, did President Obama or his predecessor go to the trouble of revoking Executive Order 11905, Executive Order 12036, or Executive Order 12333, all three of which prohibit assassinations? Or were these merely reinterpreted to mean that a ban on assassination means "not unless you really want to"? Unquestionably the latter, as someone deemed it useful to keep the old executive orders on the books as sacred artifacts one could point to as examples of our virtue—much in the way the Roman curia, ever rife with corruption and intrigue, can in a pinch pull out a handful of holy relics to pacify the querulous.

The administration has done its best to keep the specifics under wraps, maintaining a close hold on all documents while leaking a white paper that supposedly summarizes its policy.[14] Here one gets a sense of ad hoc improvisation: since then–deputy national security adviser John Brennan and other administration officials had already publicly stated that drone strikes were used only to disrupt "imminent" attacks, the white paper appears to have been engineered after the fact to prevent the administration from being constrained by Brennan's words. "Imminent" is gradually redefined over the course of several paragraphs so that it no longer means a criminal action is nigh, but rather inheres in the status of the targeted individual. Thus are certain people beneath the law: their status assumes their intended action, so they are fair game regardless of their actual conduct.

The white paper qualifies this startling legal theory (superficially similar to the German army's Commissar Order of 1941 that legalized the shooting on sight of Soviet commissars) by helpfully stating that such operations would not be conducted if civilian casualties would be "excessive." One supposes the definition of the term "excessive" is as elastic as that which constitutes an "imminent" threat. Unofficial estimates suggest civilian casualties in the thousands, including several hundred children.[15] The tragic deaths of two Western hostages of the Taliban in a drone strike in January 2015 were a vivid reminder that the targeting is hardly as painstaking or precise as our government claims.

One is tempted to conclude that there really is no administration-level drone policy, let alone one constrained by law, only a sham policy cobbled together after the fact in order to construct a plausible justification whenever complaints arise. At the operational level, drone targeting is constrained neither by the military code nor the laws of war nor by any other applicable treaty. It is just an intelligence-driven data set applied to a checklist: does target X-ray fit "terrorist signatures" alpha, bravo, charlie, and delta? If the boxes can be checked, the government operative (or contractor) hits the switch. Everything is legal by definition and the only consideration is the status of the person on the receiving end, those around him be damned.

The Supreme Court as Corporate Enabler

The United States Supreme Court, the tribunal of last resort, has shown a similar drift toward results-oriented legal interpretation. The Supreme Court's 2014 decision in *McCutcheon v. Federal Election Commission* sparked considerable outcry, as did *Citizens United,* the court's infamous 2010 decision on federal campaign financing. But the *McCutcheon* case was not strictly about setting aggregate limits on individual campaign donations to candidates in federal elections, as is widely perceived. The case was really about what constitutes a bribe, how big that bribe can be, and whether an electoral system can be corrupt even in the absence of a legally demonstrable cash payment to an officeholder or candidate for an explicit favor.

Above all, the case was about the prerogative of the rich to control the political process of the country. The Roberts court, or rather five of its nine members, adopted the misanthrope's faux-naïve pose in ruling that private money, far from promoting corruption in politics, actually causes democracy to thrive. The basic argument, boiled down, is that money being speech, the more speech (meaning money), the freer the politics. And so the court decided to strike down a law that put a limit on total donations by individuals in any one election cycle. Anatole France mocked this kind of legal casuistry by saying, "The law, in its majestic equality, forbids the rich as well as the poor to sleep under bridges, to beg in the streets, and to steal bread." And now you, according to the Supreme Court, as an American citizen, have just as much right to be influential in politics as billionaire David Koch.

After the *McCutcheon* ruling, James Fallows wrote in *The Atlantic* that during Chief Justice John Roberts's 2005 confirmation hearing, the nominee described his own judicial approach as "Humility. Modesty. Restraint. Deference to precedent. 'We're just calling balls and strikes.' "[16] Fallows went on to suggest that Roberts was being cynical, adopting that pose to get through the hearing. Now, while I believe it is true that our chief justice is a cynical man, I don't think the term "cynicism" quite captures the key quality that drives him to decide legal cases as he does. Nor is it cynicism alone that differentiates him from his jurisprudential fellow travelers Scalia, Thomas, Alito, and Kennedy.

There is unquestionably a bit of theater on the court: Scalia plays the opinionated blowhard at your local saloon; Thomas the complete cipher; Alito the pinched professional Catholic who could have come straight from the Roman curia; Kennedy, the guy who purports to be a swing vote when his mind is already made up. As chief justice of the Supreme Court of the United States, Roberts can't very well clown around in the manner of Scalia, who sometimes acts like Bill O'Reilly in a judicial robe. But for all their theatrical differences, the five conservative justices' bedrock beliefs seem to be as similar to one another as the creepy alien children of *Village of the Damned*. Roberts is different insofar as he is the more strategic front man.*

Let us consider his unexpected decision in 2012 on the Affordable Care Act (ACA). Business interests were roughly divided on the law—some disliked its mandates and thought certain provisions might drive up their costs, while others saw its potential to let them dump insured employees into pools, or to benefit from tax subsidies. Pharmaceutical and health insurance industries may have seen it as a license to print money. The ACA was a costly and convoluted way to insure more people, but Republicans saw only one thing: it was Obama's initiative, so it must be opposed. Roberts saw it as a political squabble in which there was no uni-

---

* The chief justice, and only he, is empowered to appoint judges to the Foreign Intelligence Surveillance Court. That power makes him ex officio a significant operative of the Deep State and invests him with gravitas. As such he cannot behave like a rancorous partisan, a clown, or a mental vacuum.

fied business position. It was even a law with a Republican pedigree—the Heritage Foundation had proposed something like it more than a decade before,[17] and Mitt Romney had signed a bill into law in Massachusetts in 2006 that was nearly identical to the ACA. If a Republican were president, he might have proposed a similar bill; after all, the president who had nominated Roberts engineered the costly Medicare Prescription Drug Act.

Roberts perceived a deeper dynamic beneath the ideological posturing. Overturning the entire law in one decision would cause millions to question the court's legitimacy. Roberts threw a valuable bone to the Republicans by vitiating the Medicaid mandate to the states, making it harder to implement the law and permitting Republican governors and legislatures to work all manner of mischief, but he let the bulk of the law stand. Likewise, he led the majority in upholding the constitutionality of federal health exchanges in the 2015 *King v. Burwell* case. Roberts was not about to damage the financial interests of insurers and hospitals for the sake of a patently desperate lawsuit by right-wing dead-enders, regardless of the comical heaving and sputtering by the ideologically driven Scalia.

McCutcheon was a more relevant fight, and here we see Roberts the avatar of corporations rather than Roberts the tactician. *McCutcheon* and *Citizens United* were not cases about campaign finance laws nor were they, despite the artful smokescreen, about free speech or whether money constitutes speech. They were really about upholding the superior political privileges and political access of rich interests in society. It is worth emphasizing that point: Immediately after the June 2014 ruling in *Sibelius v. Hobby Lobby,* the vast majority of press commentary saw the verdict as a distillation of the religious and cultural wars that have raged in this country for decades, with the five Catholic justices for the majority essentially ruling as factotums of the Vatican. Scalia and Alito may have seen themselves as such, but the deeper principle that united the Court's majority, as it has in dozens of cases involving corporations (in a way that they were not united on some other religious-cultural issues such as gay marriage), was the belief that when the perceived interests of business clash with those of individual employees, business prerogatives must prevail.

We now have an algorithm with which we can crack the code of the Supreme Court. Once five members of the Court accepted the nineteenth-century concept of "freedom of contract" (which stipulates that an employee must put up with whatever conditions his employer chooses to impose, or leave), they had the power to rewrite laws governing employment. This simple fact explains hundreds of cases before the Court and clarifies seeming anomalies like the ACA. It explains the Court's position in *Vance v. Ball State,* which made it more difficult to sue employers for harassment, and *Ledbetter v. Goodyear Tire & Rubber Co.,* which barred any remedy for pay discrimination (Congress in this instance subsequently saw fit to redress the self-evident bias of the Court's decision). In *Wal-Mart v. Dukes,* the Court rejected a class-action suit by women employees who had been denied raises and promotions. The Roberts court also took the side of corporations against consumers in *Mutual Pharmaceutical Co. v. Bartlett* and *AT&T Mobility v. Concepcion.* And it declared unconstitutional a 1988 law that subjected corporate officers to fraud charges if they could be shown to have deprived clients of honest services.

As Oliver Wendell Holmes suggested in his dissenting opinion on the 1905 *Lochner* case that established the concept of freedom of contract from which so many subsequent probusiness decisions have flowed, the court's majority based its decision on economic ideology rather than a plausible interpretation of the Constitution. Roberts is wise enough to know this, and to conceal his hand with strategic references to the free speech or the free exercise clauses in the First Amendment, but a careful study of his decisions reveals a more insidious rationale.

Laissez-Faire Economics Disguised as Legal Theory

The justices who currently make up the majority on the Supreme Court are not anomalies. In the last thirty years, conservative justices have become a kind of standard assembly with interchangeable parts churned out by the conveyor belt of American law schools. The University of Chicago school of economics, which gave birth to the modern American version of economic neoliberalism, also fostered the so-called law and economics movement of the 1970s, which, with the assistance of endowments from corporations and wealthy individuals, conquered the nation's law schools. The reigning philosopher king of this movement is Richard Posner, a judge at the United States Court of Appeals, a senior lecturer at the University of Chicago's School of Law, and by some accounts the most cited legal scholar of the twentieth century.

While Posner adopts a progressive stance on social issues, on the bottom-line matters of economics he shares with contemporary Republicans a rigid belief in laissez-faire. Posner uses a reductionist approach in order to define questions of justice involving economic matters as questions of efficiency rather than tort or equity, and applies a specious market valuation to issues that have traditionally been considered moral or ethical problems. Thus, if your house is worth $300,000 and you like it fine and don't want to leave, beware of the developer who can match that price and use campaign contributions to persuade a city council to declare eminent domain on your residence! According to the law and economics movement, the land on which your house sits will always find a higher and better use in the hands of someone with more money, so don't complain when the sheriff arrives with an eviction notice. Thanks in part to Posner and his fellow legal theorists, jurists and regulators have interpreted antitrust statutes virtually out of existence: if business efficiency is the overriding consideration, big companies are by definition more efficient than smaller ones, and the matter is settled. Nonquantifiable values such as the public good scarcely enter into the equation.

A friend once complained to me about a basketball game in which the referee consistently called fouls on one team when none existed and failed to call fouls on the other team when it repeatedly committed them. I asked him if he thought the referee had taken a cash bribe. "Of course not," was his answer, "he was just openly biased." But is that not also corruption? Sometimes judges can be tainted by dogma, bias, or a priori reasoning even in the absence of what Justice Roberts himself narrowly defined as quid pro quo corruption. The high court reminds us of journalist Humbert Wolfe's doggerel about the alleged incorruptibility of the British press:

> You cannot hope
> to bribe or twist,
> thank God! the
> British journalist.
> But, seeing what
> the man will do
> unbribed, there's
> no occasion to.

Congress's Subservience to Corporations

Once the law was seized at its source, it did not take much to permeate the institutions of government, whose major players have largely become subservient to corporate needs. I saw this submissiveness on several occasions. One memorable incident was the passage of the Foreign Intelligence Surveillance Act Amendments of 2008, a piece of legislation that retroactively legalized the Bush administration's illegal and unconstitutional surveillance (first revealed by the *New York Times* in 2005) and indemnified the telecommunications companies for their cooperation. The bill passed easily: all that was required was the invocation of the word "terrorism," and most members of Congress responded both to the siren call of "national security" and to the prospect of donations from the telecommunications companies.[18]

One such was Senator Barack Obama, soon to be coronated at the Democratic National Convention in Denver. He had already won the most delegates in the primary races while campaigning to the left of his main opponent, Hillary Clinton, by pointing out the excesses of the war on terrorism and denouncing the erosion of constitutional liberties. Months earlier he had even supported a filibuster against any bill that would bestow retroactive immunity on the telecoms.[19] What happened? Had Obama "grown" and become a more "thoughtful" or "serious" person—to use the language of the Beltway for anyone aspiring to conventional wisdom—or had the dawning prospect of the presidency forced him to reconsider his position in an effort not to offend powerful constituencies in a position to aid or hinder his campaign?

Obama's political conversion is a microcosm of the evolution of Congress as a whole since the Vietnam War. There was a time when Congress used to engage in serious debate and occasionally take tough stands opposing the alleged imperatives of national security. Over the last three decades, however, and particularly since 9/11, it has increasingly abdicated its powers and transferred them to the executive branch. This development makes a depressing study for anyone who takes seriously the checks and balances that the Founders designed into the U.S. constitutional system.

In 1970, both houses of Congress agreed to the Cooper-Church Amendment, which stipulated that the administration could not spend funds for soldiers, combat assistance, advisers, or bombing operations in Cambodia. In June 1973, Congress passed an amendment to prohibit the use of additional funds in Southeast Asia after August 15 of that year. Most significant of all, Congress then passed the War Powers Resolution over President Nixon's veto. The legislation imposed restrictions on the executive branch to ensure that the president would have to consult with the House and Senate before sending troops into conflict or potential conflict for extended periods.

In the post-9/11 period, by contrast, Congress has never mustered the collective will to cut off funds or force troop withdrawals, no matter how forlorn the situation. Even *after* the final withdrawal of troops from Iraq at the end of 2011 (an action taken entirely at the initiative of the president and according to his own timetable), Congress could not summon the nerve to agree to an amendment to repeal the original authorization for use of force in Iraq. The chairman of the Senate Armed Services Committee, Carl Levin (D-MI), said it was a bad idea because the amendment would (as he expressed it in the wearisome legislative cliché) "tie the hands of the president." Although Levin's bromide is now conventional wisdom, it is at variance with the view of President James Madison, the principal author of the separation of powers doctrine: "The power to declare war, including the power of judging the causes of war, is *fully* and *exclusively* vested in the legislature . . . the executive has no right, in any case, to decide the question, whether there is or is not cause for declaring war."

Congress has disempowered itself of its legislative authority and allowed a serious debasement in the tenor and decorum of its operations. I listened carefully to the debate preceding the authorization for use of force in the Persian Gulf War in 1991, and it struck me as substantive and thoughtful, accommodating a wide range of views. The same debate a dozen years later, prior to the invasion of Iraq, was the perfunctory overture to a legislative rubber stamp. Congress cannot even exercise its fundamental oversight functions anymore. The October 1982 Beirut, Lebanon, barracks bombing, which killed 241 U.S. military personnel, resulted in a thorough and mostly apolitical investigation of the serious deficiencies in the military's chain of command, rules of engagement, and medical evacuation practices—all of which were addressed. The 2012 attack on the U.S. consulate in Benghazi, Libya, by contrast, led to talking points, campaign ads, and elected officials making jackasses of themselves.

Politics Starts at the Water's Edge: Foreign Policy as a Political Football

Congress has in truth ceded the field in national security policy; only a few members remain who even recognize that other countries might have a perception of their own vital interests, and that taking these into account, along with history, geography, and trade issues, ought to inform congressional policy positions, rather than simply bowing to homegrown lobbies with vested interests. Most members in any case, preoccupied as they are with polarized domestic issues, have little interest in national se-

curity matters beyond local pork projects if they happen to have a military
or contractor presence in their districts. Beyond that, national security
policy is hardly more than a stick with which to beat the other political
party as the occasion arises. Most members of Congress do not really like
having to go on record with a clear yes or no vote on a critical matter of
foreign policy. In a rare outburst of candor, one member, Jack Kingston, a
Georgia Republican, gave an accurate assessment of the prevailing attitude when asked whether Congress would seek a timely debate on the
authorization of military action against ISIS:

> A lot of people would like to stay on the sideline and say, "Just
> bomb the place and tell us about it later." It's an election year. A lot
> of Democrats don't know how it would play in their party, and Re-
> publicans don't want to change anything. We like the path we're on
> now. We can denounce it if it goes bad, and praise it if it goes well
> and ask what took him so long.[20]

Kingston's unusual frankness may be explained by the fact that he
had lost his primary election and would not be returning to Congress. As
it turned out, Congress postponed a full debate on the military authorization until after the November 2014 midterm election: in their deathly
fear of being held accountable to voters, members preferred to wait several months until a lame-duck session for their voices to be heard on a
supposedly crucial matter of national security (as it turned out, even the
lame-duck session came and went with no congressional action).

The Republican Party is slightly ahead of Democrats when it comes
to devaluing any traditional understanding of foreign and national security policy. This is not surprising, because in all other matters of public
policy, the GOP has strictly subordinated practical governance and problem solving to the emotional thematics of an endless political campaign.
Whether the topic is Iran, Russia, or the proper level of defense spending
at a time of high deficits, the GOP's stance has little to do with the merits
of the situation; it is a projection of domestic political sloganeering. Tak-

ing a position on anything, whether it be Ukraine or the efficacy of drones, boils down to a talking-point projection of focus group–tested emotional themes: strength versus weakness, standing tall versus cutting and running, acting versus thinking.

It is sometimes confusingly contradictory: over the course of Barack Obama's presidency, Republicans have hammered on the theme that the president is an out-of-control, unconstitutional tyrant when it comes to domestic issues like health care. When the subject matter shifts overseas, however, he suddenly becomes a weak, indecisive, appeasing milquetoast. The contradiction does not matter, because no one is really proposing a meaningful solution to a foreign policy problem; it is just a dog whistle to rally an angry political base lacking the wit to notice the contradiction. Whenever a presidential wannabe like Senator Marco Rubio wishes to establish himself as a man of gravitas with what press secretaries typically bill as a "major foreign policy address," the resultant speech is a word salad of decades-old clichés that inevitably invokes Ronald Reagan, peace through strength, our men and women in uniform, everlasting friendship with Israel, eternal vigilance, and no more Munichs. Of such sketchy material is presidential timber made.

One might have hoped that this dysfunction would be confined to GOP elective officeholders, but even a Republican former secretary of state, Condoleezza Rice, has succumbed to the temptation. A couple of weeks after the eruption of the crisis over Russia's annexation of Crimea, Rice unburdened herself of the standard menu of foreign policy bromides: America must not become "war weary . . . as Ronald Reagan said, peace only comes through strength. . . . When America steps back and there is a vacuum, trouble will fill that vacuum. . . . What are we signaling when we say that America is no longer ready to stand in the defense of freedom?"[21] As for concrete steps the United States might take to address the crisis and advance its interests, none was on offer.

The self-lobotomizing of Congress is one of the chief reasons why the executive branch, and behind it the Deep State of contractors, lobbyists, and think-tank experts, has filled the void of decision making in Washington. It is less that they seized the levers of government than that they walked into an institutional void. Outrageous partisan rhetoric, specifically designed to stir up media attention and energize the party bases, has become the daily currency of visible politics in Washington. This legislative circus camouflages the fact that Congress has become a largely symbolic institution, like the French Estates-General during the ancien régime. It is ineffectual and paralyzed because significant issues can never be taken up until after the next election—and the next election is always looming. The real power has shifted to other groups, impervious to elections, beyond the control of Congress and, by extension, the American people. One of those groups, Silicon Valley, has become enormously powerful because of its impact on the economy, social habits, and the very meaning of privacy.

9

SILICON VALLEY AND THE AMERICAN PANOPTICON

It was terribly dangerous to let your thoughts wander when you were in any public place or within range of a telescreen. The smallest thing could give you away. A nervous tic, an unconscious look of anxiety, a habit of muttering to yourself—anything that carried with it the suggestion of abnormality, of having something to hide.
—George Orwell, *1984*

They're reminders to all Americans that they need to watch what they say, watch what they do.
—Presidential press secretary Ari Fleischer, September 26, 2001

Evil Is as Evil Does

Google probably never imagined that its hipster slogan "Don't be evil" would become the focus not only of irony, but of serious historians of twenty-first-century U.S. national security policy. Since Edward Snowden's revelations about the extent and depth of surveillance by the NSA, it has become evident that Silicon Valley is a vital node of the Deep State. Unlike military contractors, or intelligence contractors like Booz Allen, Silicon Valley overwhelmingly sells to the private market, but its business is so important to the government that an unusual relationship has emerged.

While Washington could simply dragoon the high-technology companies to do its bidding, it prefers cooperation with so important an engine of the nation's economy. Perhaps this explains the extraordinary indulgence the government shows the Valley in intellectual property matters—if an American "jailbreaks" his electronic device (i.e., modifies it so that it can use another service provider than the one dictated by the manufacturer, or uses an unapproved application), he can, under certain circumstances, be fined up to $500,000 and sent to prison. So much for America's vaunted property rights.[1]

In recent years, Silicon Valley has begun to rival if not surpass Wall Street as a money machine. During the last several years, the San Francisco Bay area has experienced the same symptoms New Yorkers have lived with since the unleashing of Wall Street thirty years ago: stratospheric housing prices, higher consumer prices (since a relative handful of the rich can bid up the price level of restaurants, medical care, and day care), and telltale signs of social stratification like the "Google bus" that whisks its well-heeled occupants from their tony San Francisco homes to their jobs without the indignity of using public transportation.[2]

Just as information technology has not quite lived up to its billing as a great liberating and democratizing force, neither has it entirely fulfilled its hype as an engine of American prosperity. Undeniably, the IT industry has been one of the few sectors of the U.S. economy to see impressive job growth: According to the Bureau of Labor Statistics, between 2001 and 2011, 565,000 IT-related jobs were created in America, a 22 percent increase, greatly surpassing an anemic 0.2 percent average increase in other sectors. Despite being a driver of the national economy, however, the tech industry has not produced the number of jobs one might expect: the vast majority of its touch labor is performed in outsourced and offshored factories at low wages, and the "good high-tech jobs" are not nearly as plentiful in America as the manufacturing jobs of the post–World War II era. George Packer, who has written extensively on the industry, reports that a venture capitalist told him the Valley has been responsible for more jobs lost than created.[3]

Just as with financial services, high tech has been prone to bubbles. The first dot-com mania of the 1990s gave us tech start-ups with huge market capitalizations but little or no revenue. Who would have thought an online pet food store would become the great hope of venture capitalists?

Just before its initial public offering, the revenues of Pets.com were only about one-twentieth of what it spent on advertising, but investors were undeterred. Within a month of its IPO, Pets.com shareholders lost $300 million. The puncturing of the tech bubble in 2000 was just the prelude to Wall Street's own boom and bust. In the years after the collapse of the housing market in 2008, tech stocks have once again reached dizzying heights. Some stock analysts say we could be approaching another bubble.[4]

Indulgent intellectual property laws, trade and tax policies that encourage the offshoring of production, and a knack for tax avoidance have emboldened tech companies to move several hundred billions in cash offshore. A substantial portion of the money IT makes, even domestically, is stashed abroad in low-tax or no-tax countries and not repatriated, so that it cannot be put to work in research and development, hire American workers, or declared as taxable profits. A 2013 Senate investigation of Apple revealed that it had cut its tax bill by $10 billion per year over the previous four years by squirreling away profits overseas.[5] Apple and other tech companies allocate as many of their corporate costs as possible to the United States, which offers generous corporate tax deductions, and book their profits in jurisdictions with low tax rates. Bloomberg News has estimated that the top ten U.S. companies practicing this scheme happen to be tech companies.[6] Here are the companies and their overseas profits:

1. Microsoft, $76.4 billion
2. IBM, $44.4 billion
3. Cisco Systems, $41.3 billion
4. Apple, $40.4 billion
5. Hewlett-Packard, $33.4 billion
6. Google, $33.3 billion
7. Oracle, $26.2 billion
8. Dell, $19.0 billion
9. Intel, $17.5 billion
10. Qualcomm, $16.4 billion[7]

With that kind of money sloshing around, Silicon Valley's moguls are beginning to displace the buccaneers of Wall Street as the symbols of our new gilded age: Google's Eric Schmidt, with $106 million in annual compensation, makes JP Morgan Chase's Jamie Dimon, at a mere $20 million, look like a pauper. It's hell to be the poorest member of the country club!

The Libertarian Moguls

The social liberalism of tech executives like Mark Zuckerberg is hardly the man-bites-dog story it is sometimes made out to be, nor is it particularly good news for progressive activists who envision the Valley's philanthropic contributions going to their cherished causes. Socially liberal billionaires have been with us a long time; the news media, for some reason, always swoon over a Republican who favors gay marriage. But the libertarian pose of some Silicon Valley moguls, so carefully cultivated in their public relations, is a bit of a sham.

Peter Thiel is a Silicon Valley tycoon noted for his love of Ayn Rand, his desire to build offshore "seasteading" habitations beyond the reach of law, where libertarian ideals will rule, and his belief that freedom and democracy are incompatible. Thiel, who sounds about as antisocial as a blood tick, unburdened himself in 2009 on the unfitness of his fellow Americans to live in his libertarian utopia with a Nietzschean *Übermensch* such as himself:

> The higher one's IQ, the more pessimistic one becomes about free-market politics—capitalism simply is not that popular with the crowd. . . . The 1920s were the last decade in American history during which one could be genuinely optimistic about politics. Since 1920, the vast increase in welfare beneficiaries and the extension of the franchise to women—two constituencies that are notoriously tough for libertarians—have rendered the notion of "capitalist democracy" into an oxymoron.[8]

Nevertheless, this principled antistatist built one of his start-up companies, Palantir, with the infusion of $2 million in venture capital funding from the CIA. Palantir is a purveyor of "big data" whose customers include the NSA, the FBI, and the CIA; the U.S. Chamber of Commerce, one of its corporate clients, hired Palantir (through a lobbying firm) to spy on inconvenient domestic political groups.[9] It does not require a great deal of imagination to understand why a former secretary of state, Condoleezza Rice, and a former CIA director, George Tenet, should be among Palantir's advisers, but it is puzzling why a tech company that touts itself as cutting edge and disruptive, whose corporate advertising persona is premised on hippie nonconformity and even resistance to the idea of being subject to U.S. laws, should rely on CIA funding and be advised by Washington big shots.[10]

Marc Andreessen, perhaps the most famous of Silicon Valley's venture capitalists, is a rather pure example of the high-tech visionary and libertarian. He has shared his philosophy with the public in numerous tweets. The technology of the future not only will *not* eliminate jobs: it will utterly abolish poverty. Sounding like a cross between Ayn Rand and H. G. Wells, Andreessen writes that technology will eliminate planetary resource constraints and allow each member of humanity to become his own philosopher king: "Human nature expresses itself fully, for the first time in history. Without physical need constraints, we will be whoever we want to be." And: "Imagine six, or 10, billion people doing nothing but arts and sciences, culture and exploring and learning. What a world that would be."[11] Pretty heady stuff to imagine a time when no one is stuck taking out the trash!

So how is Andreessen's utopia to be achieved? Naturally, by getting off Silicon Valley's back and letting it do its thing. He paints those critical of some of the social and economic consequences of high tech as Luddites who are opposed to technology per se: "Make no mistake, advocating slowing tech change to preserve jobs equals advocating punishing consumers, stalling quality of life improvements." He advocates no regulations on the industry and the lowest taxes possible. The only positive thing government should do with respect to technology companies, apparently, is to allow unfettered immigration: a cause for which Andreessen and his fellow tycoons have lobbied Washington. The eternal demons of poverty and income inequality will be banished by the old standby recommendation of the CEO class: "increasing access to education." Showing his softer side, Andreessen also recommends a "vigorous social safety net."

Andreessen's stirring rhetoric dodges some crucial questions: If the tech industry's business model is predicated on avoiding U.S. taxation by stashing profits overseas (a practice that other industries are rushing to emulate through schemes like "tax inversion," whereby a firm merges with a foreign company and moves its headquarters offshore), what will happen to the domestic tax base that must pay for our rising generation of philosopher kings to be educated? Despite information technology's undeniable role in the rapid diffusion of information over the past twenty years, have American educational standards made commensurate strides? What does that say about technology's alleged ability to revolutionize human learning capacity? While correlation is not causation, Andreessen's prediction that technology will eliminate poverty should give us pause: two decades of explosive dissemination of technology have been accompanied by rising, not falling, income inequality, and the number of food stamp recipients is at a record level.

The NSA and Silicon Valley: Not Always at Arm's Length

Silicon Valley has long been tracking for commercial purposes the activities of every person who uses an electronic device. It is not surprising that the Deep State should wish to hijack the data for its own purposes. Nor is it surprising that it should obtain the Valley's assistance, although it is not yet clear to what degree this assistance has been voluntary. It is of course in the companies' self-interest to make it appear that the cooperation was coerced because of widespread indignation over NSA surveillance. Some degree of coercion is undeniable: according to documents declassified by the director of national intelligence, in 2007 Yahoo faced fines of $250,000 a day, to double each week, when it balked on Fourth Amendment grounds at providing access to user information to the NSA without a judicial warrant.[12]

The documents that Edward Snowden gave to journalists suggest that some of the tech industry's cooperation has been more enthusiastic, however. According to one classified file, an unidentified corporate "partner" of the NSA was "aggressively involved in shaping traffic to run signals of interest past our monitors."[13] Other documents reveal email exchanges between NSA director general Keith Alexander and Google executives Eric Schmidt and Sergey Brin which undermine their claims that their cooperation with the agency was legally compelled. The emails suggest cordial relations with the NSA director, who arranged a four-hour classified cyberthreat briefing for them near Palo Alto.[14] It is unusual for anyone outside government to receive a classified briefing of such length, and the chairman of the Joint Chiefs of Staff even attended. This suggests a relationship in which Silicon Valley was hardly an ill-used underling. It is normal government protocol for subordinates to call on their superiors, and for the nation's highest-ranking military officer to fly across the country to attend the briefing implies a good deal of deference.

As more than one intelligence veteran has told me, the NSA has made itself completely dependent upon Silicon Valley for the technology necessary for it to do its mission. A tacit part of that mission is to keep the money flowing, and the agency is now helpless without contractors to implement that technology—about 70 percent of the agency's budget is spent on contracts. The NSA and the rest of the intelligence community are dependent upon high technology and the contractors who install, operate, and service it in exactly the same way the military is for the weapons systems it employs. The technology is so crucial—at least in the minds of senior officials and ambitious mid-level administrators, particularly since 9/11—that the entire American method of conducting warfare, intelligence, antiterrorism, and law enforcement has become predicated on it. All these sectors of the Deep State have become ensnared in the alluring concept of "big data," and information technology contractors are only too happy to sell them the gear to sort it out.

The Big Data Fallacy

A minor but telling example of this mind-set was the reaction to a fatal mass shooting at Fort Hood, Texas, on April 2, 2014. Immediately after the incident came the usual discussion of how the tragedy could have been prevented. Chris Poulin, one of the founders of the Durkheim Project, which received $1.8 million from the Defense Department's Defense Advanced Research Projects Agency, was sure he knew. It was all a matter of "finding and processing predictive signals in available data, whether those signals are overt or deeply hidden." Poulin had published a paper shortly before the incident claiming that suicidal (and possibly homicidal) motivation is predictable on the basis of language, even when suicide is not mentioned. Sounding like a character from the movie *Minority Report,* Poulin went on to say "the technology exists" to predict future events, but "we haven't worked out the civil liberties and the policing procedures to use predictive analytics effectively."[15]

It is indeed the case that in predicting homicides and suicides, just as in predicting terrorist attacks, or in "signature" targeting of potential terrorists for assassination, we haven't worked out the civil liberties issues— nor can we, for reasons linked with the limits of human knowledge and the methods by which we apply our assumed rather than definite knowledge to solve problems. The critical requirement is to eliminate "false positives," whether in detecting suicide risks, terrorist suspects, or potential military targets. The default solution in all of these cases is more data and more sifting by means of additional search criteria, which not only generates increasingly complex (and more expensive) technological solutions from which contractors obviously benefit, but also drives more data collection. That inevitably means a vicious cycle of more intrusion into personal privacy. It should not surprise us that something as benign sounding as suicide prevention requires a near-Orwellian scale of "big data."

The biggest flaw in the processing of big data is that it may not work. The algorithms on which many of these programs are based are some variant of Bayes' theorem, an eighteenth-century mathematical formula that assigns probabilities to outcomes based on prior conditions. The theorem works accurately in a classic coin-toss game (where, for example, it is known in advance that two coins are fair and one is a trick coin that always lands on "heads"), because the prior probability is exactly known and the eventual outcome of the coin tosses is beyond dispute. But if fallible human actors (in this case, the government and its contractors) are assigning a known probability to data that is itself incomplete or faulty or cherry-picked, then the prior conditions become skewed. And given the fact that the behavior of the target is incompletely known and capable of change (unlike the coins), the Bayesian algorithm breaks down.

These faulty assumptions are why (besides inevitable coding and translation errors) innocent people end up on no-fly lists.* It is also why Hellfire missiles may hit a wedding party rather than an al-Qaeda operative, and why automatic target recognition software might cause a bomb to hit an orphanage rather than a telephone exchange. Because the Deep State is so wedded to Bayesianism as a method of organization and control, the dystopia into which we are heading may look less like *Minority Report* and more like Terry Gilliam's black comedy *Brazil:* a ramshackle authoritarian state where nothing works as intended, and where innocent people are incarcerated and tortured because of silly bureaucratic errors.

Why is the Bayesian approach so seductive? It is not simply that it has become technically easier to implement as computers have grown so powerful. It is significant that it became so prevalent after 9/11. In the six-month period leading up to the terrorist strike, there was plenty of

---

* Once on the no-fly list, it is virtually impossible to get off; the government will not even tell a person why he is on the list. It may not only be a case of administrative arbitrariness: because the source of any coding and translation errors can't easily be tracked down, as well as the fact that the methodology using Bayesian algorithms is understood by few people, government officials themselves may have no genuine idea why a person is on the list.

evidence suggesting an attack was in the offing: "the system was blinking red," as the 9/11 Commission admitted. Failure to anticipate the attacks was primarily a policy failure of senior officials, including the president, whose behavior during the month prior to the attack verged on willful negligence. According to Robert Nisbet's "no fault" doctrine, failure at the top is rarely if ever admitted. The failures had to be pushed lower down, and so the blame landed on the worker bees in the agencies who allegedly "failed to connect the dots."

The solution to this imaginary problem not only entailed vast government reorganization and expansion at huge expense (and lucrative opportunities for contractors to get in on the gold rush), it also ensured that something like big data, with a patina of scientific rationality, would come in its wake. Mathematical algorithms provide the deceptive allure of detached objectivity when making judgment calls; the human element is removed and the supposed precision of high technology substituted. Government officials for the most part have no more idea of the limitations of Bayesian algorithms than they do of quantum physics or string theory, so they are easy marks for contractors with ingenious proposals.

One thing these officials do understand is that a portion of government money spent on government contracts gets recycled into campaign contributions, and postgovernment careers beckon. Creepy phrases like Total Information Awareness, the name of a 2003 DOD big data program (administered by Admiral John Poindexter, previously convicted on five counts of lying and obstruction in the Iran-Contra scandal),* are also very appealing to those people in government with an authoritarian mind-set and who crave Zeus-like powers. But saying that we can predict the future is as ridiculous as saying the *Titanic* was unsinkable.

Despite these limitations, the NSA's insatiable appetite for collecting data proceeds apace. According to a *Washington Post* study of the 160,000 NSA records of intercepted emails the newspaper obtained from Edward

---

* The convictions were reversed on appeal on the grounds that some of the witnesses against him were influenced by his immunized testimony before Congress.

Snowden, only about 11 percent were communications of targeted individuals; all the rest were third parties with no connection to an investigation. Therefore, in just this small sample of the NSA's prodigious vacuuming of communications, the daily lives of more than 10,000 people were cataloged and recorded. The *Post* described the content as telling "stories of love and heartbreak, illicit sexual liaisons, mental-health crises, political and religious conversions, financial anxieties and disappointed hopes."[16] The material includes more than 5,000 private photos. All of this personal data results from the incidental collection of information from innocent third parties in the course of the spy agency's search for a targeted individual. Anyone participating in an online chat room visited by a target or even just reading the discussion would be swept up in the data dragnet.

The NSA is not the only player at this game. Thanks to a Freedom of Information Act lawsuit, the Electronic Frontier Foundation discovered that the FBI's "next generation" facial recognition program would have as many as 52 million photographs in it by 2015—including millions that were recorded for "non-criminal purposes." The bureau's massive biometric database already "may hold records on as much as one third of the U.S. population."

Why is the collection of personal communications so indiscriminate, and why is it that government agencies cannot be more mindful of Americans' privacy? Thomas Drake, a former NSA employee, told me it was because "the NSA is addicted to data." Consistent with the information revolution, data has become the currency of the government, and particularly of the national security state. "Data is power," he said. Yet this addiction leads to some perverse results, not least of which is the violation of citizens' Fourth Amendment rights. It also can impede, rather than assist, in the national security state's ostensible mission of "keeping us safe."

I asked Drake why, if his omniscient former agency really claims to know where the sparrow falls anywhere on earth and in real time, it took the federal government twelve days to inform Target that its systems were being hacked, and why, seven months later, the perpetrators had not been caught. "The NSA is incentivized to collect data, not to prevent cyber-intrusions," he said. "In any case, they have little incentive to share information with the other agencies. They would prefer to keep the data flowing and collect it rather than interrupt it by triggering a law enforcement action."[17] So much for keeping us safe.

The Unintended Consequences of Surveillance

In much the same way that the CIA's covert arming of the Afghan Muja-hidin in the 1980s created a sharply negative blowback in the form of mu-tating and evolving terrorist groups, so has the NSA's pervasive surveillance led to negative outcomes. The Center for Strategic and International Studies has estimated the annual cost of cybercrime and economic espionage to the global economy at more than $445 billion: about 1 percent of gross world product.[18] This activity ranges from sophisticated state-backed efforts, like those of China, to extensive private rings of cybercriminals stealing credit card data, to individual hackers. Obviously, cybercrime is a major global problem, and it would exist with or without the NSA. But some unquantifiable portion of that activity may be due to the agency's practice of creating cyberimplants that disable security and encryption software, allowing the agency complete access to a target computer.

William Binney, a former top code-breaker and later whistle-blower at the NSA, told me that these implants are a two-edged sword. He said he has argued for the U.S. government "not to do backdoors or weaken en-cryption and firewalls or operating systems. The NSA goes around think-ing they are the only ones who can see and exploit these weaknesses. This is of course false. What they have done and continue to do is make all of us more vulnerable to hackers and other governments cracking into our data centers and networks. And, by placing more than fifty thousand im-plants in the worldwide network, they have put in place a potential for others (including governments) first to isolate these implants, then analyze the code, and in turn discover how to manipulate them. This would mean that others can take over those implants and start to use them as their own. This I have called shortsighted and finite thinking."[19]

It is unclear exactly to what extent these implants and backdoors are something the agency creates on its own and covertly disseminates without the knowledge or consent of the technology companies, and to what extent the NSA coerces the companies either to accept them or develop backdoors of their own for the agency to exploit. A third possibility is a regime of voluntary cooperation between government and industry, with the industry even receiving contracts to weaken the security of their own products. As with other aspects of the Silicon Valley–NSA relationship, the technology industry is extremely reluctant to acknowledge any collaboration.

Reuters reported in late 2013 that the computer security firm RSA received a cyberimplant from the NSA and distributed it very widely by incorporating it into software ostensibly used to safeguard security in personal computers and other devices. According to the news service, RSA received $10 million to establish an NSA algorithm as the default method for number generation in the bSafe encryption software.[20] This sort of relationship is hardly surprising: as we have already seen, Silicon Valley start-ups routinely received money from the government. The New York Times has reported that the CIA pays AT&T $10 million a year for access to data on overseas phone calls.[21]

The uproar resulting from Snowden's disclosures led to a predictable sequence of responses by the White House. First, denial that there is a problem: everything that has been done is within the law. Second, when the hullabaloo fails to subside, the president and his spokesmen profess to welcome a vibrant debate by the American people. Finally, when the legislative gears at last begin to turn, the administration offers a proposal that is called reform and whose substance is its antithesis. Such was the legislative solution proposed by the White House in May 2014. Responding to concerns that the NSA was collecting and storing vast amounts of telecommunications metadata, the administration suggested that the telecoms could maintain the data themselves. The proposal was structured in such a way that the NSA could legally obtain even more metadata than it sweeps up now. As one anonymous intelligence official told the *New York Times,* "It's a pretty good trade. All told, if you are an NSA analyst, you will probably get more of what you wanted to see, even if it's more cumbersome."[22]

Corporations Are Spying Too

Government surveillance is only the tip of the iceberg of what Americans must contend with. During the 1990s, tech moguls and their fan club of technology writers propounded glowing and idealistic predictions about how the Internet would democratize everything it touched and empower everybody. A notable one was Howard Rheingold's 1993 book *The Virtual Community,* in which he described his "utopian vision" of the Internet as an "electronic agora" with "democratizing potential." Although Rheingold had the good sense to temper that prediction with a warning against corporate commodification of the new information technologies, few of the prognosticators of that time were able to imagine the ability of the Internet, cell phones, and global positioning systems to keep track of citizens' every move, whether at the order of the government or for a tech industry seeking to commercialize all of our private behavior.

As for high technology's democratizing properties, the example of China should throw cold water on that notion. The country has over a half-billion Internet users, but its political leadership has succeeded in controlling the content that Internet subscribers may see and is carefully policing the web for signs of nonapproved opinions. Although it is true that electronic social media may have played a role in the so-called Arab Spring of 2011, the results show that while it may have helped channel discontent, the movements that played a significant role in challenging despotic regimes were not necessarily aiming at democracy in the traditional Western sense. In any case, the affected governments, like Egypt, were perfectly capable of shutting down nonapproved Internet sites and monitoring cell phone traffic.

As information technologies matured, their user base expanded, and the ability to exploit information grew by an order of magnitude, millions of Americans learned from experience that corporations were keeping tabs on them. As we have seen in the cases of Target or the hacking of Blue Cross–Blue Shield, tens of millions of us have had to deal with financial loss and frustrating inconvenience as our credit card or Social Security numbers have been compromised and other personal identifiers have been stolen. Beyond the overtly criminal activity of hackers and thieves, merely going online and using social media generates an array of personal data that companies assiduously collect and sell to others. One of the ironies of the digital age is that even as American citizens have become worth less and less to businesses as paid employees, their value as living repositories of commercial data is becoming greater by the day.

In 2014, the Federal Trade Commission issued a report about the increasing pervasiveness of this practice and the activities of commercial data brokers who facilitate it.[23] Companies like Acxiom, RapLeaf, and the appropriately named PeekYou have compiled volumes of data on customers and sell or barter that data to other firms. Just as the NSA, FBI, and other federal agencies compile massive amounts of data and winnow it according to algorithms that result in numerous "false hits" of the kind that can land an innocent person on a terrorist watch list, the nine data brokers the FTC reviewed were not only assembling billions of pieces of information, they were also categorizing consumers in ways that could be inaccurate. The brokers have characterized persons according to income, ethnicities, hobbies, and other traits in ways that may be incorrect or misleading. These categories become red flags for financial institutions or insurers, and can cause a person unfairly to receive a poor credit score or be turned down for insurance. One of the firms the FTC reviewed has information on 1.4 billion consumer transactions and 700 billion aggregated data elements.

Most of us have only the most shadowy concept of what goes on in the intelligence agencies. Nor do we know the full extent of the intelligence community's collaboration with the commercial information technology companies to whom we entrust so much personal information. Almost all of what we know comes from inference, the occasional leak, and the government's own sanitized and self-aggrandizing accounts. We can judge the significance of the Snowden material by how it has roiled the public and forced politicians, much against their will—they would rather do nothing and go back to sleep—to take baby steps in the direction of making intelligence agencies accountable to their nominal masters, the American people. I shall leave the last word to Thomas Drake, who knows more about this secret world than I ever will, and who learned at great personal cost, as we shall see in the next chapter, how difficult it was to try to hold it to account: "Obama—like any president—is literally a captive of the people who brief him on secret intelligence."

10

PERSONNEL IS POLICY

I cannot accept your canon that we are to judge Pope and King un-like other men, with a favourable presumption that they did no wrong. If there is any presumption it is the other way against the holders of power.

> —John Dalberg-Acton, First Baron Acton, in a letter to
> Mandell Creighton, author of *History of the Papacy During
> the Period of Reformation,* April 5, 1887

Larry leaned back in his chair and offered me some advice. I had a choice. I could be an insider or I could be an outsider. Outsiders can say whatever they want. But people on the inside don't listen to them. Insiders, however, get lots of access and a chance to push their ideas. People—powerful people—listen to what they have to say. But insiders also understand one unbreakable rule: They don't crit-icize other insiders.

> —Elizabeth Warren, describing a meeting with Lawrence Summers,
> director of the National Economic Council, Spring 2009

Holding Officials Strictly Unaccountable

If the Deep State is an institution that hides in plain sight, the same holds true for the people who run it. While there are countless operatives in and out of government with beyond-top-secret clearances who toil away in anonymity on projects we will never hear about, they are usually the order-takers. The individuals who drive the policy are mostly people we know about, or whose names are at least publicly assessable. What distin-guishes these leaders from those of similar rank who do not drive the Deep State agenda is their gravitational attraction to power, their agenda-setting ability regardless of which party is in power, and their remarkable longevity.

The historic—and disastrous—national security policies of the George W. Bush administration were established by men who were already senior officials in the Ford administration thirty years before. The change agent Barack Obama picked as the most important member of his national security team was an individual who was a key operative in secretive, questionable activities as far back as the first term of the Reagan administration. Many of Obama's other national security picks had been high-level Bush administration officials, carrying out policies he had sharply criticized in his campaign.

Perhaps the most characteristic quality of these senior personnel is their imperviousness to accountability. However responsible they might be for misbegotten policies, they are usually able to walk away from the train wreck unscathed, with their future job prospects intact. Lesser mortals do not enjoy these privileges.

The Deep State Is Not Quite *House of Cards*

One of the surprises of recent years has been the immense popularity of a television drama set in Washington called *House of Cards*. The series is an American knockoff of a British drama of the same name from two decades ago. Both series vividly depict the swinish behavior and Machiavellian scheming that film directors now consider mandatory for depicting politicians, albeit in an oddly decontextualized political and social environment. The principal characters, Francis Urquhart in the British version and Frank Underwood in the American, are central casting's up-to-date representations of the conniving politician on the make: coldly cynical, sociopathically amoral, not even blanching at the cold-blooded murder of an inconvenient witness. President Obama himself is a fan of the show. He has even told the producers, "I wish things were that ruthlessly efficient . . . this guy's getting a lot of things done."[1] So a TV show about politics has channeled Walter Mitty fantasies even in the president of these United States.

Such depictions understate the social ecology in which these characters function. *House of Cards* presents the arcane rigmarole of Washington politics through a prism that people who have been conditioned by decades of TV crime dramas can readily understand: the lone psychopath, the Hillside Strangler of a hundred cop shows, from *Dragnet* to *CSI*. The establishing shot has now gone upscale, to Capitol Hill, and the references are to cloture motions in the Senate rather than drug busts in the tenderloin district, but the machinery of the plot is familiar and comprehensible. It is digestible in a way that the less telegenic reality of Washington is not.

Would similar numbers of viewers sit still for a straightforward documentary on the skullduggery that went into the introduction and passage of the Authorization for Use of Military Force Against Iraq, or Wall Street's efforts to buy off politicians so as to blunt the force and effect of financial reform? Would they generate the same buzz of social media chitchat? Let's unpack the contrasts. During the decades of my tenure on the Hill, I was aware of no elected official skulking in the corridors of Capitol Hill or the adjacent Metro system looking for ambitious reporters to murder. But these same politicians rubber-stamped legislation that led to the needless deaths of 4,500 U.S. soldiers in Iraq and countless hundreds of thousands of Iraqi civilians. The narrative arc of financial deregulation over the last thirty years would be far too tedious to explain in a TV miniseries to a public used to dramatized bank heists and ordinary embezzlements.

Art is not always truth. Elected officials are not the kind of people who would commit a murder with their bare hands. As dim a view as I hold of a lot of them, I do not believe most of them are cynical in the way Frank Underwood is cynical. Through conditioning and assimilation, they come to believe what they say, at least most of the time, and vote accordingly. With appropriate adjustments, the unelected officials of the shadow government, be they cabinet secretaries, generals, or corporate senior executives, respond to the same stimuli in roughly the same way. The man becomes the mask. That metamorphosis, combined with peer pressure, groupthink, and confirmation bias, makes them what they are. The mixture of such traits in otherwise "good" persons discharging what they hold to be their public or corporate duties can sometimes result in a far more subtle but consequential evil than the obvious amorality of a lone criminal.

Meet the Characters Who Run the Deep State

Only a few of those who come and go (and always seem to come back again) in our permanent government rate as genuinely toxic. On his departure in 2006, Donald H. Rumsfeld was one of the most reviled figures in government. It is difficult to plumb the depth of the distaste with which the members of the congressional defense committees viewed him. As the Iraq casualties began to mount, this walking vacuum of human empathy could not even be bothered to sign condolence letters to the next of kin to the fallen. He assigned his office staff to sign them by autopen. Yet this was likely just a lack of imagination and self-reflection, rather than a conscious capacity for the violent malevolence of Frank Underwood.

Most people have forgotten that Rumsfeld was a player during another American disaster. He was President Ford's chief of staff during the final military collapse of South Vietnam. When asked in 2013 about which lesson he drew from America's misadventure in Vietnam, he answered with lapidary succinctness: "Some things work out, some things don't, that didn't."[2] Even looking from four decades' distance, his answer was like his off-the-cuff remarks during the Iraq war: Why did the U.S. military that he was in charge of have no plan to prevent the looting at Baghdad's museums? "Stuff happens." Why, irate combat infantrymen asked him on a later occasion, were the troops not provided proper body armor? "You go to war with the army you have."

Rumsfeld is an egregious example of a character type that seems to be magnetically drawn to the upper levels of the government and corporate world. Actual competence is often less important than boundless self-confidence and a startling lack of reflectiveness about what one is actually doing. That, and being sheep-dipped and credentialed in the proper elite colleges and politically connected think tanks. One of the major counts of the conservative bill of indictment against public education is the claim that American public schooling fills children with a sense of unearned self-esteem while failing to instill core competence. You can fault a child for not knowing algebra, but that dereliction is not in the same league as invading the wrong country. And what about the perennial cry against grade inflation in schools? If one were to apply that criterion for judging competence, how did Paul Wolfowitz, the deputy secretary of defense who blithely predicted before the committee I was serving that there would be no insurgency in Iraq and that the war would pay for itself, ever earn a Presidential Medal of Freedom and a sinecure at the World Bank?*

An overweening sense of self-importance and a capacity for self-satisfied assertion seem to be all that are required. Such persons, whether appearing as cabinet heads or corporate CEOs, make splendid witnesses for their organizations in front of congressional investigating committees. Their bluff bonhomie combined with bottomless obtuseness allows them to sail through a hearing without visibly betraying any personal consciousness of responsibility for whichever foul-up is under investigation. They can also mouth the party line without any feeling of cognitive dissonance. No doubt they sincerely believe it, at least in the moment they say it. Rumsfeld's statement that he never read the so-called torture memos generated by the Justice Department's Office of Legal Counsel is believable in view of his imperturbable incuriosity. He is a shining example of what David Owen, a former British foreign secretary and a medical

---

* Wolfowitz's career arc appears to represent a bipartisan solution to what to do with exalted personnel who make grossly misleading assessments about wars. After years of giving sunny estimates about the situation in Vietnam that he himself did not believe, Lyndon Johnson's secretary of defense, Robert McNamara, also got a gold watch in the form of the presidency of the World Bank. (Incredibly, Wolfowitz is back—he is now one of presidential candidate Jeb Bush's national security policy advisers.)

doctor by training, has called "hubristic incompetence," the narcissistic habit of seeing the world as an arena for achieving power and glory rather than as a place for pragmatic problem solving.

The Deep State as an evolved social organism is optimized to achieve certain things: power, money, and career security for its major players; and a preservation of the status quo for the system within which they operate. What it is not well adapted to achieving is useful solutions for society as a whole. Iraq and Libya were never "problems" crying out for American answers, certainly not by means of a full-dress ground invasion or an armed intervention leading to regime change. As a consequence, potential difficulties needed to be concealed and purported facts constructed in order for the leadership class to get its preferred outcomes.

Likewise, the existence of the Glass-Steagall Act separating commercial and investment banking was hardly a problem in the real world: it was a firewall against recurrence of the financial calamity of 1929, and it had worked well for more than six decades. But by the 1990s, the lords of finance, in their own hubristic quest to make their corporate empires bigger and bigger, and to stuff more money into their pockets, convinced themselves—along with a compliant Congress and a collusive Treasury Department—that the law was anachronistic and a hindrance to the complex, competitive, and globe-girdling financial industry. A moment's thought should have suggested that the huge market leverages, global reach, and instantaneous transactions of modern finance did not make the risks inherent in gambling with depositors' money go away—they increased them exponentially.

This pattern has played out over and over again: once one or a handful of the leadership class get a notion about something that appeals to their acquisitive or grandiose instincts, most of the rest of the elites, their staff underlings, and their troubadours in the think tanks and op-ed pages troop behind them like a flock of parrots, all squawking the same tune.

The Career Path

Once a senior operative has completed his job in one sector of the Deep State, it is usually time for promotion to another—at a considerably higher salary. The corridor between Manhattan and Washington is a well-trodden highway for the personalities we got to know in the period since the massive deregulation of Wall Street: Robert Rubin, Lawrence Summers, Henry Paulson, Timothy Geithner, and many others. Perhaps the most notorious was Rubin. President Clinton tapped the Goldman Sachs cochairman to be his treasury secretary, and in that role Rubin lobbied assiduously for the repeal of Glass-Steagall. When he left his government job, Clinton called him "the greatest secretary of the Treasury since Alexander Hamilton."[3] Rubin promptly landed a job as director of Citigroup, the conglomerate that had just been formed as a result of the merger of Citicorp and Travelers Insurance; it was only because of Glass-Steagall's repeal that the merger of a commercial bank and an insurance company was legal. Thereafter, he pocketed $126 million in salary and bonuses, including during the period that Citigroup was being bailed out by taxpayer money. Like the other senior executives of bailed-out institutions, Rubin did not have to disgorge any of his earnings, thanks to his friend and former Treasury subordinate Timothy Geithner's insistence that the sanctity of contract prohibited government-imposed compensation limits on the officers of rescued financial entities (for some reason, sanctity of contract never seems to apply to lesser fry like hourly workers or municipal pensioners).

Not all the traffic to and from Wall Street involves persons connected with the financial operations of the government: in 2013, General David Petraeus joined KKR (formerly Kohlberg Kravis Roberts), a private equity firm with $40 billion in assets. The firm specializes in management buyouts and leveraged finance. General Petraeus's expertise in these areas is unclear; his ability to peddle influence, however, is a known and valued commodity. Unlike Cincinnatus, the military commanders of the Deep State do not take up the plow once they lay down the sword. He has also obtained a sinecure as a nonresident senior fellow at the Belfer Center for Science and International Affairs at Harvard. The Ivy League is the preferred bleaching tub, charm school, and postretirement sinecure of the American oligarchy.*

Petraeus's fellow army general, NSA director Keith Alexander, who several members of Congress claimed misled them about the scope and legality of his agency's collection of Americans' private information, and who has recommended legislation to restrict the media's First Amendment rights, has also reached for the big payday on Wall Street. After retiring in 2014, Alexander set himself up as the head of a consulting boutique called IronNet Cybersecurity. His principal client is one of Wall Street's largest lobbying groups, the Securities Industry and Financial Markets Association (SIFMA), from which he receives $600,000 per month.[4]

Barely a month after he landed on SIFMA's payroll, the banking group proposed a government-industry cyberwar council that would include financial industry executives and deputy-level representatives from at least eight U.S. agencies, including the Treasury Department, the National Security Agency, and the Department of Homeland Security, all led by a senior White House official.[5] Is better cybersecurity a good idea? Sure. But hiring the man who presided over a top-secret agency when the unauthorized removal of millions of electronic documents from that agency occurred certainly is a head-scratcher. And what does Wall Street really want with this council? Ultimately, they want legislative relief from liability for exposing their customers' data to hackers. One congressman, Alan Grayson of Florida, was skeptical: "This could in effect make the banks part of what would begin to look like a war council. Congress needs to keep an eye on what something like this could mean."[6]

Petraeus, Alexander, and most of the liegemen of the Deep State—

---

* Beginning in 1988, every U.S. president has been a graduate of Harvard or Yale (or both). Beginning in 2000, every losing presidential candidate has been a Harvard or Yale graduate, with the exception of John McCain in 2008.

the White House advisers who urged Obama not to impose compensation limits on Wall Street CEOs, the contractor-connected think-tank experts who besought us to "stay the course" in Iraq, the economic gurus who perpetually demonstrate that globalization and deregulation are blessings that make us all better off in the long run—are careful to pretend that they have no ideology. Their preferred pose is that of the politically neutral technocrat offering well-considered advice based on profound expertise. Expertise is what they sell, but that pose is nonsense.

Domestically, whatever they might privately believe about essentially diversionary social issues like abortion or gay marriage, they almost invariably believe in the "Washington consensus": financialization, outsourcing, privatization, deregulation, and the commodification of labor. Internationally, they espouse twenty-first-century American exceptionalism: the right and duty of the United States to meddle in every region of the world, coercive diplomacy, boots on the ground, and the right to ignore painfully won international norms of civilized behavior, such as the prohibition of torture. To paraphrase what Sir John Harrington said over four hundred years ago about treason, now that this ideology has prospered, none dare call it ideology. That is why describing torture by using the word "torture" on broadcast television is treated less as political heresy than as an inexcusable lapse of Washington etiquette: like smoking a cigarette on *Face the Nation,* these days it is simply not done.

What Bipartisanship Means

To a greater degree than in domestic agencies, the organs of national security retain high-level appointed personnel who serve under both Democratic and Republican administrations. Putting the best face on the practice, one could say it is an attempt to make politics stop at the water's edge, and to maintain a cadre of senior people with policy experience. But that is not quite right, because policy experience has a very specific meaning in Washington: an operative is supposed to toe the line on subjects like national security. Victoria Nuland, Obama's assistant secretary of state for European and Eurasian affairs, who made headlines for a bugged phone call in which she made highly undiplomatic remarks about the countries in her diplomatic portfolio, also served as a foreign policy adviser to Dick Cheney and as U.S. ambassador to NATO in the administration of George W. Bush.* Her husband, Robert Kagan, a well-known Washington neoconservative and dogged advocate on op-ed pages of U.S. military intervention, was highly regarded by the Bush administration and remains a fellow at the Brookings Institution. One never lacks for employment opportunities in Washington if one advocates involvement in overseas mayhem.

John Brennan, Obama's current CIA director, was director of the National Counterterrorism Center under George W. Bush. When Obama took office, he intended to appoint Brennan CIA director, but he had to withdraw when awkward charges surfaced about his possible advocacy of torture—the very practice that Obama had so vigorously campaigned against in 2008. Obama then appointed him deputy national security adviser, a post not requiring Senate confirmation. By early 2013, the controversy had subsided, and Obama nominated him for CIA director once more—this time successfully. In a less labyrinthine environment, one might consider a Bush administration holdover alleged to have engaged in practices the current president campaigned against to be a millstone rather than an asset. Is it any wonder that Democratic national security policies differ somewhat in tone but not in fundamental practice from those of the Republicans?

---

* In the phone call, Nuland disparaged the European Union's efforts to mediate the brewing crisis in Ukraine by saying "F*ck the EU," thus providing one more piece of evidence that the U.S. government, or at least some players in it, did not want a calming of the growing disorder in Ukraine's capital city.

The Strange Case of Bob Gates

This flexibility in personnel is hardly an innovation of Obama's presidency. George Tenet served as CIA director for both Clinton and Bush, and Robert Gates served as secretary of defense under both Bush and Obama. Gates made heavy weather of his nonpartisanship after leaving the job, saying in response to a question about his party affiliation, "Well, I'm actually not a registered Republican." When asked where he stood on the subject of abortion, he replied, "I don't have a stand on abortion. Somehow that's never come into the national security arena." A clever and disarming answer. Contrived dog-whistle themes like abortion or gay marriage are designed to mobilize voters to support one party or another, but senior servants of the Deep State are above that kind of petty partisan issue-mongering, because they know that the only ideology worthy of their effort is one that will keep the right people in the real positions of power and the cash flowing into the hands of those who matter.

It is worth lingering over Gates's career. He is a prime example of the longevity of senior operatives of the Deep State and their characteristic habits of mind. Now that he is retired, Gates has seen fit to criticize his former bosses, Barack Obama and Joe Biden, in his memoirs. Fair enough; they are hardly immune from criticism. What generated controversy was his claim that President Obama did not believe in the military's strategy for Afghanistan that Gates pressed him to adopt. Given everything that has unfolded in Afghanistan since this decision to escalate the war, one can only conclude that it is a peculiar species of candor to criticize Obama for accepting, however grudgingly, advice that Gates himself tendered, advice that was based on flawed assessments. It is, perhaps, a variant of Robert Nisbet's "no fault" doctrine: the advice that generals offer is sacrosanct, and those criticizing it show ill grace even if the critics are eventually proved right.

The real mystery is why Obama, who campaigned so effectively in 2008 against the national security policies of George W. Bush, decided to keep Gates on as secretary of defense. One defense industry source told me in early 2009 that Gates was essentially able to dictate the terms under which he would serve. If true, it speaks volumes that Obama was so eager to placate the Washington consensus that he would allow an old Bush family retainer to write his own job description for a crucial cabinet port- folio. If there was any early sign that the candidate of hope and change was actually going to be the avatar of stay-the-course, his reappointment of Gates was a glaring one.

Obama ought to have known what he was getting into. A cursory ex- amination of Gates's past performance would have revealed that he was a Soviet specialist and deputy director for intelligence at the CIA in 1982, early in the presidency of Ronald Reagan, when the agency issued greatly overstated estimates of the Soviet threat. Those estimates unleashed a military spending spree that seriously impacted the federal deficit.

Shortly after that, the world learned about the arms-for-hostages scandal known as Iran-Contra. That tragicomic, illegal operation re- quired an assessment by the CIA that moderate factions in Iran were ready to make a deal. This assessment was conveniently forthcoming from the CIA as Gates moved up to deputy director of the agency (his influence was greater than his title indicated as the director, William Ca- sey, was fading into senescence). A man in his position was also situated to know exactly what sort of freedom fighters we were sending arms to in Central America and Afghanistan. Lawrence Walsh, the independent counsel who investigated the Iran-Contra affair and indicted several of the principal actors, did not indict Gates, but Walsh later wrote how frus- trating Gates's slipperiness was in making sworn statements.[7] The sharp and incisive Bob Gates could develop amnesia on cue.

The agency in which Gates, the Soviet expert, played a pivotal role somehow missed one of the epochal events of the twentieth century: the collapse of the Soviet Union. The CIA failed to anticipate events in the one country it was set up to focus on. But the information was available for anyone willing to listen. In 1985, I attended an unclassified sympo- sium on the Soviet Union. One of the experts, Murray Feshbach, was a demographer for the U.S. Census Bureau. Rather than interpreting Soviet power from satellite photographs of missile fields, he looked at available data about life expectancy, fertility rates, infant mortality, and nutrition. The implication was clear: the USSR was a walking corpse. Gates and his team of experts greatly exaggerated the Soviet threat and left U.S. policy makers unprepared for the crumbling of the Warsaw Pact, yet later he demanded that presidents accept his assessments of Afghanistan at face value.

Gates's cultivated public image as a no-nonsense truth teller is a perfect example of how Deep State operatives are able to fashion artificial personas. Ray McGovern, a Soviet analyst at the CIA for twenty-seven years who presented the president's daily White House briefing and was awarded the Intelligence Commendation Medal, has a somewhat different recollection of Gates than is available in his official biography. At one time, McGovern was his supervisor in the agency's Soviet division. He recalled Gates being intelligent and a good writer, but said he had to hedge when he wrote his performance evaluation: "He was perpetually cultivating senior officials elsewhere in the agency." The young analyst had already understood the old Washington chestnut that "know-who" trumps "know-how." McGovern recalls that Gates was so visibly ambitious that he was a disruptive influence among his colleagues.[8]

Gates is an example of something that has often puzzled me: the incongruous sentimentality that ruthless American men of affairs frequently show. Like Citizen Kane's longing after Rosebud, it is a psychological quirk that can be depicted but never quite explained. Gates's emotions about combat soldiers, feelings he has so visibly demonstrated in public, are perfectly genuine. His record in shaking up the military's medical command and forcing it to reduce the maximum time allotted to evacuate a wounded soldier to a hospital from two hours to one was surely proper and to his credit. Praiseworthy, but that action does not nullify the crux of the matter: his execution of policy.

Was the surge in Iraq that gave rise to the casualties Gates has so publicly mourned wise or necessary given that it reinforced failure in a war launched on false pretenses in a country that was bound to lapse into sectarian violence after the United States' inevitable withdrawal? Was Gates accordingly justified or unjustified in excoriating then–Senate majority leader Harry Reid for saying that the war was lost? Was the surge in Afghanistan with its attendant casualties wise or necessary, given that the United States had already remained too long, and that the number of U.S. troops was irrelevant so long as Afghanistan was saddled with the corrupt Karzai regime? It is questions like these that should compel us all to keep a firm grip on our reason and our wallets whenever members of the political class choke up as they invoke Old Glory or the blood of patriots. Samuel Johnson's hoary statement that patriotism is the last refuge of the scoundrel is no less true for being a cliché.

Mark Leibovich's exposé of the permanent Beltway class, *This Town*, reads like Thackeray's *Vanity Fair* as annotated by Tina Brown, but he makes several valuable observations—albeit shorn of their deeper political significance. When a lobbyist in a lucrative partnership with a colleague of the other political party tells Leibovich, "Everyone involved in the world in which we operate is a patriot," he expresses the tacit, wink-and-nod understanding among the permanent operatives, short-term contract players, and hangers-on of the Deep State that the daily politics of the stereotypical "issues" that agitate the public are basically bread and circuses for the cheap seats. Leibovich focuses on the limos, greenroom chitchat, and after-parties as titillating aspects of the Beltway class. But his tale is like a history of World War II as told by a stateside troupe of USO entertainers: the reader is left to infer the meaning and the mayhem of the epic event. Alan Greenspan's attending a reception for Maria Bartiromo indeed shows us that "everyone, ultimately, is playing for the same team," but what is that team, and what do the players want beyond an appearance on *Meet the Press* to raise their market value on K Street?

Leibovich harps on the Scrooge McDuck level of greed of the average Washington player, who moans that he is having a terrible year when he makes only ten times the national median household income. There is a good deal of truth to that characterization, but it is not the whole truth, and it may invert cause and effect. Corruption does not always require an immediate cash nexus. Justices of the Supreme Court, who have lifetime tenure and fixed salaries, receive no bribes from corporate America to rule in its favor. They do so because they believe in a certain ideology with dogmatic faith, and accordingly backfill their rulings with whichever legal arguments more or less hang together. It is not corruption so much as bias confused with principle.

The New Nomenklatura

The personnel of the Deep State in some respects resemble the old Soviet nomenklatura, the officials who held key administrative positions in the important sectors of the USSR's government and economy. They obtained their positions with the approval of the Communist Party apparatus. Lenin laid down the principle that appointments were to take the following criteria into account, in descending order of importance: reliability, political attitude, qualifications, and administrative ability.

The nomenklatura evolved over time into a patronage system that the Tammany Hall cronies of Boss Tweed would have recognized: in return for assistance in promoting his career, the subordinate in the Soviet system carried out and defended the policies of his patron. The nomenklatura became a privileged class in a country that had allegedly abolished the class system. Political reliability was valued over technical competence, so it is no wonder that the system drifted inexorably toward stagnation and decline.

The Deep State is less formal in personnel matters than was the Soviet Union, but parallels remain. The same type of cronyism, political litmus-testing, and mutual back-scratching that pervaded Kremlin politics during what Soviet historians call the "Era of Stagnation" of the 1970s prevails in much of our shadow government. In early 2001, just before George W. Bush's inauguration, the Heritage Foundation produced a policy document designed to help the incoming administration choose personnel (ever since the Reagan administration, Heritage has been very influential in formulating Republican policies, notwithstanding its nonprofit 501c(3) "charitable" tax status). In this document the authors stated the following: "The Office of Presidential Personnel (OPP) must make appointment decisions based on loyalty first and expertise second, and . . . the whole governmental apparatus must be managed from this perspective."[9] The Leninist principle in a nutshell!

Americans have paid a high price for our Leninist personnel policies, and not only in domestic matters. In important national security concerns such as staffing the Coalition Provisional Authority, a sort of viceroyalty to administer Iraq until a real Iraqi government could be formed, the same guiding principle of loyalty before competence applied. The administration scoured the database of the White House Office of Personnel, the Republican National Committee's donor lists, and evangelical college graduating classes for likely candidates with suitable motivation and loyalty to the company line. Jim O'Beirne, the husband of Kate O'Beirne, a *National Review* columnist much esteemed by conservatives, was the Pentagon political appointee in charge of screening prospects. The *Washington Post* reported that "O'Beirne's staff posed blunt questions to some candidates about domestic politics: Did you vote for George W. Bush in 2000? Do you support the way the president is fighting the war on terror? Two people who sought jobs with the U.S. occupation authority said they were asked their views on *Roe v. Wade*."

Such vetting techniques resulted in appointments like these: "A 24-year-old who had never worked in finance—but had applied for a White House job—was sent to reopen Baghdad's stock exchange. The daughter of a prominent neoconservative commentator and a recent graduate from an evangelical university for home-schooled children were tapped to manage Iraq's $13 billion budget, even though they didn't have a background in accounting."[10] This riotous incompetence extended far beyond the Coalition Provisional Authority itself and pervaded the entire Iraq effort, both in the theater of war and in Washington.

In 2006, I attended a small staff briefing on Iraq by Anthony Cordesman of the Center for Strategic and International Studies. Tony is a highly knowledgeable defense analyst who is relatively free of political agendas.

He revealed in the course of his depressing *tour d'horizon* that Rumsfeld's DOD actually disqualified candidates if they were Middle East area experts or knew Arabic. Not certain that I had heard him correctly, I asked him if he wasn't perhaps exaggerating for effect. His deadpan reply, with a touch of irritation, was "No, unfortunately, I'm being completely serious."

Job-qualified or not, whatever mischief these neophytes were doing wasn't their own idea. The incompetent management of postinvasion Iraq came from the people at the very top, the Cheneys, Rumsfelds, and Wolfowitzes, because they held with the dogmatic rigidity of a religious zealot that a crash program of laissez-faire economics and privatization of Iraq's state assets were just what the doctor ordered for a fragile, sect-ridden state reeling from years of draconian sanctions and a violently imposed occupation. In that belief they were hardly discouraged by the corporate donors they consorted with, or the numerous service contractors like Halliburton who stood to benefit.

Then there is the matter of L. Paul Bremer. As chief administrator in Iraq, he was a kind of imperial sovereign who could rule by decree. Among his more unfortunate diktats were the following: the disbanding of Iraq's army, thereby creating roughly 400,000 desperate, unemployed people possessing AK-47s in a collapsed economy; the firing from government jobs of all members of the Ba'ath Party, including schoolteachers, which meant most of the people who knew how to keep the fabric of civil order intact; and implementation of radical privatization, which greatly complicated the job of restoring Iraq's state-run water, sewer, and electricity systems.

To top it off was the little matter of $12 billion in unfrozen Iraqi state assets, which were supposed to be returned to the country for the benefit of the Iraqi people. Of that amount, $8.8 billion was unaccounted for. Even the former House Speaker, Newt Gingrich, no mean author of administrative chaos himself, called Bremer "the largest single disaster in American foreign policy in modern times."[11] It is easy to see why President Bush bestowed on Bremer the Presidential Medal of Freedom, which has become a twenty-first-century equivalent of the Order of Lenin, for his services beyond the call of duty. In Bush's world, it was the appropriate gold watch for the loyal hired help.

The same principle of trying to use unqualified personnel to implement ideological policy was on display in the Bush administration's bungled response to Hurricane Katrina. White House misuse of the Federal Emergency Management Agency as a dumping ground for Republican campaign operatives is well known. What exacerbated the poor response to the disaster, however, was not just incompetence—it was deliberate, ideology-driven choices made at the top.

After the hurricane hit New Orleans, while thousands were trapped in the fetid and unsanitary conditions of the Superdome, the key railroad lines leading out of New Orleans remained intact. A contact in the inspector general's office at Amtrak told me that the company's president called the White House and offered—free of charge—to send trains into New Orleans to evacuate the stranded residents. His offer was rejected. Why? My contact did some follow-up with the White House and discovered that the Bush administration, which had been trying to eliminate Amtrak from the budget, was not eager to see the passenger railroad get any favorable publicity from the rescue effort. Human need had better not stand in the way of ideology.

Both Parties Do It

This Leninist approach to recruitment of personnel is not confined to the Republican Party, although the Bush administration went to extravagant lengths in its implementation. Obama has nominated ambassadors who appear barely to have heard of the country to which they are being sent. The president's nominee for ambassador to Norway, a former campaign fund-raiser, referred in his confirmation hearing to the "president" of Norway, although the head of state is the king. Colleen Bell, producer of the soap opera *The Bold and the Beautiful,* was chosen as ambassador to Hungary—where the recent emergence of a far-right government and neofascist movements has been a cause of international concern. Her testimony revealed a depressing lack of knowledge about her assignment. It is telling that neither candidate bothered to study up for the job. The days of Charles Francis Adams or George Kennan, ambassadors who were deeply knowledgeable of the world, are long gone.

The Deep State runs on money, and these ambassadors, unqualified though they may be, help make the wheels go around in their own minor and farcical way. For services courageously rendered in raising cash for politicians, they receive a short-term, honorary membership in the nomenklatura. Ambassadors have relatively little de facto power, but an ambassadorship is a prestigious job that allows a campaign contributor from, say, the axle-grease business, to rub shoulders with a lot of high-level international business contacts who could be very helpful to his postdiplomatic career. Being able to append "ambassador" to one's name allows a person to dine out on the title for the rest of one's life: a useful prop for getting onto the masthead of directorships and charities or to break into the right social circles. As for the sausage making back at the embassy, those operations are generally run by the deputy chief of mission—normally a career foreign service officer—and the CIA station chief in a kind of informal interagency diarchy. If the embassy is in a politically critical country or a hardship post where no self-respecting Hollywood social climber would deign to serve, the ambassadorial position will be filled by a career State Department employee.

Geoffrey Pyatt, the U.S. ambassador to Kiev and the voice on the other end of the line of Assistant Secretary of State Victoria Nuland's notorious "hacked" phone call, fits the template for this type. Armed with the mandatory Ivy League credentials, he worked his way up both in crime-ridden hardship posts like Honduras and in critical posts like the U.S. mission to the International Atomic Energy Agency in Vienna, where a former career in movies would be a jobs-skills mismatch.

The United States has had a policy to fish in the troubled waters of Ukraine by overtly and covertly working with political opposition groups there (Nuland boasted in a speech to the U.S-Ukraine Foundation on December 13, 2013, that the United States had spent $5 billion since

Ukraine's independence to influence politics there). Pyatt was a more appropriate choice for Kiev than some glad-handing campaign bundler. On the other hand, postings that are popular tourist destinations, or have a lot of social cachet like London's Court of St. James's or Paris, are sinecures where figurehead ambassadors can reign rather than rule.

Different Spanks for Different Ranks

We have seen what happens to the higher-grade nomenklatura when they bungle or neglect the job they are supposedly uniquely qualified to perform: Wolfowitz, for botching the Iraq invasion and misleading Congress about the likely outcome of the occupation, got the World Bank presidency; and Bremer, for disastrous policy errors and losing track of $8.8 billion, got a Medal of Freedom. Under Barack Obama, the practice has not changed appreciably: Victoria Nuland, for the severe indiscretion of proposing regime change over an unencrypted phone in a country bordering Russia and giving Vladimir Putin the veneer of a pretext to occupy Crimea, continued in her high-level job without even having to explain her actions. CIA director John Brennan has repeatedly embarrassed Obama over torture and misleading Congress, yet he remains at his post. America's de facto three-tiered system of justice and accountability always seems to allow the great and the good to slip off the hook.

What happens to the foot soldiers who do not dwell in these charmed circles? While the case of NSA contractor Edward Snowden has captured worldwide attention, the example of Thomas Drake, the former NSA employee we met in the previous chapter, should be better known to Americans. Even before 9/11, the NSA was developing systems to capture the rapidly expanding data of the Internet. Drake grew concerned about the NSA leadership's choice of the so-called Trailblazer Project over another system, ThinThread. Drake and a number of other NSA employees favored ThinThread because it met requirements while being cheaper and, he believed, better at protecting U.S. citizens' privacy.

Trailblazer was far more intrusive and would potentially violate privacy rights. In addition, Trailblazer's full implementation would cost billions of dollars, greatly exceeding the cost of ThinThread. But instead of selecting the agency-developed ThinThread, the NSA's director, General Michael Hayden, selected Trailblazer, which used outside contractors like IBM, SAIC, and Boeing. (Hayden's deputy director, William Black, was a former NSA employee who had left for SAIC, and then returned to the NSA to manage Trailblazer for Hayden in 2000).

Drake and several other NSA employees complained to their bosses, the NSA inspector general, the Defense Department's inspector general, and finally the House and Senate Intelligence committees (he was not "going over the heads" of the NSA, as the role of the committees was to provide oversight for the NSA). The Pentagon's inspector general found in 2004 that Trailblazer was poorly executed and overly expensive. Defects included improper contract cost increases, nonconformance in the execution of the statement of work, and excessive labor rates for contractor personnel.[12] The NSA finally canceled the project in 2006. But that was not the end of the story for Drake.

For having communicated with journalists—although he did not give them classified information—the FBI raided Drake's house and confiscated his computers, documents, and books. The government then engaged in blatant police-state chicanery, such as retroactively classifying unclassified documents he had retained, and he was eventually charged under the Espionage Act and faced thirty-five years in prison. Finally, in May 2011, after media exposure of the case, the government dropped all the major charges against him. But since federal prosecutors always need to salvage something for their expensive efforts and their expansive egos, they continued to press a misdemeanor charge of misusing the NSA's computers. He was sentenced to one year of probation and community service. At the sentencing hearing the judge slammed the prosecution: it was "unconscionable" to charge a defendant with a list of serious crimes that could land him in prison for decades, only to drop them just before the trial. The prosecution pressed for a large fine, but the judge rejected that on the grounds that Drake had been made practically destitute, having lost his job and pension.

Thomas Drake's case makes nonsense of the claims by Edward Snowden's critics that he should have brought evidence of the NSA's abuse to his superiors, or informed Congress. Drake and many other whistleblowers have found themselves ostracized, fired, bankrupted, or even criminalized for going through appropriate channels.

Hayden had a softer landing. After leaving the NSA in 2005, he became principal deputy director of national intelligence and then CIA director, where he developed quite an enthusiasm for waterboarding. He is currently a principal at the Chertoff Group, a security consultancy cofounded by former homeland security secretary Michael Chertoff, who is also chairman of the board of BAE Systems, Inc.* Hayden is a frequent guest of news programs, where he advocates for mass surveillance. On Fox News, he opined that Senator Dianne Feinstein's revelation of the CIA's intimidation of her staff was "emotional": as if serious legal and constitutional issues should be dismissed with a patriarchal wave of the hand.

It must be conceded that no one has accused Hayden of leaking or mishandling classified information, however objectionable his favoritism toward the contractors responsible for the gold-plated Trailblazer. But that cannot be said of all the exalted members of the nomenklatura. David Petraeus, the most celebrated general of the last decade, ended his career on a note that was not only ignominious but potentially criminal. His adulterous relationship with his biographer, Paula Broadwell, drew so much attention that the Obama administration saw fit to seek his resignation. Less well known was the fact that he had shared highly classified "code word" documents with her so that she could write the book.

Lesser persons accused of such crimes have faced jail time and forfei-

---

* "Security consultant" is a Washington term of art for influence peddlers who stand astride the cash pipeline between their old employers in government and the major contractors.

ture of their pensions. John Kiriakou, a CIA employee who revealed the existence of his agency's torture program (a program violating U.S. law, the Constitution, and the Geneva Convention), was not hailed as an exposer of government wrongdoing—he received a sentence of two and a half years in federal prison. Petraeus, by contrast, got off with a suspended sentence and a fine that was derisory in light of his seven-figure compensation at KKR on top of his four-star general's pension of approximately $250,000 a year. As they say in the military, different spanks for different ranks.

The Deep State as Bizarro World

There are so many cases of virtue unrewarded—or even punished—while bungling, incompetence, and grandiose dishonesty are richly compensated with promotion and money, that one is almost tempted to believe that the Deep State operates on some inverted principle, like Superman's Bizarro World. Occasionally, though, hubris encounters nemesis exactly as it is supposed to.

I first heard of Richard Fuld sometime in 2001. My old boss, Congressman John Kasich, who had rounded out his congressional career as chairman of the House Budget Committee, retired at the end of 2000 to seek his fortune elsewhere. He ended up at Lehman Brothers on Wall Street, in keeping with the trend of public servants going into lobbying or banking. Shortly after landing the job, Kasich offered a journalist a flattering picture of Fuld, Lehman's CEO, that would have made Caesar blush: "Fuld is an awesome guy. He is the kind of guy you want to go into battle with. He is a great leader. I like people who are really smart and who are great leaders."[13] Fuld sounded like a name to conjure with, I thought, whereupon I promptly forgot about him for the next seven years.

As everyone now knows, things didn't turn out to be quite so awesome after all. The collapse of Lehman Brothers on September 15, 2008, tipped an already sliding economy into the abyss. Bear Stearns, Merrill Lynch, and other financial institutions at least avoided bankruptcy through shotgun marriages forced by the Treasury and the Fed. Lehman was different—the biggest corporate collapse in U.S. history led to the worst international liquidity crisis of the last eighty years within a week of the bankruptcy.

Why didn't Lehman get bailed out? For one thing, Fuld was blinkered, narrow, and lacked a sense of proportion, like so many senior operatives in and out of government. He saw Lehman as his personal mission, and he would not sell the wildly overleveraged firm when he had a chance to do so. Like Rumsfeld or Bremer, he believed in staying the course, even when the course was leading to disaster. Once the financial dominoes started falling, from the desert McMansions of Victorville, California, to the vaults of the New York Federal Reserve Bank, Fuld's opportunity to rescue his firm was gone.

Even in the Wall Street domain of cutthroat egomaniacs, Fuld was singular. Known as "the gorilla," he once informed an audience about his strategy for dealing with short-sellers: "I am soft, I'm lovable but what I really want to do is reach in, rip out their heart and eat it before they die." Fuld's sociopathic reputation was such that his retrospective claim that Treasury Secretary Paulson, an old rival from Goldman Sachs, declined to bail out Lehman because of personal animosity may have a glimmer of truth, however self-serving it might be. If there was only limited room in the Treasury's lifeboat and someone had to drown, that guy was going to be Fuld.

Lehman went down, and the Dow Jones average fell over five hundred points that same day. That same week, investor panic threatened to cause an unprecedented run on money-market funds as liquidity dried up. I could grasp something of the urgency of the situation at the time because the Senate Budget Committee gave me the ad hoc assignment to monitor and report on the Treasury's effort to shore up the market by using its Exchange Stabilization Fund, a little-known facility established during the New Deal, to insure money-market mutual fund accounts.

While Jamie Dimon of JPMorgan Chase, Lloyd Blankfein of Goldman Sachs, and other titans of Wall Street came out of the catastrophe with their positions and fortunes largely intact, Fuld became the Jesse Livermore of the 2008 crash, albeit without his grisly finale. He did manage to win *Condé Nast Portfolio*'s number-one ranking on their "Worst American CEOs of All Time" list. Not only did he forfeit his lucrative position on Wall Street; he lost his securities license and wound up as a defendant in more than fifty lawsuits.

The exalted do sometimes come down with a thump, although that is the exception rather than the rule, even in Lehman Brothers' case. Kasich was an executive at Lehman until the collapse, and, according to the *Columbus Dispatch,* he "tried to persuade two state pension funds in 2002 to invest with Lehman Brothers while he was the managing director of the investment banking house's Columbus office." According to an April 2, 2010, Associated Press story, after the Lehman Brothers implosion, Ohio pensions took a $480 million hit as a result of having Lehman investments in their portfolio.

When running for the Ohio governorship in 2010, Kasich successfully fended off charges that he had anything to do with the management of the fallen investment house. Whenever disaster strikes an institution, its leading executives, for once, minimize their importance in their organization's pecking order, and such was his strategy: "Blaming me for Lehman Brothers is like blaming a car dealer in Zanesville for the collapse of General Motors."[14] As a native Ohioan, I might have predicted what forgiving natures and short memories my fellow Buckeyes possessed: Kasich was duly elected governor and is now a contender for the Republican presidential ticket in 2016. On the eve of his entering the presidential campaign, Kasich gave an interview to CNBC in which he defended the lack of prosecutions on Wall Street, saying, in the face of all evidence, "It's not like the system was rigged."[15] All of which proves very little, other than that elected officials, for the most part, are the carnival barkers whose job it is to bring the rubes into the big top.

The Psychopaths Next Door

Numerous psychological studies have revealed a significantly higher quotient of psychopathy in corporate CEOs than in the population at large, and give us a further clue beyond mere hubristic incompetence to explain why these operatives engage in risk seeking and even reckless behavior and have an inability to internalize social norms.[16] Psychopaths can be visibly antisocial in their behavior: when Donald Rumsfeld was appointed secretary of defense the first time in 1975, his immediate Pentagon staff presented him with a bouquet of flowers. Rumsfeld instantly threw the gift in the trash can in front of the staff in order to humiliate them and show them who was boss.[17]

Psychopaths can also be obsessively organized and give the appearance of being normal in their social relationships, often forming mutually dependent or parasitic relations with peers or superiors; this is known in Washington as "networking." Such people feel little empathy for the less fortunate or remorse for the people they have harmed, and they can never feel genuinely contrite about the messes they make. This trait explains why, rather than having the decency to shut their mouths, many of the authors of the Iraq disaster of 2003 took to the airwaves and op-ed pages in June 2014, when Iraq's security deteriorated, to justify their prior actions by advocating the expenditure of even more American blood while often insinuating that holders of other views were unpatriotic. John Bolton (Fox News), Dick Cheney (Fox News, ABC News, and the *Wall Street Journal*), L. Paul Bremer (CNN), and convicted Iran-Contra conspirator Elliott Abrams (*Politico*) all held forth before a largely supine and complicit media.

Likewise, after the collapse of the housing market in 2008, Angelo Mozillo, the Countywide Financial CEO whose greedy machinations played a significant role in creating the preconditions for the financial crash, blamed unions and the media for demonizing brilliant entrepreneurs like himself. It was as if Wrong Way Corrigan had come to the microphone to explain aerial navigation.

Did ambitious psychos like Rumsfeld and Mozillo scramble to the top of the heap against the will of the American people? To some extent they did. The political game is so rigged, and corporate malfeasance so inadequately policed, that their rise within the system was to a degree foreordained. But what about the system itself? Just as Americans console themselves with the belief that Washington is not the real America when it is only a distillation of all the best and worst qualities of any American town, so do people routinely condemn politicians and big shots of all stripes without noticing an uncomfortable resemblance.

It is one thing for pundits to denounce Dick Cheney and his henchmen for authorizing torture as if they were somehow disembodied from society at large, but it is more painful to reflect upon the results of a 2014 Amnesty International poll, which found that 45 percent of Americans believed that torture can be justified on public safety grounds, a significantly higher percentage than in any other country in what used to be called the civilized world.[18] By contrast, respondents in countries like Chile, Argentina, and Greece, where public knowledge of torture was much more up close and personal, gave sharply lower affirmative responses to the question than Americans did. The snarling face of Dick Cheney, some Americans would be shocked to find, is a grotesque reflection of their own countenance, distorted as in a funhouse mirror.

11

AUSTERITY FOR THEE BUT NOT FOR ME

The family which takes its mauve and cerise, air-conditioned, power-steered and power-braked automobile out for a tour passes through cities that are badly paved, made hideous by litter, blighted buildings, billboards, and posts for wires that should long since have been put underground . . . may reflect vaguely on the curious unevenness of their blessings.
    —John Kenneth Galbraith, *The Affluent Society,* 1958

Every gun that is made, every warship launched, every rocket fired signifies, in the final sense, a theft from those who hunger and are not fed, those who are cold and are not clothed.
    —President Dwight D. Eisenhower, farewell address, January 17, 1961

Is America a Poor Country?

On February 26, 2014, during the Obama administration's presentation of its budget proposal for the upcoming fiscal year, Secretary of State John Kerry made an unintentionally illuminating statement. Decrying the slight decline in his department's planned budget resulting from a bipartisan congressional budget deal reached the previous December, Kerry launched into a ritual denunciation of one of the Beltway's favorite villains: "isolationism." Since the days of Kerry's cold war predecessor Dean Acheson, secretaries of state have dutifully knocked down this straw man every time the public has grown tired of military interventions and the endless entanglements that follow in their wake. That is predictable fare from Foggy Bottom. But Kerry's next comment was more original: "We are beginning to behave like a poor nation."[1]

Yes, John, you might think so. A 2011 study by the Bertelsmann Foundation concluded that in measures of economic equality, social mobility, and poverty prevention, the United States ranks twenty-seventh out of the thirty-one advanced industrial nations belonging to the Organization for Economic Cooperation and Development.[2] The U.S. ranked ahead of only Turkey, Chile, and Mexico. *The Economist* Intelligence Unit's 2013 quality-of-life index, using different criteria, rates the United States a bit better but still only in sixteenth place. While Kerry's statement was an argument for more spending on foreign aid, meaning, among other things, the payment of baksheesh to compliant foreign despots, kleptocrats, and warlords, he inadvertently put his finger on the fact that by many measures, the United States really *is* becoming a poor country.

The result of the economic inequality that has become a predominant feature of the American social structure over the last three decades is not simply a forced choice between sirloin and ground chuck. An international health study has found that maternal mortality rates in the United States are not only falling behind improvements made in other countries; they are rising in absolute terms. In 1990, the U.S. maternal death rate was 12.4 per 100,000 cases; and by 2013, it had risen to 18.5. Other countries showing a similar rise include Afghanistan, Belize, and El Salvador. One of the authors of the study says that the sinking state of U.S. maternal care probably reflects "the performance of the health system as a whole."[3] The overall national rate masks even greater disparities in some regions of the United States: in Texas, the maternal mortality rate quadrupled over the last fifteen years to almost 25 out of 100,000 births, according to data from the state's Department of State Health Services.[4] This is comparable to a country like Lebanon and roughly five times the rate in Japan.

Such disparities can be found in other international metrics of health and well-being as well. According to the World Health Organization, the

United States ranks thirty-fifth among nations in life expectancy at birth. Easier and cheaper access to first-class health care is one of the major factors in lengthening life expectancy. In much of Western Europe, where such health care access is the norm, people live longer than Americans.

According to the World Health Organization, average life expectancy in the United States is 79 years compared to 83 in Switzerland; 82 in Italy, Sweden, France, Spain, Iceland, and Luxembourg; 81 in Norway, Austria, the Netherlands, Germany, Finland, and the Republic of Ireland; and 80 in Malta, the U.K., Belgium, Portugal, and Slovenia. In the impoverished areas of the United States, life expectancy is well below that. A 2013 study by the Institute of Health Metrics and Evaluation at the University of Washington discovered that in McDowell County, West Virginia, life expectancy for males was only 63.9 years. This is comparable to male life spans in such beacons of social advancement as Kazakhstan and Papua New Guinea.

This subpar performance in perhaps the most basic measures of national well-being underlines the political choices that our leaders have made for us: in 2014, the U.S. government gave $3.1 billion in direct grants and $3.8 billion in taxpayer-guaranteed loans to Israel—a country whose inhabitants have a greater life expectancy at birth than the donor country.[5] The NSA's grants to British intelligence organizations subsidize a country whose population lives longer on average than Americans.[6]

The United States is taking halting steps at redressing its health and longevity deficit. The Affordable Care Act of 2010 aims at getting every American insured, but as we have seen, the Supreme Court has already struck down key provisions in the law. This circumstance points to the fact that the absence of universal health care in the United States is not a question of resources—we certainly have enough money to wage expensive and futile wars, and can afford to equip our domestic police with armored behemoths—or of technical difficulty, but one of ideology. Even if Obamacare were to be implemented completely as written, it would still be too expensive, with its bribes to the pharmaceutical industry and subsidies to insurers. Every country in Western Europe has some form of universal health care, which might be implemented in different ways. The United Kingdom and Spain have single-payer systems, while Germany, with an employer-based, regulated, and fee-for-service approach, looks superficially similar to the American system, but it distinguishes itself from American health care by being significantly cheaper.

The Rutted Road to Ruin

As with longevity and health, so with transportation infrastructure. One wag was quoted in the *Washington Post* as saying that Amtrak has "Russian quality at Swiss prices. It is the shame of the developed world." But it turns out that the comment was a little too charitable: rail travel in Switzerland, a high-wage, high-cost country whose currency is above parity with the dollar, is more affordable than Amtrak. A round trip between Geneva and Zurich costs about 53 cents per mile. A round-trip ticket from Washington, D.C., to New York will cost nearly double that, at 98 cents per mile. And Amtrak is on time on only 72 percent of trips.[7]

This lamentable record is not entirely Amtrak's fault. Ever since the Reagan administration, Republicans have starved the system of capital funding, resulting in antique, worn-out rail infrastructure and high operating costs. Travel on the Northeast Corridor, where the *Post* made the cost comparison, is also expensive because operations there effectively help subsidize routes in places where passenger train travel is uneconomical, but where Congress forces Amtrak to operate (as with the U.S. Postal Service, congressional Republicans maintain a weird relationship with Amtrak—they hate it on ideological principles, but fight to maintain service in their *own* districts, and the health of the system as a whole be damned). When one of Amtrak's trains derailed at high speed in May 2015, causing eight deaths, many safety experts said the crash could have been averted had the system had the funds to install automatic train control technology to supplement the seventy-year-old signaling system of the Northeast Corridor. But the very day after the tragedy, Republicans on the House Appropriations Committee, on a party-line vote, cut Amtrak's budget request, which included such safety upgrades, by 18 percent.

As good a metaphor as any for the legislative gridlock and policy paralysis that have beset Washington can be found in a rail tunnel that skirts the southern edge of Capitol Hill. The tunnel carries the main north-south freight rail corridor on the densely populated East Coast, yet it is only a single-track tunnel built 110 years ago. It is also too low to accommodate the double-stacked containers on flatcars that are standard in most of the country. The old D.C. tunnel bottlenecks freight shipments between Maine and Florida; with luck, it may be replaced by a double-tracked, high-clearance tunnel by 2020. The contractors had better hurry, because the present tunnel is in terrible shape: already in 1985, a three-hundred-foot section of it collapsed.

The American Society of Civil Engineers, in its 2013 "report card" on the state of American infrastructure, rated it overall as a D+. Decades of boutique wars costing trillions and money wasted on reckless pork barrel projects or siphoned off into overseas tax havens appear to have taken their toll: in some places, money is no longer available even to maintain properly paved roads. Reversing a century-long trend in developed countries, many rural jurisdictions in Ohio, Michigan, North Dakota, and other states are grinding up their rutted and dilapidated paved roads and reusing the ground-up asphalt as a gravel-like surface. John Habermann of Purdue University's College of Engineering has called it "back to the stone age."[8]

Brian J. O'Malley, a former counsel with the Michigan legislature's Joint Special Committee on Pollutants and Contaminants, pointed out to me that gravel roads need maintenance, too, and entail additional costs. "The gravel wears out. When the stone is not replaced it grinds down to dust which sends up a choking cloud with each passing vehicle. Then ruts and permanent holes appear which fill with water, which breeds mosquitoes, and potentially malaria and yellow fever. The state of Michigan was oiling gravel roads to keep down dust and kill mosquitoes in stagnant pools well into the 1970s at the insistence of the Department of Public

Health, overruling the concerns of the Department of Natural Resources about polluted groundwater runoff. The gravel dust itself was considered a health hazard similar to mesothelioma. It was also an ideal refuge surface for diseases like tuberculosis, given the rapid airborne propagation of the dust. State health officials told me about bronchial illnesses in people who lived near gravel roads. To go back to gravel roads now reminds me of how you can trace the decline of the Roman empire by the increasing decrepitude of its land communications."[9]

I talked to O'Malley about America's failure to invest in infrastructure a few days after President Obama had requested $500 million to arm and train rebels attempting to overthrow the Syrian regime. This time, Obama assured us, we would be able to distinguish good insurgents from bad insurgents. At the same time as the president made this extraordinary request, the House and the Senate gridlocked on a long-term reauthorization of domestic surface transportation programs that would contain a mechanism to replenish the rapidly depleting Highway Trust Fund.

The expiration of a domestic authorization like the highway bill is an entirely predictable event. One merely requires knowledge of the calendar to enact a new authorization in a timely fashion. Yet Congress is incapable of doing more than passing temporary extensions of the current authorization, a stopgap that leaves the question of perennial underfunding unaddressed. The present federal gasoline tax, which has not been increased since 1993, is inadequate to cover costs anymore due to the increasing fuel efficiency of motor vehicles. Raising the tax appears to be out of the question because Republicans—the self-described party of personal responsibility—have a phobia about asking their electoral base to pay for the roads they drive on. Thus does the Appian Way begin to crumble even as the empire embroils itself in yet another messy conflict beyond its borders.

America First?

Congress's present slug-like lassitude is not always in evidence; as we have seen with the bank bailout, the institution can act expeditiously, even precipitately, at the behest of Deep State interests. When the stars align, Congress can even act decisively on its own initiative: within days after yet another resumption of the decades-long Israel-Palestine conflict during the summer of 2014, the Senate Defense Appropriations Subcommittee doubled U.S. funds for the Israeli Iron Dome missile defense system. There are disputes about the system's combat effectiveness,[10] but there is no dispute over Congress's speed in stepping into an intractable foreign conflict with even more money than the executive branch has thus far lavished upon it.

The chairman of the subcommittee, Senator Richard Durbin of Illinois, won some notoriety as a moderately candid truth teller in 2009 when he said of the Senate that the banks "frankly own the place." Apparently, the senator was not averse to fostering a similar relationship with the American lobbying affiliates of the Likud Party. Among some factions of the Deep State (being chairman of a defense subcommittee confers ex officio membership), the intensity of that relationship is considered a touchstone of good old American patriotism.

As the bill containing the Iron Dome provision proceeded to debate in the full Senate, other business intervened. A bill to address the Central American migration crisis, which had churned domestic politics during the summer of 2014, failed. So did a bill to extend a large number of popular tax provisions: it garnered 96 out of 100 Senate votes on a motion to proceed, but nevertheless fell to a Republican filibuster when majority leader Harry Reid refused to allow a vote on an amendment to repeal the medical device tax provision contained in the Affordable Care Act. The Iron Dome measure, however, miraculously survived when the otherwise terminally dysfunctional Senate considered it. Acting in lockstep, senators rolled over the lone objector, Senator Tom Coburn (R-OK), who protested that the $225 million for Iron Dome was not offset by spending reductions elsewhere. The bill cleared the chamber by unanimous consent. Senators were ecstatic, according to *Politico:* "Reid [D-NV], [Senator Mitch] McConnell [R-KY] and Sens. Lindsey Graham (R-S.C.) and John McCain (R-Ariz.) all shook hands after the Iron Dome money finally passed—an uncommon kumbaya moment in a bitterly divided Capitol."[11]

This profile in senatorial courage was very touching, and must have been deeply satisfying to billionaire political contributor Sheldon Adelson, who funds newspapers in Israel for the express purpose of supporting the Likud Party, and who has "auditioned" prospective GOP presidential candidates for their conformity with his views. As columnist Jim Newell wrote with minimal exaggeration, "It doesn't matter which Congress it is, or how dysfunctional things get. If there was another Civil War and a batch of states seceded from the union but Israel still needed its war money, the two sides would call a cease-fire, the seceding states would temporarily rejoin the union, go to Congress to pass the funding, and then re-secede and continue fighting."[12]

Prisons and Stadiums: The Infrastructure of Choice

Since about 1980, America's domestic infrastructure has become less and less the envy of the world and more often a cautionary tale about the perils of social disinvestment. In the past, examples of the American-built environment were wonders in their own right: Hoover Dam, the Golden Gate Bridge, the Saint Lawrence Seaway, the interstate highway system. That era has ended. One of the few examples of large-scale infrastructure investments today is prisons.

The ten states leading the nation in incarceration—Texas, Florida, California, New York, Michigan, Georgia, Illinois, Ohio, Colorado, and Missouri—operated more than three times as many prisons in 2000 as in 1979, with the total number of facilities increasing from 195 to 604.[13] In many poor rural counties in America, prisons are one of the few sources of stable full-time employment. Already by the mid-1980s, booming prison construction was outrunning state resources to operate them; the states turned to private contractors to manage the facilities in public-private partnerships. Private prisons had previously been done away with around the year 1900 because of widespread abuse, but neoliberals saw an opportunity for Lady Justice and Adam Smith to serve the same ends. As of 2011, there were 107 privately operated prisons in America.[14]

Another example of accelerated public infrastructure investment is sports stadiums and arenas. Dodger Stadium in Los Angeles is one of the last major professional sports facilities that was privately financed—and it was finished back in 1962. Ever since then, municipalities with failing school systems, rutted streets, and ramshackle public transit have lavished hundreds of millions of dollars each on professional sports stadiums. The financial benefits accrue almost exclusively to the wealthy franchise owners while the employment created consists mostly of seasonal, low-wage jobs. Cities typically use skewed economic analyses claiming that the proposed stadiums will have an economic multiplier effect, but, as economist Mark S. Rosentraub writes in his book *Major League Losers,* stadium receipts usually represent little or no net addition to a metropolitan area's economic activity, merely redirecting the local population's entertainment dollars from existing activities to a new one. Furthermore, the cities obtain inadequate shares of stadium revenue, since they usually submit to the extortionate terms of the franchise owners who threaten to leave town if those terms are not met.

All these practices culminated in the 2000s in the $1.5 billion boondoggle of New Yankee Stadium, a project replete with gimmicky tax breaks and suspect land transactions. And now bankrupt Detroit, a crumbling monument to the decay of once-thriving industrial America, will kick in $283 million of public money to build the Detroit Redwings a new arena. This fulsome contribution came as the city moved forward to cut municipal retiree pensions.[15] I suspect there are millions of American sports fans who would claim they'd die on the barricades against alien socialism, yet they seem to accept America's preferred form of socialism: the transfer of billions of dollars from municipal taxes into the hands of wealthy developers and franchise owners.

One such die-hard antisocialist sports fan is Wisconsin governor and Republican presidential hopeful Scott Walker. In 2015, the same year his budget slashed $250 million from the University of Wisconsin, one of the nation's premier state universities, Walker handed the identical amount of public money to two hedge fund managers who own the Milwaukee

Bucks basketball team in order to build them a new arena. Walker rationalized the scandalous deal by saying that keeping the team in Milwaukee
would garner $6.5 million in state tax revenues per year. That means it
will require almost forty years for the state to recoup Wisconsin taxpayers' initial outlay, and we can be sure the Bucks' owners will be clamoring
for another new public-financed arena decades before the state's expenditure on the 2015 deal is amortized. Walker's math skills would seem as
deficient as his sense of responsibility to the public interest—but the evidence that Jon Hammes, a major investor in the sports franchise, is also a
heavy political contributor to the governor, and that only a month before
the arena deal he was appointed co-chairman of Walker's presidential
fund-raising committee, suggests there is more to it than just poor political judgment on Walker's part.

Why We Fight

American elites do not like to address the contradictions between the extravagance of overseas adventurism and penury at home except in the
form of ritual denunciations of bogeymen. The *Washington Post* editorial
page, which has increasingly become the Beltway's cheerleader for reflexive interventionism, from time to time sees fit to explain ever so patiently
to the public why they must be obliged to intervene abroad, fight, die, and
spend. A typical argument goes like this: first, the sorrowful and conde-
scending acknowledgment by the adult in the room that the children are
indeed tired of the strain of intervention, war, and being forced to eat
their spinach: "As the toll, physical and financial, of the most recent U.S.
military engagements undeniably reminds us, that role imposes a price on
this country and its people. . . . It is natural that many Americans would
wish to lay down that burden. . . . It is equally natural that politicians
would compete for votes by promising to give a world-weary electorate
what it says it wants."[16]

Of course the public only *says* it wants less involvement in war and
intervention, but if they were as well informed as the *Post*'s editorial

board, they would grasp that the benefits are far greater than the burdens, such as having the dollar remain the world reserve currency and the enjoyment of free trade. The *Post*'s editors see the bright side: the bloody struggle of the Korean War and sixty years of U.S. military presence in that country gave us the Samsung smartphone! The editorial then takes a swipe at Senator Rand Paul for entertaining isolationist heresies, chides President Obama for failing to show leadership, and ends with the ritual invocation of General Maxwell D. Taylor's phrase about how the people will not "rally to the sound of an uncertain trumpet," a cliché these editorials use almost as frequently as their vow of no more Munichs.

Is it true that maintaining the dollar as the world reserve currency depends on having military forces in dozens of countries, fighting wars in Iraq and Afghanistan, and keeping large garrisons in Korea or Germany for decades on end? Since the 1960s there have been concerns about the U.S. dollar losing its leading status, but those concerns originally arose from heavy deficit spending, of which military spending was a significant portion; the growing trade deficit; and the direct foreign drain of dollars as a result of wars and the large expenditures abroad by our garrison forces.

It is a shaky system as well as a Faustian bargain that has many domestic policy downsides, not the least of which has been a hollowing manufacturing base and declining hourly wages. Economist Jared Bernstein believes the advantages of maintaining the dollar as the world reserve currency under the present circumstances are not worth the economic and social costs at home.[17] In any case, the dollar's future status will be determined far more by our domestic fiscal and monetary policies and the general health of the economy than by whether the United States sends troops to Ukraine, South Sudan, or the Persian Gulf. The failure of alternative currencies such as the euro to replace the dollar as the world currency has much more to do with their own persistent structural problems than our global military activities and Europe's lack of them.

The *Post* was equally unpersuasive with its free-trade argument. So-called free-trade (actually managed-trade) agreements like NAFTA, the

World Trade Organization, and granting most-favored-nation status to China are at bottom a recipe for the international arbitrage of labor to the lowest possible price. The whole editorial argument suggests slipshod reasoning at best. It does not point to any direct benefit resulting from America's extraordinary martial exertions in the Middle East and South Asia, but instead concocts secondary benefits (such as securing free-trade agreements) that turn out on examination to be tenuous if not nonexistent.

Driving to the Poorhouse in a Gold-Plated Tank

Another perennial backhanded justification for the Deep State and its foreign interventions is the claim that the military-industrial complex generates jobs. It is certainly a rationale Congress embraces on a bipartisan basis. But in reality the wildly uneven concentration of defense contracts and military bases means that some areas, like Washington, D.C., and San Diego, benefit greatly from DOD spending, but in most of the country the balance is a net negative: more is paid out in taxes to the Pentagon than comes back in local contracts. Economic justifications for Pentagon spending are even less persuasive when one considers that the $600 billion spent every year on the DOD generates comparatively few jobs per dollar spent. The World War II days of Rosie the Riveter are long gone; most weapons projects now require little touch labor. Instead, a disproportionate share of the contract price is siphoned off into high-cost research and development.

It was once the case that national defense research spun off many high-payoff technologies, such as commercial airliners with intercontinental range, or jet propulsion, to the civilian economy, but as defense R & D becomes more specialized and exotic, this is now less often true. One could make the case for drones, but given the highly problematic civil liberties issues entangled in the use of this technology, this gift may be a two-edged sword. The rest of the cost of defense contracts goes to exorbitant management expenditures, whopping overhead, and out-and-out padding—including, of course, a small but crucial percentage of the money that flows back into the coffers of political campaigns. A dollar appropriated for highway construction, health care, or education will create many more jobs than a dollar appropriated for Pentagon weapons procurement. The jobs argument is specious.*

The same cost-benefit ratio applies to Wall Street in its effects on the economy, albeit in an even more concentrated fashion. As the financial services industry has grown from 4.9 percent of America's gross domestic product in 1980 to 8.3 percent at its 2006 peak just before the crash, wealth has become more unequal. The public at large has faced stagnating or falling wages over the last three decades, and has only been able to maintain its standard of living by taking on more household debt. But the public's debts are the financial sector's assets. In New York, the headquarters of the financial services industry, we see the imbalance at its starkest. Despite the staggering wealth in the city that allows for new penthouse suites around Central Park to sell for close to $100 million and one New York restaurant to offer $95,000 truffles on its menu, New York's poverty rate rose to 21.2 percent in 2012.[18]

The contradiction between the power and majesty of the Deep State and the decline of public services and infrastructure is not an abstraction, as a tour of the rotting, decaying, bankrupt cities of the Midwest will attest. It is not even confined to those parts of the country like Detroit or Cleveland that have been left behind by a Washington consensus that favors the financialization and deindustrialization of the economy in the interests of shareholder value. This paradox is evident even within the Beltway itself, the richest metropolitan area in the nation. Although demographers and urban researchers invariably count Washington as a "world city," that is not always evident to those who live there. Virtually every time there is a severe summer thunderstorm, tens or even hundreds

---

* A University of Massachusetts study claims that several alternative ways of spending money would produce anywhere from 35 percent to 138 percent more jobs than spending the same amount on the DOD (http://www.peri.umass.edu/fileadmin/pdf/published_study/PERI_military_spending_2011.pdf).

of thousands of residents lose power, often for many days. There are occasional water restrictions over wide areas because water mains, poorly constructed and inadequately maintained, burst. The Washington metropolitan area considers it a Herculean task just to build a rail link to its international airport—with luck it may be completed by 2019, fifty-seven years after the airport opened.

Contrast that with the $103 billion the United States government has spent to date in direct aid to Afghanistan along with more than a half-trillion dollars on the U.S. military mission in that country, much of which flows to the local economy. By 2010, U.S. direct and indirect spending accounted for three-quarters of Afghanistan's gross domestic product, and produced economic growth rates of up to 14 percent per year.[19]

It is as if Hadrian's Wall was still fully manned and the fortifications along the border with Germania were never stronger, even as the city of Rome disintegrated from within and the life-sustaining aqueducts leading down from the hills began to crumble. The governing classes of the Deep State may deceive themselves with their dreams of omnipotence, but others beg to differ. A 2013 Pew poll that interviewed 38,000 people around the world found that in twenty-three of thirty-nine countries surveyed, a plurality of respondents said they believed China already had or would in the future replace the United States as the world's top economic power.[20]

Washington is the headquarters of the Deep State, but its time in the sun as a rival to Rome, Constantinople, or London may be term-limited by its overweening sense of self-importance and its habit, as Winwood Reade said of Rome, to "live off its principal till ruin stared it in the face." Living off its principal in this case means extracting value from the American people in vampire-like fashion and siphoning it off into hubristic and unnecessary military expenditures.

We are faced with two disagreeable implications. First, that the Deep State is so heavily entrenched, so well protected by surveillance, firepower, money, and its ability to co-opt resistance, that it is almost impervious to change. Second, it is populated with leaders whose instinctive reaction to the failure of their policies is to double down on those same policies in the future. Iraq was a failure briefly camouflaged by the fictitious success of the so-called surge. This public relations deception helped justify the surge in Afghanistan, which equally came to naught. Undeterred by that failure, the functionaries of the Deep State plunged into Libya. The smoking rubble of the Benghazi consulate, rather than discouraging further misadventure, seemed merely to incite the itch to get involved in Syria. Will the Deep State ride on the back of the American people from failure to failure until the country itself, despite its huge reserves of human and material capital, is slowly exhausted? The dusty road of empire is strewn with the carcasses of former great powers that exhausted themselves in like manner.

12

A STOPPED CLOCK IS RIGHT TWICE A DAY

Democracy is a pathetic belief in the collective wisdom of individual ignorance.
—H. L. Mencken, *Notes on Democracy* (1926)

Keep your government hands off my Medicare!
—Statement by a constituent to Representative Bob Inglis at a town hall meeting in Simpsonville, South Carolina, 2009

The Deep State and the Tea Party

While it seems to float above the constitutional state, the Deep State's essentially parasitic, extractive nature means that it is still tethered to the formal proceedings of governance: it thrives when there is tolerable functionality in the day-to-day operations of the federal government. As long as appropriations bills are passed on time, promotion lists are confirmed, secret budgets rubber-stamped, special tax subsidies for certain corporations approved without controversy, and too many awkward questions are not asked, the gears of the hybrid state will mesh noiselessly. But now that Congress increasingly reflects the ideology of the Tea Party, life for the ruling echelon has become more complicated.

That said, the gradual rightward journey of the Republican Party from a political group invested in orderly governance to a hyperpartisan cult with little interest in constructive solutions has on balance deepened the entrenchment of the Deep State. The core commitment of the present-day GOP, and particularly that of its extreme Tea Party wing, involves worship of individual wealth and rejection of civil government as a democratic mechanism for collective problem solving. This attitude generally suits the vested interests of the Deep State's governing elite, who wish not only to keep their own fortunes intact, but to profit from the dismantling and privatization of government institutions, whether they are state highways, public schools, or Social Security.

The Republican Party has come to embrace a paradoxical worldview that can best be described as antidemocratic populism. The GOP's rhetoric is stridently populist, and the party has perfected propaganda themes that set it on the side of "real Americans" (as it defines them) and against the so-called elites. The fact that Republicans identify their elite bogeymen as university professors (many of whom are now adjuncts making hamburger flipper wages), unionized public school teachers, or GS-9 government employees rather than hedge fund managers or oil company executives is quite satisfactory to the hedge fund managers and oil company executives who fund the party. "Real Americans," a phrase popularized by 2008 Republican vice presidential candidate Sarah Palin, generally refers to a white, increasingly elderly, and ever-more-rural segment of the voting population. Real America is a diminishing proportion of the electorate, and that fact provides a vital clue to the seeming contradiction between the current GOP's rabble-rousing populism and its antidemocratic instincts.

The demographically limited nature of real America explains the Republican Party's eagerness to restrict ballot access and gerrymander districts to a degree that infringes on many voters' rights to fair representation. Given the logical impossibility of gerrymandering U.S. Senate seats, some Tea Party adherents have even called for the repeal of the Seventeenth Amendment to the Constitution, which provides for the direct popular election of senators. Representative Ted Yoho of Florida has gone further, suggesting that the franchise ought to be limited to property owners.[1] Tea Partyers tend to see any electoral outcome that does not put them on top as inherently unfair and legally actionable: Chris McDaniel, the losing candidate in the 2014 Mississippi Republican primary, bitterly challenged as fraudulent and unconscionable the idea that any registered voter could vote in a Republican primary, mainly because they tended to vote for his opponent.

Just as the early-twentieth-century populist Left trotted out Joe Hill as an example of an American Everyman fighting for his political rights, so the modern antidemocratic populist Right has constructed its own flesh-and-blood avatars of real America for the TV and Internet age. Samuel "Joe the Plumber" Wurzelbacher, George Zimmerman, the characters on *Duck Dynasty*, Cliven Bundy, Josh Duggar—all won nominations to the pantheon of conservative superherodom for their purported averageness, grit, plain speaking, and most of all, for being victimized by the pitiless liberal system. But no sooner was each one nominated than he (it has always been a he) has come down with an ignominious thump. The rough-hewn populist Everyman from central casting inevitably slips up under public scrutiny and reveals opinions that at best elicit an embarrassed cough and eye-roll from the audience, and at worst border on clinically insane. But there is something in the nature of antidemocratic populism—principally the need to distract voters from the regressive nature of its platform—that requires these lurid parodies of Tom Joad, so we may expect talk radio and Fox News to generate many more. These ideological symbols of a pure American have at least brought one small benefit: they refute the more naïve schools of democratic theory which hold that the raw, untutored voice of the people is the voice of wisdom.

As a congressional staff member, I heard Republicans say that the whole point of obstruction in the Senate was not so much to derail any particular piece of legislation as to lower the favorability rating of Congress as an institution by showing that it doesn't work. Fostering public cynicism and apathy will lower voter turnout, which in turn is supposed to redound to the GOP's advantage. Republicans can usually count on high turnout by its older, motivated electoral core, particularly in midterm elections. It is this electoral strategy—winning elections by lowering overall voter turnout, rather than adding adherents to their own party—that makes the Tea Party the true heirs of Karl Rove's technique of the "politics of subtraction."* But ginning up the hopeless feeling that government is beyond redemption and that voting (at least by anyone who is not a real American) is pointless also benefits those in the invisible sphere of government who really do not want the public meddling with the ground rules.

Plutocratic Populism

The Tea Party has been the most politically effective upwelling of American populist anger in decades, but instead of besieging the prince's manor house, the pitchfork-wielding peasants have agitated against food stamps, health care, and increased oversight of banks. With a black comicalness worthy of an O. Henry short story, the creation myth of the Tea Party sheds a devastating light on its real objectives and its relation to America's plutocratic elites.

On February 19, 2009, a reporter for the financial network CNBC named Rick Santelli delivered an impassioned, high-decibel rant on the floor of the Chicago Mercantile Exchange denouncing the Homeowners Affordability and Stability Plan, which the Obama administration had announced the previous day. Santelli claimed that the legislation, which was supposed to encourage lenders to reduce mortgage interest payments for homeowners, was about "promoting bad behavior." To the approval of the futures traders on the floor, he suggested that a "Chicago Tea Party" might be an appropriate response, because borrowers stuck with bad mortgages were "losers" who deserved foreclosure. The *Chicago Sun-Times* later declared Santelli's outburst to be the opening round of the Tea Party political movement.

The Troubled Asset Relief Plan, the Term Asset-Backed Securities Loan Facility, quantitative easing, and all the other government programs

---

* The post-2012 spat between Karl Rove and Tea Party groups has been for the most part not a fight about ideology but about control of money, patronage, and valuable mailing lists with the names of suckers on them.

that pumped trillions of dollars into the bankers' pockets did not garner the same hyperthyroid level of indignation. The one government program that did was ostensibly designed to assist homeowners, or as Santelli put it, losers. So the CNBC reporter's bottom line was that Wall Street CEOs get a pass, but ordinary citizens must not. Yet his indignation was founded on a misconception that the administration's mortgage relief program was genuine. Timothy Geithner, Obama's treasury secretary, later told Neil Barofsky, the inspector general overseeing the integrity of TARP funding, that the administration's mortgage relief programs were merely intended to "foam the runway" for the banks—that is, to slow the rate of foreclosures just enough so that they did not overwhelm the lenders' capacity to process them.[2] Thus, if we believe Barofsky's recollection, the programs were mere window dressing for the convenience of the banks. Thus the Tea Party may have been launched as a result of the category error of believing the Obama administration's handling of the economy was fundamentally different from that of the preceding Bush administration. Accordingly, the newly minted Tea Party believed Obama had to be stopped at all costs.

How the Tea Party Drags Everybody to the Right

This surreal backstory underlines the principal political legacy of the Crash of 2008. Despite the ferocious partisan mudslinging, the actual policy differences in the Democrats' and Republicans' response to the crash were far narrower than the public narrative suggested. Yet the emergence of the Tea Party has been far from inconsequential, even if it was based on mistaken premises. Its huge influence within the GOP has had the effect of pulling both parties to the right, and by distorting the terms of political discourse and civic engagement, the Tea Party movement has further entrenched the wealthy elites, at least in the short term.

The majority of present-day Republican officeholders, operatives, and their large network of conservative media supporters hardly bother anymore to formulate public policy or comment constructively on current issues. Their function is identical to that of an Internet troll—to attack, get attention, and hijack the debate so as to render any attempt at intelligent discussion pointless. Whether the issue is the economy, health policy, or foreign affairs, they seize attention with hyperbolic attacks and use focus group–tested catchphrases and odd conspiracy theories (like insinuating that Hillary Clinton was somehow responsible for the rampages of the Nigerian terrorist group Boko Haram).

Even George Will, for thirty years the voice of boring and respectable conservatism and a lot of pompous balderdash about Edmund Burke, has seen the need to keep up with Rush Limbaugh and Ann Coulter so as to appeal to readers who prefer entertainment to constructive proposals. Will claimed in one column that victims of sexual assault on college campuses enjoyed a "coveted status that confers privilege."[3] Note that Will, a fey, bow tie–wearing patrician from Chevy Chase, Maryland, by way of Princeton, defends rape by the populist tactic of intimating that those claiming to have been raped are elitist snobs who have wangled an unmerited, privileged position. Since the less politically engaged public hardly knows where to begin to refute these idiotic canards—would you really waste your breath rebutting a neighbor who was adamant that the sun goes around the earth?—their arguments usually go unrefuted, and thanks to endless repetition in conservative media, Republican talking points lodge themselves in the national political discourse like a tapeworm in the digestive tract. Donald Trump has mastered this technique.

The GOP's political strategy may do little to gain new party adherents—it is mainly preaching to the converted and mobilizing them—but its strategic effect, intended or otherwise, is to suck out of the room any oxygen that might support more intelligent political discourse, and reduce debate to the lowest common denominator.

The so-called IRS scandal of 2013 might have been the occasion for a serious national discussion about the proper role of tax-exempt nonprofit organizations in the United States. There are more than a million of them, their rate of growth has surpassed that of the business sector, and they now constitute 5.4 percent of the economy.[4] Do they all support legitimate

charitable, educational, or social welfare purposes? Many so-called charitable organizations pay their CEOs seven-figure salaries. Why do these
entities pay no taxes? It is difficult to justify the National Football League's
nonprofit status when its commissioner, Roger Goodell, made $44.2 mil-
lion during 2012, the most recent year to be reported by the NFL, and
virtually all the team owners that make up the league are billionaires.*[5]
Many so-called educational foundations are nothing more than overt political advocacy organizations for wealthy donors like the Koch brothers
or George Soros. Some military contractors, such as the Logistics Management Institute, have organized as nonprofits. It makes you wonder, on
which planet has a defense contractor suddenly become uninterested in
profit? It is a bit difficult to associate the name Karl Rove with the cause of
social welfare, but he is nevertheless the head of a nonprofit 501(c)4 "social
welfare organization" whose sole purpose is to raise money for political
activities. Yet all the media reports revolved around the question whether
the Obama administration was victimizing Tea Party organizations because the IRS, amid an avalanche of applications, took so long to decide on
whether those groups merited nonprofit tax status.

A similar principled debate might have taken place after the attack on
the U.S. consulate in Benghazi, Libya, in 2012. What were the premises
of an armed intervention in Libya to overthrow its government, an intervention far exceeding the terms of the United Nations resolution mandating only a no-fly zone? Was there no provision for the law of unintended
consequences? What about investigative reporter Seymour Hersh's allegations that Benghazi was the focal point of a covert U.S. effort to smug-
gle arms from Gaddafi's inventory into Syria in support of insurgents
trying to overthrow the government there?[6] What we got instead was a

---

* The NFL announced in spring 2015 that it will give up its nonprofit status the following year. The league determined that there was no difference in the way it would
operate—raising the question of how many restrictions nonprofits must observe if
they can function just like a for-profit business. The only real difference is that by
running a for-profit, Goodell will no longer have to disclose his compensation.

supremely uninformative partisan political tribunal conducted by the same chicken-hawk politicians who only recently had been cheering the Libya misadventure.

These hearings are typical of the Tea Party era. They act as a political theater to bait the media into representing them to the public as the legitimate issues of the day. Meanwhile, the fundamental social questions— Who gets what? How sound is our democracy in a period of increasing economic inequality? What are the limits of U.S. military power abroad?—are swept under the rug. Thus the Tea Party–influenced GOP, by seizing the megaphone and stridently repeating its increasingly deranged memes, has made intelligent debate and the search for constructive solutions a fool's errand.

Tea Party Versus GOP Establishment: A Phony Conflict

Since Obama won his second term, one of the dominant media narratives has been the supposed war between the Tea Party and the GOP establishment. While a factional struggle to nominate candidates has led to considerable internecine brawling, we should not make too much of it. In almost every case where there has been a contest between a self-described Tea Party contestant and an establishment candidate, the issue was not over policy but over the personal presentability of the candidate. The only significant result of this intraparty struggle, over which Democrats take such gloating satisfaction, has been to drive the Republican Party even further to the right, which, by a law of political physics, drives the Democratic Party, conscious of its donor base, to the center-right. The Tea Party–establishment conflict is a mortal struggle mainly in the minds of Tea Party followers themselves, who thrive on conflict and a sense of their own victimization.

A *Washington Post* piece recounts a meeting of Tea Party candidates, elected officials, and operatives in Tysons Corner, Virginia, at the Ritz-Carlton Hotel, which is not normally a venue for peasant uprisings. There the Ritz revolutionaries drew up their manifesto, which the *Post* describes as follows: "In the 10-page pamphlet finalized Thursday, they called on party leaders to champion lower taxes, a well-funded military, and the idea that 'married moms and dads are best at raising kids.' The document warns Republicans against signing on to an immigration overhaul unless the U.S. border is 'fully secure,' and it argues that support for school prayer, a balanced-budget amendment and antiabortion legislation should remain priorities."[7]

While the *Post* presents this meeting as an effort by the conservative wing of the GOP to regain control of the party's agenda, there is hardly a single Republican candidate or officeholder throughout the country who could not have enthusiastically endorsed every single one of those agenda items. Moreover, with the exception of immigration legislation (corporate America wants changes in immigration law to ensure a large reservoir of foreign workers whose presence will keep wages down and render unionization more difficult), most business interests would endorse the Tea Party's stated agenda. Tax cuts and a flush military budget are the gravy that makes up for the Tea Party's immigration stance, and social issues like school prayer are just rube bait that doesn't affect corporate America's bottom line at all. The manifesto is less the symptom of a split within the GOP than a device to pump up a feeling of group solidarity and inch the party as a whole further to the right.

Is Gridlock Inconveniencing the Deep State?

If the business elite has no real problem with most of the ideological program of the Tea Party—after all, it was born of a financial reporter's rant at a commodities exchange—the dogmatic and heedless consequentiality with which the movement's devotees have pursued their apocalyptic vision has been unsettling to them. For if there is anything the Deep State requires, it is silent, uninterrupted cash flow and the confidence that things will go on as they have in the past. It is even willing to tolerate a degree of gridlock: mud wrestling over cultural issues may in fact usefully distract voters from its own agenda.

But recent antics over sequestration, the government shutdown, and the threat of default over the debt ceiling have disrupted that equilibrium. And an extreme gridlock has developed between the two parties such that continuing some level of budget cuts, including defense cuts, may be politically the least bad option for both parties. As much as Republicans may wish to give budgetary relief to the organs of national security, they cannot fully reverse agreed-to cuts without giving in to Democrats' demand for revenue increases. And Democrats wishing to spend more on domestic discretionary programs cannot eliminate reductions of domestic discretionary spending programs without Republicans insisting on entitlement cuts.

For the foreseeable future, the Deep State must restrain, if ever so slightly, its enormous appetite for taxpayer dollars going to the Pentagon: limited deals have softened the effect of sequestration, but it is unlikely that agency requests will be fully funded. Even Wall Street's rentier operations have been affected: after helping finance the Tea Party to advance their own interests, at least some of America's big-money players are now regretting the monster they have created. Like children playing with dynamite, the Tea Party's compulsion to drive the nation into credit default alarmed the grown-ups commanding the heights of capital, some of whom are now telling the politicians they thought they had hired to knock it off. In late 2013, as the possibility of another debt limit apocalypse approached, a senior political strategist of the U.S. Chamber of Commerce announced, "We are going to get engaged. The need is now more than ever to elect people who understand the free market and not silliness."[8]

The House vote to defund the NSA's illegal surveillance programs in July 2013 was equally illustrative of the disruptive nature of the Tea Party insurgency. Civil liberties Democrats alone would never have come so close to victory. Tea Party stalwart Justin Amash (R-MI), who has also upset the business community in his Michigan district as a result of his debt-limit fundamentalism, was the lead Republican sponsor of the NSA amendment, and most of the Republicans who voted with him were aligned with the Tea Party. Whether their vote was a sincere reaction to abuses of the Fourth Amendment protection against unreasonable searches and seizures or whether it was a partisan response to a program of which Obama happens to be the temporary steward would make interesting speculation, but the objective result was a challenge to the authority of the Deep State. The amendment lost narrowly, but in my experience, it has been very rare for an amendment promoted by junior members of the House and opposed by the leadership to come that close to passage on the first try.

Less than a year later, the House passed by an overwhelming margin of 293 to 123 a bill to restrict the NSA's collection of electronic records generated by Americans. While the final House bill came in for significant criticism from some civil liberties groups because the House leadership watered down several provisions just before it was called up for debate, it was still noteworthy as a sign of how much the congressional mood has changed since the days of the PATRIOT Act. This change of tenor was in part due to the militant attitude of the Tea Party congressmen—who for once did something constructive.

The Tea Party and Congress's Power of the Purse

The 112th Congress of 2011 to 2013 and the 113th Congress of 2013 to 2015 were the two least productive congresses since records started being compiled in 1948.[9] But the Tea Party has also profoundly shaken up the system in ways that the national media have barely noticed. Since the days of the Founders, Congress has used its power of the purse under Article I of the Constitution to set spending levels and priorities. This practice inevitably led to congressmen who would specify, or earmark, projects that would benefit their district or state. Over time, granting earmarks became standard strategy to get members of both parties to support appropriation bills.

By the 1980s and 1990s the practice had become so ingrained, and public perception of it as wasteful "pork barrel spending" had become so widespread, that organizations like Citizens Against Government Waste sprang up to denounce it and publicize egregious examples. Politicians like John McCain made a cottage industry of inveighing against earmarks.

It got worse. Disgraced Speaker of the House Dennis Hastert set up an anonymous trust to buy land, and then inserted earmarks in legislation directing the building of highways in the area to increase the value of his property. As Bret, a good friend who worked on the Hill at the time as a specialist on transportation issues, recalled: "One of the first things Hastert did as Speaker—I mean within a day or two [of his 1998 election as Speaker]—was to have hundreds of millions of transportation funds shifted to projects benefiting Illinois and his district—or more specifically to projects which would enhance the value of land he owned. When I pointed that out, I was called in by a senior Hastert aide who told me to 'shut the f*ck up.'"[10]

Outrageous cases like the late Senator Ted Stevens's $398 million "bridge to nowhere" in 2005 finally ignited a strong backlash against earmarks. By the time the Tea Party freshmen took their seats in January 2011, the move to drastically curtail such spending was in full swing. Now earmarks of the traditional kind are virtually extinct.* Does that mean Congress has finally banned pork barrel spending?

The first problem is a fundamental institutional one: if Congress is not competent to set its own spending priorities (and unfortunately there are rogues in the institution who will grab for their district anything that isn't nailed down), who is? The only alternative is the executive branch, which actually spends the funds Congress appropriates. But are self-interested bureaucracies the best judge of the wise expenditure of taxpayer dollars? Executive agencies, and particularly the Office of Management and Budget,

---

* The House's 2011 "ban" on earmarks has been occasionally honored more in the breach than in the observance. During the February 2011 deliberations on that fiscal year's defense funding, Speaker John Boehner inserted a provision to continue funding for the F-35's alternative engine, which happened to be partially manufactured in an Ohio GE plant employing many of his district's electorate. But the new Tea Party House of Representatives demonstrated its antiearmarking fervor when the full body voted for an amendment to kill the provision.

which writes the president's annual budget request, certainly believe they are: they want their recommendations, which now total almost $4 trillion annually, to be passed by Congress unamended. Executive branch budget requests, however, are no more sacrosanct than congressional earmarks.

Take the new F-35 fighter aircraft, panned by the Government Accountability Office and the Pentagon's own Office of Operational Test and Evaluation. But the Department of Defense insists it is its top priority, and has proposed scrapping proven, effective (and much cheaper) aircraft such as the A-10 and the F-16 in order both to make room in the budget for the F-35 and to burn its bridges by eliminating any alternatives. The total cost to buy the F-35 is now estimated at $399 billion—almost exactly a thousandfold greater than the most egregious congressional earmark in memory. In addition, the operation and support costs over the projected life span of the aircraft fleet exceed $1 trillion!

The F-35 does, however, possess one crucial advantage: it supports the policy objectives and cash-flow requirements of the Deep State far better than any number of freeway on-ramps, bridges, or irrigation projects that are typical examples of congressional earmarking. In order to garner more congressional votes for the F-35, the Air Force and Lockheed Martin have politically engineered the project's subcontracting to firms in every state except Alaska, Hawaii, Nebraska, and Wyoming.[11] Industrially, that is inefficient and drives up costs, but politically it is enormously effective. How is that any better than congressional earmarking?

There is no direct causal relationship between the decline of congressional earmarks and limits on government spending. Earmarks are carve-outs from an already agreed-upon budget. One can argue that earmarked projects are often inefficient spending, but they do not increase the deficit: Congress had already decided on the overall spending level in an annual budget resolution, and it was only a question of whose priorities, the legislative's or the executive's, would be funded. Earmarks also served an underrated purpose: while not a large percentage of appropriated funding—they were generally less than 1 percent—they acted as a lubricant for the legislative wheels and helped ensure a bipartisan buy-in so that bills would be passed by majorities of both parties. In today's highly partisan and ideological Congress, cooperation is the exception rather than the rule. This ideological approach has begun to have an impact on the smooth operation of the Deep State.

How the Tea Party Rattles the Lobbyists

When I asked a former colleague who had staffed the House Armed Services Committee and is now a lobbyist whether the new members of the House who are either explicit Tea Party candidates or sympathizers are really sincere about their principles, he told me the following: "About half of them go native and suck up the lobbyist contributions just like any other member. They understand the quid pro quo, and you don't have to explain the benefits of your proposal to them as long as your check clears the bank. About half, though, do not. They actually seem to believe what they're saying." A former Senate colleague, now employed by a major defense contractor, concurred, telling me that some Tea Party incumbents would not shift their positions about spending on military projects even when told there were jobs in their district or state dependent on the continued flow of money. Campaign contributions had little or no impact on their actions. Why?

Tea Party politicians' peculiar ideological orientation renders them relatively immune to the blandishments of lobbying so long as the electoral base that has sent them to Washington is happy. Thanks to the scientific gerrymandering of House districts and the voluntary "social sorting" of people with similar political beliefs into the same zip codes, incumbents are roughly 96 percent safe in general elections. So it is highly unlikely that a Tea Party Republican will ever be defeated by a Democratic candidate in the general election. *The Economist* has pointed out that House members, both Democratic and Republican, are safer in their districts than the crowned heads of the European monarchies, who have had a higher rate of turnover through death or abdication.[12]

The only threat to an incumbent Republican is a primary challenger who stands even further to the right. Thus has ideology replaced money, by no means in all races, but in the contests for a crucial fifty or sixty seats in the House of Representatives. This new reality has disrupted the business model of many K Street lobbyists who have specialized in obtaining earmarks for their clients. Van Scoyoc Associates, whose clients included public universities and municipalities, has seen its revenue fall 25 percent since 2010.[13] Lobbyists, as the middlemen between wealthy interests and Congress or the executive branch, have long reinforced antidemocratic and unrepresentative tendencies in American governance; their current distress over the no-earmarks rule is one more indication that the Tea Party already is upsetting, if only so far to a minor degree, the smooth functioning of the Deep State.

A Tea Party–Progressive Coalition?

One should not, however, make too much of these symptoms as a predictor of future politics. Ralph Nader, after decades on the left-hand fringe of American political discourse, has had an epiphany and believes an anti-establishment Left-Right alliance has the potential to overcome the oligarchical rule of the establishment that has smothered American politics over the last three decades. In his book *Unstoppable,* Nader sees evidence that populist conservatives—just like progressives—abhor the too-big-to-fail banking system, distrust the surveillance state, and are weary of foreign adventurism. It is possible he also detects a faint cultural resemblance between Left and Right.

Ever since it formed, the Tea Party has struck me as a kind of weird generational echo, forty years on, of the young leftists of the late 1960s. The 1960s leftists, like the Tea Party now, had unrealistic goals and were hostile to compromise. Both saw themselves as cultural forces up against a shadowy establishment. Both treated politics as street theater and had a curious fondness for using violent rhetoric and making apocalyptic pronouncements. Generationally speaking, the 1960s Left and the Right of today are the same group. It was the trailing edge of the Silent Generation and the leading edge of the Baby Boomers who overwhelmingly made up leftist organizations like Students for a Democratic Society. Circa 2015, the core demographic of the Tea Party, Rush Limbaugh, and Fox News are those over the age of sixty—early Boomers and late Silents. Indeed, they may even be the same people! One has only to think of former liberal operatives like Pat Caddell and Bob Beckel, who have settled comfortably into their new role as resident right-wing cranks on Fox News. Erstwhile leftist bad boy David Horowitz is now a second-string neoconservative, and former civil liberties lawyer Alan Dershowitz has since 9/11 advocated the imposition of legalized torture. If LSD was the gateway drug for the adolescent sixties Left, Fox News is the gateway drug for the senescent Right of the present day.

But Ralph Nader's belief that the populist Right in its present form could enter into a viable coalition that would enact the kinds of reforms that he advocates is wishful thinking. The populist American Right, particularly in its Tea Party incarnation, is too schizophrenic and deranged to make a reformist political coalition partner or engage in coherent governance, even if its theatrical behavior and brinkmanship have already disrupted some of the Deep State's operations. For all its histrionics about Wall Street banks, 95 percent of candidates whom Tea Party voters elect would never countenance a root-and-branch reform of the financial sector that would place compensation limits on executives and tax some of its operations. After all, the politicians chosen by a motivated Republican electorate have already voted en bloc against the tepid improvements of the Dodd-Frank financial reform bill.

The Tea Party distrusts the surveillance state under the guidance of Barack Obama, but these same Patrick Henrys who wave the Gadsden flag showed no similar agitation over George W. Bush's depredations against the Constitution. Their weariness of endless war on foreign shores betrays a comparable partisan dynamic; it only takes one minor-league incident like the prisoner swap that released Sergeant Bowe Berg-dahl for the populist Right to start snapping like rabid dogs (and for a few deranged individuals even to send death threats to Bergdahl's family).

Beyond the substantive issues of war, the economy, and civil liberties, the populist Right comes freighted with the baggage of the culture war: a mania for controlling people's private consensual relations as well as habitual conspiracy theorizing about death panels, birtherism, or whether the U.S. Army is trying to take over Texas. The spectacle of Tea Party members ranting against a bill to provide other Americans with health care makes Nader's dream of a Left-Right coalition achieving a single-payer health care system seem unrealistic.

The contemporary populist Right is a bastard child of corporate America, which has subsidized the Tea Party via front groups like Americans for Prosperity and the Club for Growth ever since the movement's beginning on the floor of the Chicago Mercantile Exchange. Its real, as opposed to stated, purpose was to distract and channel the inchoate popular longing for a change in the status quo. That this movement has not always pleased its benefactors is one more example of the fact that corporate rollouts are not always successful: for every Apple iPhone that fully lives up to the expectations of marketing strategists, there is a New Coke.

Nothing could mask the shock of the Washington pundits when Republican House majority leader Eric Cantor lost his primary election to an underfunded, unknown Tea Party candidate. It was the electoral equivalent of Pearl Harbor, mainly because they failed to predict it. The following day, the *Wall Street Journal* at least partially attributed a 102-point drop in the Dow Jones Industrial Average to Cantor's defeat.[14] But did it materially change anything? One intransigent Republican was replaced by an even more intransigent one, albeit with less seniority. The successful challenger, David Brat, employed populist and antiestablishment themes for the same reason that wolves don sheep's clothing.

Brat's previous job was teaching Ayn Rand–style economics at Randolph-Macon College. The position was endowed by the "charitable" foundation of a bank, BB&T, whose former CEO, John A. Allison IV, set up the endowment expressly to propagandize in favor of extreme laissez-faire ideology. Allison's philosophy is exemplified by his comment that merely requiring corporations to disclose the ratio between the compensation of their CEO and their median employee would be "an attack on the very productive."[15] If Tea Partyer Brat is a populist insurgent, I wonder what a reactionary would look like.

The Recurring American Cycle of Right-Wing Movements

Democratic pundits console themselves with the belief that the Tea Party's extremism has driven the GOP so far to the right, and made it so captive of an older, angrier voting demographic whose antics repel independents, that the Republican Party has locked itself into a death spiral. But a quick look at history suggests that their thesis is flawed.

Since World War II, America has seen a series of backlash populist movements—McCarthyism, the New Right that propelled Goldwater's 1964 candidacy, the backlash against the civil rights movement and campus disorders that gave birth to Nixon's Southern Strategy. And after Senator Joseph McCarthy's censure, Goldwater's election debacle, and Watergate, the wise men of the op-ed pages saw the right wing of the Republican Party as an electoral dead end and opined that the GOP must become a moderate, centrist party or face electoral suicide. And each time, the right wing of the party recovered with surprising speed and won elections, always on some sham populist platform opposing whichever elitist bogeyman the party's spin doctors had manufactured for that election cycle.

The external enemies might have changed from communists to Muslims, and the internal enemies from Nixon's campus protesters to Romney's 47 percent of Americans who were allegedly "takers," but from election to election the underlying dynamic has been strikingly similar. According to their narrative, the billionaire and the shoe clerk always have the same interests because both are taxpayers, and both are menaced by the same parasitic, un-American forces that use the government to prey equally on the billionaire and the shoe clerk. The Tea Party is a particularly well organized and heavily funded manifestation of this recurring theme, and neither it nor the Republican Party is going away anytime soon. Some quirk in the American psyche made up of nostalgia, resentment, anti-intellectualism, and fear makes backlash populism an abiding presence on the national political scene. It appeals, as Corey Robin writes in *The Reactionary Mind,* to people motivated by "the felt experience of having power, seeing it threatened, and trying to win it back."

The Tea Party cannot topple the Deep State both because it is a financial dependency of wealthy donors and AstroTurfed Washington organizations, and because it is incapable of coherent governance either alone or in coalition. Speaker of the House John Boehner's resignation vividly illustrates the irrational and cannibalistic nature of the movement. He was a staunch conservative by any objective standard, but also a politician who accepted the necessity of compromise in a divided government. Yet Tea Party extremists in the House drove Boehner out of power, demonstrating their implacable hostility not only toward liberals and moderates but toward anyone who refuses to swallow their exotic flavor of Kool-Aid.

Like Frankenstein's monster, the Tea Party is not entirely amenable to the will of its creator: the dangerously insane candidacy of Donald Trump, which infuriated the GOP establishment, was merely the logical culmination not only of the Tea Party's toxic ideology but of deep-seated trends in the broader Republican Party. To be sure, the Tea Party is a repository of discontent with the status quo, but there is little that it can do other than intermittently disrupt and inconvenience the Deep State.

13

SIGNS OF CHANGE?

Few will have the greatness to bend history itself, but each of us can work to change a small portion of events. It is from numberless diverse acts of courage and belief that human history is shaped.
—Robert F. Kennedy, address at the University of Cape Town, South Africa, June 6, 1966

Is Congress Getting a Backbone?

In certain quarters there have been a few green shoots of pushback to the Deep State and its demands. When Edward Snowden revealed the NSA's collection of sensitive data on U.S. citizens, I suspected that it would be at most a two-week story, like the disclosure of torture at Abu Ghraib prison in Iraq, or James Risen's exposé in the *New York Times* of the complicity of the telecoms in NSA spying. Yet Snowden's disclosure continued to build, gain resonance with the public, and even stir a somnolent Congress. Barely a month afterward, the House of Representatives narrowly failed to agree to an amendment that would have defunded the NSA's warrantless collection of data.

A month after that, the president, advocating yet another military intervention in the Middle East (this time in Syria), met with overwhelming public rejection. As Reuters reported on August 24, 2013, "Americans strongly oppose U.S. intervention and believe Washington should stay out of the conflict even if reports that Syria's government used deadly chemicals to attack civilians are confirmed. . . . About 60 percent of Americans surveyed said the United States should not intervene in Syria's civil war, while just 9 percent thought President Barack Obama should

act."[1] Even if the government were to produce proof that Syrian government forces had used chemical weapons, just one in four Americans favored intervention. Obama could obviously read public opinion polls and
the congressional mood, and he quickly changed the subject and grasped
at a diplomatic lifeline thrown to him by Vladimir Putin (of all people)
and changed the subject. While over the next two years the administration continued to push around the edges of involvement in Syria, the idea
of a full-dress military campaign to depose the regime appeared to be off
the table.

Has the visible, constitutional state, the one envisaged by Madison
and Jefferson, containing a Congress that is actually responsible to voters,
finally begun to reassert itself? Yes, to some extent, although the debate
about ISIS that unfolded in the summer of 2014 showed much of the same
reflexive hysteria that has characterized the whole period since 9/11. Still,
the scope of the NSA's warrantless surveillance is so vast that even habitual apologists have begun to backpedal from their knee-jerk defense of
the agency. As more people begin to awaken from the fearful and suggest-
ible mental state induced by 9/11, it is possible that the Deep State's de-
cade-old tactic of crying "Terrorism!" each time it faces resistance will no
longer elicit the same Pavlovian response.

The CIA Versus the Senate

On March 11, 2014, Senator Dianne Feinstein, chair of the Senate Intelligence Committee, delivered one of the more consequential congressional speeches of the last decade. She was addressing the committee's
investigation into allegations of torture by the CIA. A report on the findings, running to over 6,300 pages, had been completed more than a year
earlier. Her floor speech amounted to a bill of indictment of the spy
agency, which had been holding up the report's release on the pretext of a
declassification review. Floor speeches by members of Congress condemning this agency or that program are routine, but this one was a blis-
tering attack on the CIA—albeit in lawyerly language and maintaining

every institutional decorum—by a senator who had long been a reflexive defender of the intelligence community. Here are the most significant points that we can tease out of her speech:

- Torture, as practiced by the CIA, was worse than the conventional Beltway wisdom had believed. Her purpose in exposing it was to bring to light the "horrible details of a CIA program that never, never should have existed," so as to prevent torture from ever again becoming American policy.
- The agency misrepresented the results of its interrogations. The CIA claimed that "enhanced interrogation" (in ordinary English, torture) had extracted information from detainees, when in many cases the prisoners had already supplied the same information before being tortured.*
- The torture was conducted in "black sites" (unacknowledged facilities) in several countries. The Intelligence Committee redacted the names of the countries so as not to embarrass those governments, but given what went on at those sites, it is reasonable to believe that the host governments know certain things that the Intelligence Committee was unable to discover. Those governments now have leverage over a United States government that is not eager to see further details disclosed.
- The CIA spied on a congressional committee that was lawfully engaged in oversight of it, making the agency in violation of the statutory prohibition on domestic spying.
- Private contractors not only had access to secret documents to which the Intelligence Committee was not privy, they were actually in

---

* "Enhanced interrogation" is a literal translation of the German *verschärfte Vernehmung*, a term introduced by a Gestapo directive of June 12, 1942, to describe permissible methods of interrogating prisoners. Post–World War II war crimes tribunals judged the techniques described in the directive—techniques strikingly similar to those employed six decades later by the CIA—to be war crimes.

charge of vetting what the committee was permitted to see. The CIA thus granted more access to private contractors than to its own constitutional overseers, and gave them veto power over what Congress could know.

- To compound it all, the CIA was considering prosecution of Senate committee staffers for the "crime" of carrying out legitimate constitutional oversight.

What are we to make of all this? First let us consider the gravity of the issues at stake. Despite claims that torture was necessary to protect Americans, in reality it became a recruiting tool for terrorists and endangered the lives of U.S. soldiers. We do not need to rely on statements by senators operating from the comfort of their well-appointed offices that torture was counterproductive: Matthew Alexander, a veteran of U.S. Air Force counterintelligence who served as an interrogator in Iraq, reports that torture was the principle motivator for foreign jihadists to come to Iraq and fight Americans. He also says, "What I saw in Iraq still rattles me—both because it betrays our traditions and because it just doesn't work." Alexander found that old-fashioned police techniques like building rapport with detainees brought much better information than physical duress.[2]

The most important point is one that Feinstein never addressed. She said that the White House had supported her committee's probe of the CIA. It is hardly beyond the realm of possibility that Obama or one of his aides would have suggested as much while tolerating, or even encouraging, CIA obstruction. But suppose the president did support the committee's probe. That would suggest that the White House does not really control the CIA. In either case, whether from obstruction or lack of control, the situation merits Senator Feinstein's description as a constitutional crisis.

Our elected representatives were fighting an uphill battle, with every advantage in the hands of the CIA. The vast majority of the rules governing classification are generated by the executive branch rather than Congress, but they bind Congress as well—a potential breach of separation of powers. In order to make a declassified summary of the report public, the committee would thus have to submit it to the Obama administration for declassification. The government's security classification regime is daunting: in a single year, it makes about 183,000 original classification decisions.

It also classifies material referred to in newly classified files. This is called "derivative classification." In 2009, in its first year as the most open and transparent administration in history, the Obama administration took about 55 million derivative classification decisions.[3] The process by which material is classified was convoluted even during the cold war, but after 9/11 it morphed into a wilderness of mirrors. The rules for declassification are incoherent and contradictory, and can be arbitrarily twisted so that classifying material more often becomes a means of advancing the executive branch's political agenda or of suppressing embarrassing or downright criminal information.

Now no president—other maybe than Richard Nixon—would be so brazen as to issue an executive order instructing his agencies to classify documents to cover up a crime. And sure enough, the current top-level directive, titled "Executive Order 13526: Classified National Security Information," dated December 29, 2009, states the following:

SEC. I.7. CLASSIFICATION PROHIBITIONS AND LIMITATIONS.

(a) In no case shall information be classified, continue to be maintained as classified, or fail to be declassified in order to:

(1) conceal violations of law, inefficiency, or administrative error;
(2) prevent embarrassment to a person, organization, or agency;
(3) restrain competition; or
(4) prevent or delay the release of information that does not require protection in the interest of the national security.

This all sounds perfectly innocent, but any document disclosing illegal acts can still be classified by asserting that it contains information relevant to national security. It can then be redacted so as to conceal the crime. Recently declassified documents about events that took place decades ago often have so many blacked-out passages they look like player-piano rolls. It is often impossible to gain a coherent picture of the document's subject matter. To challenge the administration's classification decision, the Senate would have to know the details of what was being withheld and also contest the administration's decisions on classification, something the legislative branch has traditionally been reluctant to do. Even then, the CIA, the agency originating the material on which the report is based, would have the first cut at deciding what to reveal and what to keep classified—a clear conflict of interest when the issue is the legality of its own conduct.

As it happened, the CIA made its own referral to the Justice Department for potential prosecution—not against employees who may have hacked into Senate-controlled computers, but against the very Senate staffers who were the hacking targets, for supposedly accessing CIA documents they were not authorized to see. In Pontius Pilate fashion, the Justice Department decided to wash its hands of the whole issue, closing the case on July 9, 2014, without finding sufficient evidence either that the CIA had hacked the Senate's computers or that the Senate staffers had accessed forbidden documents. Later that same month, the CIA's own inspector general issued a report confirming that the agency's employees had engaged in hacking, and explaining that its lawyer, Robert Eatinger, had based his referral letter on inaccurate information.

John Brennan, the CIA director, who had earlier said that any senator who dared accuse the CIA of malfeasance would regret it, was forced to issue a rare personal apology to Dianne Feinstein and her Republican counterpart on the Senate Intelligence Committee. President Obama then expressed his full confidence in Brennan, despite calls from some senators for his resignation. This was only to be expected from a president who has smoothed Brennan's career path at every opportunity since taking office in 2009. Obama's statement did contain one mild surprise—a clear admission that the government had in fact used torture: "My hope is that this report reminds us once again that the character of our country has to be remembered in part not by what we do when things are easy, but what we do when things are hard. And when we engaged in some of these enhanced interrogation techniques, techniques that I believe and I think any fair-minded person would believe to be torture, we crossed a line."[4]

Perhaps in some breezy, sunlit alternate universe, Obama would actually allow the American people to read all the facts in the full report and judge for themselves what the government—the government he nominally leads—did in their name, but the president's statement did not quite put an end to the intelligence community's gamesmanship. The intelligence community was not going to give up without a fight. The next struggle predictably occurred over the agency's redactions of classified material in the report. While the CIA claimed it had redacted only 15 percent of its content, Intelligence Committee members complained that it was precisely the 15 percent that was key to understanding both the extent of the torture and the insignificance of its results. Committee member Mark Udall of Colorado complained that although the director of national intelligence, James Clapper, "may be technically correct that the document has been 85 percent declassified, it is also true that strategically placed redactions can make a narrative incomprehensible."[5]

Finally, in December 2014, still reeling from the midterm elections that had swept the Democrats from their Senate majority, the Obama administration cleared for release a 525-page summary of the torture report. Even this carefully redacted fragment told a story of deception, incompetence, and ultimate futility. The summary said that the CIA had outsourced the program to two psychologists, James Mitchell and Bruce Jessen. The two had never witnessed a real interrogation before and had no other relevant experience. At $2 million per interrogation, the program they oversaw had produced negligible intelligence of any value and many false leads.

Classified Foul-ups

My first serious professional brush with the puzzle of runaway classification came in 1988, after three B-1 bombers were written off in fatal
crashes shortly after the $280 million aircraft entered service. Two of
these accidents were later found to have been caused by poor design of the
fuel and hydraulic lines near hot engine components, a dangerous flaw.
My boss, John Kasich, represented a congressional district heavily involved in the manufacture of the plane, and he was naturally concerned
by the accidents. As a member of the Armed Services Committee, he assumed he would be granted access to the Air Force's accident investigation reports as a matter of course. He guessed wrong: the reports were not
available to Congress. It soon became evident that needless secrecy surrounded the crash reports: the services hid the details even from Armed
Services Committee members with the requisite clearances and an obvious need to know what had happened. Why the secrecy?

Excuses ranged from supposed ostensible concerns of the next of kin
to the need to protect proprietary contractor data to "just because." We
will probably never know why the Air Force chose to withhold the crash
reports, but my guess is that it was to prevent relatives of casualties from
filing liability suits for defective equipment. As we have seen, the genesis
of the state secrets privilege was to allow the Air Force in 1953 to render
inadmissible as evidence the report on the crash of a B-29 during a routine
training flight.

Classifying information protects legitimate secrets, to be sure, but
the process has gradually transmuted into a blunt instrument of political
control. It separates the sheep from the goats in Washington: the political insiders with access to classified information from the rank outsiders
without it. Kafkaesque actions like retroactive classification allow bureaucracies to demote, fire, or prosecute whistle-blowers who complain
about agency malfeasance. Paranoia has reached the point where workers in federal cafeterias must now undergo extensive (and expensive)
background checks. Some agencies even require a top-secret clearance

for their cooks.[6] But classification is also used as a tool to shape political debate.

The ship of state, the only known vessel to leak from the top, discreetly feeds to journalists tidbits of classified information that make the administration look good and its political opponents look bad. The practice has the tendency to make journalists dependent on their sources and inclined to depict them favorably. Congressmen on the Intelligence committees who are "read in" to "beyond–Top Secret" programs cannot discuss them even with their colleagues off the committees, thus stifling debate and impairing informed decision making on national security matters. There is no more potent sign of the triumph of the Deep State than the fact that contractor personnel are empowered to vet the secrets our elected officials are allowed to see. It remains to be seen whether the Senate's challenge to the cult of secrecy marks the beginning of a pushback against an out-of-control national security state, or whether it was merely an episodic spat occasioned by the bruised egos—which I can assure the reader are often as big as supernovas—of our current crop of senators.

Will the Supreme Court Rein In the Surveillance State?

A handful of senators does not a revolution make, but there are some indications that across the street from the Capitol, the justices at the Supreme Court are beginning to have reservations about the Panopticon state that has metastasized since 9/11. In June 2014 the court made a surprising ruling on the legal admissibility of cell phone data obtained without a judicial warrant. Law enforcement organizations naturally argued that warrants were not needed, in line with their perennial contention that unless the courts grant them police-state powers and complete immunity from wrongdoing, public safety will be endangered and officers' lives will be at risk. Since the demise of the Warren Court, and particularly since 9/11, America's court of last resort has normally found in favor of an authoritarian interpretation of police and national security powers.

This time, however, was different. The court ruled unanimously that a judicial warrant was required because the vast amount of personal data on a cell phone renders it qualitatively different from inspecting the contents of a wallet.

The ruling was carefully hedged to avoid inviting challenges to the admissibility of NSA surveillance, but it was nevertheless significant both for the unanimity of the verdict and its unambiguousness. It was certainly surprising to find that the most reactionary high court since the Gilded Age had ruled in favor of individual liberties against the prerogatives of the state. Perhaps the fact that the case did not involve corporate interests permitted it (one might have expected the phone manufacturers and carriers to have filed an amicus curae brief to demonstrate their newfound concern for their customers' privacy; alas, that did not happen).

Beyond the plain constitutional arguments on the narrow matter of domestic law enforcement, it is also possible that after an entire year's headlines about the fragility of personal privacy in the computer age, the justices just may have been spooked by the implications of the surveillance state. Or perhaps, despite the hackneyed government slogan that if you have nothing to hide you have nothing to fear, the truth is that *everybody*—even a robed chief justice on his alabaster throne in the temple of the Supreme Court—has something to hide and something to fear.

Silicon Valley Challenges the NSA

The final player challenging the Deep State is Silicon Valley. Owing to secrecy and obfuscation, it is hard to know how much of the NSA's relationship with the Valley is voluntary, how much is legally compelled through Foreign Intelligence Surveillance Act warrants, and how much is the NSA surreptitiously breaking into the tech companies' systems. Given the Valley's need to mollify customers with privacy concerns, it is difficult to take their protestations at face value. But evidence is accumulating that the Valley is losing billions in overseas business from companies, individuals, and governments that want to stop using the services of

American tech companies.[7] For high-tech entrepreneurs, the cash nexus is ultimately more compelling than the Deep State's demand for patriotic cooperation. Even legal compulsion can be combated: unlike individual citizens, tech firms have deep pockets and batteries of lawyers with which to fight government diktat. Silicon Valley is now lobbying Congress to restrain the NSA, and some tech firms, such as Microsoft, Google, and Yahoo, are moving to encrypt their data.[8]

This pushback has borne fruit. On January 17, 2014, President Obama announced several revisions to the NSA's data collection programs. These included withdrawing the NSA's custody of a domestic telephone record database, expanding requirements for judicial warrants, and ceasing to spy on (undefined) "friendly foreign leaders." Critics have denounced the changes as a cosmetic public relations move, but still they are politically significant. The clamor was loud enough for the president to feel the need to address it.

Microsoft is fighting the government's effort to access its email storage overseas. The Justice Department has issued a search warrant demanding access to the data in its servers in Ireland, and the company has challenged the warrant's legality in a lawsuit. Microsoft's motive is obvious and an amicus brief made it explicit: if the United States can legally obtain customer data physically located in a foreign country, foreign individuals and businesses will abandon Microsoft in favor of non-U.S.-based competitors. However self-interested the suit may be, Microsoft is fighting on behalf of a principle: does the United States have the right to extend its jurisdiction to other countries on a routine basis without gaining that government's approval?

Ordinarily, the United States must abide by its mutual legal assistance treaties with other countries. In the Microsoft case, an Irish court would have to approve the request for the email data. The administration has argued that the location of the servers holding the data is irrelevant because a U.S.-headquartered company, Microsoft, is subject to the warrant. Such an expansive interpretation, if upheld, would mean that the United States purports to exercise legal jurisdiction over the entire planet. Several hundred years of international law and state treaties would be invalidated by this novel precept. For the courts this will be a difficult conundrum to unravel: the Deep State, which has so far mostly gone undefeated in judicial venues, will be pitted against the claims of corporations, which have prevailed in most legal disputes over the last thirty years.

Silicon Valley is clearly ambivalent toward the NSA. It has collaborated with the agency on surveillance, and has even benefited in past years from seed money from the intelligence community; yet it has now experienced the downside of a hostile public reception at home and lost sales abroad. Apple has reacted by making the data encryption of its iPhone 6 so advanced as to be very difficult to crack; James Comey, the FBI director, has publicly complained that it will greatly complicate law enforcement's ability to access user data.[9]

Comey's concern is not a trivial one: our country should have the means to intercept the communications of criminals or violent extremists, subject to proper safeguards. But the legal and constitutional overreach of America's spy agencies and their contempt for congressional oversight made a scandalous revelation like Snowden's almost inevitable. That, in turn, was bound to force Silicon Valley's hand. With the public agitated over the security of their electronic devices, the IT industry did what any business must: respond to its customers, in this case by offering enhanced data encryption.

Silicon Valley's ambivalent position is reflected in the fate of the Stop Online Piracy Act (SOPA), which has been pending since 2011. While some segments of Silicon Valley, like the Business Software Alliance, supported this sweeping expansion of copyright privileges for intellectual property claimants, others grew leery of the bill's legal requirement for heavy-handed policing of the web by search engine providers like Google. Among the provisions in the bill was an authorization of court orders prohibiting advertisers and payment facilities from transacting with websites that infringed copyright, a ban on search engines displaying those websites, and court orders blocking Internet access to those websites. While Google has no compunctions about collecting user data on its own for profitable commercial purposes, it has no desire to be held liable if a pirate website happens to turn up in its search results. Parallel to this, a significant grassroots movement welled up to kill the legislation. The public reaction was quite unlike the 1990s, when telecommunications and copyright legislation sailed through Washington while the public hardly noticed. This time, Congress was forced to listen, and for now at least, SOPA is dead.

Whatever we might think of the moral propriety of Edward Snowden's theft of mountains of data from the NSA, it was one of the most politically consequential acts of recent years. It partially woke a lethargic Congress, prodded a Supreme Court normally subservient to national security claims to give more weight to individual privacy concerns, and shook Silicon Valley from its incestuous relationship with the intelligence community. But is that enough? Can this tentative rethinking gain enough momentum not just to score a few sporadic victories but to change the course of the national security state?

Overcoming the accumulated errors of our recent political path will require coming to terms with who Americans are, and who we want to be. It also means we will have to change the deeply ingrained habits of mind of our leadership class and the manner in which they look at the outside world.

14

AMERICA CONFRONTS THE WORLD

Great nations need organizing principles—and "Don't do stupid
stuff" is not an organizing principle.
  —Hillary Clinton, interview with *The Atlantic*, August 8, 2014

Mit der Dummheit kämpfen Götter selbst vergebens. (The gods themselves contend in vain against stupidity.)
  —Talbot in *Die Jungfrau von Orleans*, by Friedrich von Schiller, 1801

Doubling Down on Failure

America's future course is uncertain: whatever Bayesian analytics might
claim, the future is not scientifically predictable. The Deep State has until
recently seemed unshakable, and the latest events may only be a temporary perturbation in its trajectory. But history has a way of toppling the
altars of the mighty.

While the two great materialist and determinist ideologies of the twentieth century, Marxism and neoliberalism, respectively decreed that the
dictatorship of the proletariat and the dictatorship of the market were inevitable, any such determinism is illusory. Deep economic and social currents
may create the framework of history, but those currents can be channeled,
eddied, or even reversed by circumstance, chance, and human action.

Throughout history, state systems with outsized claims to power
have reacted to their environment in a peculiar way. Their strategy, re-
flecting the ossification of their own ruling elites, consisted of repeating
that nothing is wrong, that the status quo reflected the nation's unique

good fortune in being favored by God, and that those calling for change were merely subversive troublemakers. As in the cases of the French ancien régime, the Romanov dynasty, and the Habsburg empire, the strategy worked splendidly for a while, and then it didn't. To rephrase Hillary Clinton's statement, stupidity *was* their organizing principle, just as it has been for the American foreign policy Mrs. Clinton helped administer for four years. The final results in all such cases are likely to be disappointing.

Why do powers behave this way? Like the functionaries of empires of the past, the administrators of the Deep State have grown so used to getting their way through payoffs, backstairs maneuvering, force majeure, and the absence of anyone calling them to account that they have grown complacent, self-referential, and inwardly focused on their own processes. This mind-set is clearly visible in foreign policy. Whether the issue is Syria, Ukraine, or Iran, the framing device through which America's power elite sees the particular problem is lacking both a dispassionate examination of the complex history of the dispute and a pragmatic search for a solution.

As seen through the lens of Washington, other countries are not permitted to pursue their own conceptions of their legitimate national interest. Any foreign action perceived to conflict with America's grandiose conception of its destiny is automatically deemed hostile. As reflected through the media (which takes its cues and many of its commentators from the power elite), the picture becomes even more distorted, to the point that a crisis in a foreign land is not about that country at all; it's about us: Is the president "standing tall" or will he "cut and run?" How will it affect the New Hampshire primary?

This distorted framing device of course applies to domestic issues as well. Hank Paulson and Timothy Geithner rejected putting banks into receivership and replacing their executives because people with their backgrounds could not conceive of such a thing. The only thing to do was to bail out the banks and let top management keep their bonuses. Likewise, a global tax on financial transactions, which could go some distance toward curbing pernicious activities like high-frequency trading, was instantly off the table: Geithner was as incapable of grasping its merit as Hillary Clinton was blind to the merits of using diplomacy rather than force in Libya. President Obama hobbled his own health care proposal by declaring from the outset that a single-payer system was a nonstarter. He could have gotten a better bill, even if he did not envision legislation containing a single-payer system, by keeping it as a bargaining chip till later in the game. But he was a prisoner of the Washington consensus, which decrees that the wiser course is to cave to the lobbyists at the outset.

This intellectually incurious and self-referential aspect of the American elites makes them appear autistic to the observer. How else to account for Secretary of State John Kerry's impassioned tirade after Russia's takeover of Crimea: "You just don't, in the twenty-first century, behave in nineteenth-century fashion by invading another country on a completely trumped-up pretext."[1] Now most Americans might think twice about making such a statement in view of our own recent military record: after all, Kerry spent the better part of 2004 having to explain why he voted to invade Iraq if he was so critical of George W. Bush's war. Of all people, he should have been able to avoid that minefield when discussing Russia's aggressive actions. But the American press rarely asks our leaders to account for such statements; the moderator of Face the Nation, where Kerry made the comment, failed to call him out.

Kerry was at it again a couple of months later, showing how our national security establishment projects its own less admirable qualities onto those it considers rivals or threats. In an interview with the Wall Street Journal, he laid into Russian president Vladimir Putin: "You almost feel that he's creating his own reality, and his own sort of world, divorced from a lot of what's real on the ground for all those people, including people in his own country."[2] The Russian president is many things, a lot of them unpleasant, but delusional he is not; the diagnosis would seem perfectly applicable to Kerry himself and the rest of the national security establishment in Washington, whose benchmark for understanding international crises typically arises from domestic considerations. The tangled, millennia-old story of Syria and Iraq or Afghanistan, or the complex ethnic hatreds of the Balkans vanish before a few sonorous phrases like "regime change," "responsibility to protect," or "humanitarian intervention." This mind-set leads to predictable disasters from which the political establishment never learns the appropriate lessons.

In an interview with *The Atlantic* in August 2014 in which she distanced herself from Obama's foreign policy, Hillary Clinton downplayed recent Middle East disasters (and her role in supporting them) with a sweeping generalization, suggesting that everything will come out right in the end if we just stay the course: "You know, we did a good job in containing the Soviet Union but we made a lot of mistakes, we supported really nasty guys, we did some things that we are not particularly proud of, from Latin America to Southeast Asia, but we did have a kind of overarching framework about what we were trying to do that did lead to the defeat of the Soviet Union and the collapse of Communism. That was our objective. We achieved it."[3]

To describe the debacle of Vietnam as a "mistake" is like saying that contracting Ebola is equivalent to getting the sniffles. Our cold war policy of arming and training the Mujahidin in Afghanistan, which merely weakened a Soviet Union already in terminal decline, helped give rise to the very problems in the Middle East and South Asia that she thinks we can solve by employing the cold war model. Clinton goes on to complain that too many people fail to grasp the subtle genius of U.S. foreign policy because policy makers don't bother to explain it. "We don't even tell our own story very well these days," she said, suggesting that a corporate rebrand is all that is needed.

Bombing Syria to Impress Japan

Kerry and Clinton are by no means the worst exemplars of these tendencies. Anne-Marie Slaughter, Clinton's director of policy planning at the State Department from 2009 to 2011 and now president of the New America Foundation, a 501(c)3 nonprofit that receives contract money from the U.S. Agency for International Development and a handful of rich donors, responded to the Ukraine crisis with a call for action that was mystifying and reckless at the same time. In a commentary titled "Stopping Russia Starts in Syria," Slaughter argues that in order to show Putin that he means business, President Obama should lay on an intervention in Syria. And not some namby-pamby drone strike or covert actions, either, but a full-on, shock-and-awe military attack. The result, she says, "will change the strategic calculus not only in Damascus, but also in Moscow, not to mention Beijing and Tokyo."[4]

Bombing Damascus will change the strategic calculus in Tokyo?

Slaughter, who made her way up through the foreign policy establishment vetting system by way of Princeton (the Woodrow Wilson School), Harvard Law, and even in the bosom of the imperial mother country with a stint at Oxford, is an unusually pure example of the Eastern Seaboard foreign policy intellectual. The argument in her commentary boils down to saying that in order to punish Country A and make it desist from doing something your foreign policy establishment doesn't like, you should bomb Country B; the action will also impress Countries C and D.

Slaughter has all the credentials of what is usually considered a liberal internationalist, but her argument is no different from the foreign policy recommendation made a dozen years before by the very same neoconservatives who later came in for so much criticism from the liberals: "Everyone wants to go to Baghdad. Real men want to go to Teheran."* While these two foreign policy labels, that of the "liberal internationalist" and the "neoconservative," appear to contest each other on ideological grounds, the only real difference is who gets the spoils of high office and the attendant private sector rewards afterward. Anne-Marie Slaughter's brand of foolishness is bipartisan and enjoys a long pedigree. In 1975, our country squandered forty-nine service members to "rescue" the SS *May-*

---

* Ironically, this warmongering epigram was coined by an unnamed "senior British official" in an interview with *Newsweek* just before the Iraq invasion. It was endlessly and approvingly repeated by the Beltway's flock of chicken-hawk neoconservatives as evidence of their foreign policy machismo.

aguez when steps were already under way to gain the peaceful return of the ship and its crew. Why? Because Secretary of State Henry Kissinger felt that "the United States must carry out some act somewhere in the world which shows its determination to continue to be a world power." These foreign policy recipes remind one of the British quip that became common after a long string of military disasters in 1942: "When all else fails, invade Madagascar."

There is something darkly humorous in all this, but the public would find it less amusing to contemplate how the knee-jerk policy reflexes of our foreign affairs mandarinate frequently diminish, rather than enhance, our actual physical security. The U.S. government's overt and covert meddling in Ukrainian politics has stirred up a hornet's nest and threatens to maneuver the United States and Russia into an open cold war. This may be good news for the people leading governments in Warsaw, Tallinn, or Riga, who for good reasons of geography and history dislike and distrust the Russian state and who may wish to have an American senior partner to aggressively defend their interests, but it all but guarantees that for the foreseeable future, Russian intercontinental ballistic missiles carrying nuclear warheads will be targeted on Washington, D.C., New York, or Chicago, rather than on Teheran, Islamabad, or Beijing. It also greatly diminishes the chances that those Russian missiles might be scrapped after an arms agreement. We were all very lucky that the cold war ended without the nuclear trigger being pulled, but that does not ensure that our luck will always hold should there be a new cold war. Our foreign policy elites nevertheless cling to a superstitious belief in divine protection for America. As German chancellor Otto von Bismarck famously put it: "It has been said that a special Providence watches over children, drunkards, and the United States."

The quality of blind self-absorption is not confined to our national security elites. Many Wall Street and Valley billionaires, living a hermetically sealed existence surrounded by sycophants and coat holders, appear genuinely surprised that their public reputation is not that of heroic entrepreneurs selflessly creating jobs for employees and value for shareholders, but rather of greedy buccaneers who are not above exploiting labor and shortchanging investors or depositors.

Since these superrich elites are beyond reproach in their own minds, they interpret the criticism as victimization. When Obama suggested eliminating the "carried interest" loophole so that hedge fund managers would have to pay the same federal tax rates on their income that ordinary Americans pay, Stephen Schwarzman, the Blackstone Group CEO, said, "It's war. It's like when Hitler invaded Poland in 1939."[5] Pretty strong stuff, considering that Obama's suggestion went nowhere, nor did he even push it very hard. Silicon Valley venture capitalist Tom Perkins continued with the Nazi trope, writing a letter to the *Wall Street Journal* to "call attention to the parallels to fascist Nazi Germany in its war on its 'one percent,' namely its Jews, to the progressive war on the American one percent, namely the 'rich.' "[6] Oh, the humanity!

ISIS: Iraq War 3.0

The national security sector of the Deep State achieved a zenith of incoherence in June 2014, during the advance toward Baghdad of the insurgent group ISIS. Having already committed advisers and drones to shore up the corrupt and incompetent Iraqi government of Nouri al-Maliki, the Obama administration announced on June 26, 2014, that it was asking Congress to appropriate half a billion dollars to arm and train rebels fighting Syrian dictator Bashir al Assad.

The request meant that the United States government would be giving lethal support to Syrian rebels, the most effective military element of which was ISIS—a group we were bombing just across the border in Iraq. Put bluntly, the operatives of the Deep State committed the American people to supporting both sides of a transnational Sunni-Shi'a religious war. Accompanying the request were the predictable useless assurances that we would be able to distinguish between armed factions in a sectarian conflict whose origins most of the so-called national security experts in Washington patently do not understand.

Obama, like his predecessors, had fallen prey to the hubristic theory—disproven in venues as widely separated as the mountains of Afghanistan and the jungles of Central America—that he and his advisers possessed the intelligence and the moral sensitivity to select between "good" and "bad" terrorists. Thus, having already been burned by a near-intervention in Syria the year before, Obama was ready to place his hand on the red-hot stove once more. He hinted to the press that he was taking the step reluctantly, which raised the larger question of whether Obama was really in charge of the national security functions he nominally commanded, or whether he was a mere chairman of the board who ratified the prevailing consensus. To crown this masterpiece of confused thinking, a spokeswoman for the National Security Council released a statement full of Orwellian doublethink, which justified sending a huge quantity of arms into a war zone while insisting that "we continue to believe there is no military solution to this crisis. . . ."[7]

In the following months Obama pulled back slightly from his position, emphasizing the difficulty of distinguishing nascent democrats from jihadists among the Syrian rebels—a fair point, because it happened to be true. Such is the Alice in Wonderland nature of Washington, though, that Obama was attacked by Republicans, op-ed columnists, and his own former secretary of state, Hillary Clinton, for not being sufficiently hawkish either in Syria or Iraq. The mainstream media, as usual, failed to note that ISIS, however horrible its rampages, was an outgrowth of al-Qaeda in Iraq—a group that itself had arisen as a direct consequence of the U.S. occupation of Iraq a decade earlier. The media, therefore, gave strategic cover to the whole crowd of American know-nothings, from John McCain and Dick Cheney to Hillary Clinton, to revive their habitual war advocacy as if the previous decade's events had not discredited them. Sounding a shrill note of unmanly hysteria, Lindsey Graham even insisted we act militarily "before we all get killed here at home."[8]

Obama soon shifted positions once again, committing the country to a prolonged air campaign in Iraq and Syria. He cobbled together a coalition of convenience which included dubious regimes like Saudi Arabia that had funded and encouraged ISIS in the first place.[9] The rote and re-active nature of the national security establishment's response to events in the Middle East calls to mind the words of journalist Edward Peter Garrett, written more than sixty years ago: "We are no longer able to choose between peace and war. We have embraced perpetual war. We are no longer able to choose the time, the circumstances or the battlefield."

Every Problem Looks like a Nail

Why do people in high positions behave in such a manner? For years, journalist Carlotta Gall investigated the Pakistani government's covert role in manipulating terrorist groups within Pakistan and across the border in Afghanistan for her book *The Wrong Enemy.* She says that Pakistan's military and intelligence services have been at this shadowy and duplicitous activity for decades. Even though attempting to stage-manage such dangerous groups as the Taliban has brought ordinary Pakistanis nothing but grief, Pakistan's security services persist in the effort because it is basically all they know how to do—to a man who has only a hammer, every problem looks like a nail. And since Pakistan's senior military officers and intelligence officials personally benefit from these activities with increased power, money, and influence, they have every reason to continue, even if doing so wrecks the society they lead. Because of this kind of pervasive dysfunction, the Fund for Peace consistently ranks Pakistan very high in its Failed States Index.*

Our national security elites seem little different from the Pakistani military: it is only that our vastly bigger tax and resource base means the mischief can go on longer before a day of reckoning arrives. They are slowly sawing off the limb on which they sit and refuse to change their behavior. Psychologists call stubborn and irrational persistence in repeating an act or behavior "perseveration," defined as the attempt to overcome

---

* For public relations reasons, the think tank recently renamed its annual ranking the "fragile states index."

past failures by trying again at the same task. Our elites have become as accomplished at this in domestic as in foreign policy: despite thirty years of empirical evidence that tax cuts neither pay for themselves nor have any measurable effect on economic growth, large numbers of our political leaders keep on proposing the same policy and hoping for a different result.

Possibly the most discouraging result of this syndrome, however, is in foreign policy, as the irrational panic over ISIS has made painfully clear. More than a decade of war in the Middle East had discredited the authors of the Iraq invasion, disillusioned the public, and made further foreign adventurism thoroughly unpopular. The American people and their representatives in Congress were growing increasingly suspicious of the post-9/11 surveillance regime. Yet all that was required was for a terrorist group to bait us deliberately, just as Osama bin Laden had baited us years before, into reacting militarily as a tactic to aid their own jihadist recruiting. It is probable that Iraq and Syria will consume the rest of Barack Obama's presidency, consign his cherished domestic agenda to the back burner, and create a long-term burden that Obama will hand down to his successor.

The Deep State Has Unleashed Irrational Cultural Forces

Another problem the Deep State faces, although it is not yet an imminent threat, is the contradiction between the means of its survival and the cultural forces it has either unleashed or played a part in amplifying. At bottom, the military-industrial complex, Silicon Valley, and Wall Street are what Max Weber would have described as components of the process of modernization and rationalization of life: systematizing, quantifying, and bureaucratizing the spheres that they control. They are all dependent on the progress of science and technology, whether for the next generation of smart weapon, the virtual-reality glasses that Silicon Valley needs to obtain even more commercial data from the consumer, or the next financial algorithm (and the computers that can use it) in order to extract rents from a stream of investment capital. They are all creatures of science and technology, as well as the scientific method of rational inquiry that underlies them.

The cultural forces that help politically sustain both the militaristic and the corporate functions of the Deep State, however, are growing more irrational and antiscience. A military tradition that glories in force and appeals to self-sacrifice is the polar opposite of the Enlightenment heritage of rationality, the search for peace, and a belief in the common destiny of mankind. The warrior-leader, like the witch doctor, ultimately appeals to irrational emotionalism; and the cultural psychology that produces the bravest and most loyal warriors is a mind-set that is usually hostile to the sort of free inquiry on which scientific progress depends. This dynamic is observable in Afghanistan: no outside power has been able to conquer and pacify that society for millennia because of the tenacity of its warrior spirit; yet the country has one of the highest illiteracy rates on earth and is barely out of the Bronze Age in social development.

A similar paradox is observable in the relations between the business elites and the political movements they have funded. Rich corporations and their executives have spent decades egging on the foot soldiers of the conservative coalition to get the electoral results they desire: low marginal income tax rates on the wealthy, even lower tax rates on capital, and antiregulatory and antilabor governance. Along with the laissez-faire economic agenda that the oligarchy wants, however, the contemporary conservative coalition has brought a cultural agenda the CEOs may sniff at as retrograde and silly, and that incidentally has the potential to undermine the rationalist foundations of the society they command.

Will Anti-Intellectualism Undermine the Deep State?

The Deep State's own cynical political calculations have stirred up and sustained political movements that reflexively oppose, on ideological principle, the modern findings of many fields of science, such as evolutionary biology, geology, and climate science. Just as Islamic fundamentalist fanatics in Pakistan and Nigeria oppose polio vaccinations, a 2012 GOP presidential primary candidate, Michele Bachmann, attacked an opponent, Governor Rick Perry, for mandating that some of his state's public school pupils receive vaccinations against human papillomavirus. Conspiracy theorizing about vaccines has recently become a favorite topic of America's influential kooks from the mansions of Beverly Hills to the halls of Congress.

It is also unlikely that any other country in the developed world would have a sufficient base of antiscience sentiment to support institutions like the Creation Museum in Petersburg, Kentucky, which depicts human beings and dinosaurs coexisting in time, or the well-funded Discovery Institute in Seattle, Washington, which exists solely to advocate the pseudoscience of "intelligent design." The Creation Museum recently put on display dinosaur remains which, it claims, prove that Noah's flood occurred 4,500 years ago and that dinosaurs lived till then. Radiometric dating, according to sources like the National Park Service and Yale's Peabody Museum of Natural History, puts the age of the remains at about 145 million to 155 million years. The Creation Museum is run by Ken Ham, who is also the president and founder of the organization Answers in Genesis.

It would also appear that Ham is the inventor of a whole new form of mental illness: on the forty-fifth anniversary of the *Apollo 11* moon landing, Ham wrote that NASA should abandon space exploration—first, because it is a conscious rebuke to God, and second, because if NASA somehow found extraterrestrial life, it wouldn't matter anyway because those creatures are going to hell. Efforts like these to undermine science, whether they are the outcome of some obscure psychological trauma, or whether they stem from con artistry that preys on the gullible and uneducated, have not been without consequence. A study by the journal *Science* polled on public attitudes about evolution in the United States, thirty-two European countries, Turkey, and Japan; the only country where acceptance of evolution was lower than in the United States was Islamic Turkey.[10]

The United States now has the most prestigious institutions of scientific higher learning in the world. It also produces the greatest number of Nobel prize winners in science of any country. Both conditions have obtained ever since Germany, which had a comfortable lead in scientific research during the first three decades of the twentieth century, succumbed to political irrationalism and started condemning relativistic physics as Jewish science. As a result, scientists emigrated and Germany lost its position on the cutting edge of research.

This degeneration has occurred in historical civilizations as well. During its golden age from the eighth to the thirteenth centuries, the Islamic world was the world leader in science, mathematics, medicine, and philosophy, and far outstripped contemporary Europe in these fields. But by the thirteenth century, the Islamic world was already beginning to run out of intellectual energy. There was no single cause for this stagnation and decline, but antirationalist movements began to challenge scientific cosmopolitanism. The Islamic world became more and more opposed to scholarship and scientific inquiry that did not directly aid in the religious ordering of life. During the succeeding centuries, according to the noted Islamic history scholar Bernard Lewis, "The Renaissance, the Reformation, even the scientific revolution and the Enlightenment, passed unnoticed in the Muslim world."[11]

Recent outbursts of know-nothingism on the American Right are not confined to marginal issues in the conservative movement—they affect basic matters of national security. The largest single constituency of the Republican coalition is made up of self-identified evangelical Christians, a large percentage of whom believe in the rapture, a doctrine invented during the last two centuries by religious fundamentalists. This dogma holds that true Christians will be wafted into heaven when a cataclysmic battle in the Holy Land occurs, heralding Christ's return to earth. Proponents of this belief magnify the worst instincts of Republican policy makers, whose naturally aggressive military plans for the Middle East receive additional encouragement from a significant portion of their political base, which believes war in that region will trigger the fulfillment of a (fictitious) biblical prophecy. In a sense, the apocalypse is the right-wing fundamentalist's equivalent of the Muslim extremist's caliphate: a rule of the righteous, preceded by rivers of blood.

Fundamentalist preachers such as John Hagee of Texas, who claims almost two million followers, advocate the most extreme hard line in the Middle East; Hagee has called for a preemptive nuclear attack on Iran. GOP political figures such as Sarah Palin and Mike Huckabee publicly avow end times mythology, and in April 2015, Michele Bachmann claimed that the rapture was coming and Obama was responsible—which would presumably make him the Antichrist.[12] Some may suggest that lunatic-fringe politicians like these are unlikely to affect national security policy, but such thinking may already have influenced the decision to invade Iraq. According to a French journalist, then-president Jacques Chirac was "stupefied" when George W. Bush told him a reason for the 2003 invasion: "This confrontation is willed by God, who wants to use this conflict to erase his people's enemies before a New Age begins." Afterward, poor Chirac supposedly sought counsel from a professor of theology at the University of Lausanne as to what Bush possibly could have meant.[13]

Such intellectual obscurantism can also impair understanding of the technical details of vital national security issues. One additional reason for Republicans' adamant opposition to the Iran agreement may be that it touches on scientific issues and requires a passing familiarity with nuclear physics. How can a senator grasp the agreement's details about uranium enrichment or plutonium reprocessing if his ideology commands him to dispute the scientific age of the earth, a fact well established by (among other things) an understanding of nuclear physics based on the rate of decay of radioactive isotopes?

On May 22, 2014, on a near–party line vote, the Republican-controlled House of Representatives agreed to an amendment to the defense authorization bill that would ban the Department of Defense from participating in climate research. This vote came despite the department's own judgment in its most recent strategy document, the 2014 Quadrennial Defense Review, that disruptive climate change effects can produce new global instability and complicate the department's missions. The ban is similar to past edicts that prohibit government-funded institutions like the National Institutes of Health from studying the public health impacts of violence involving firearms.

As obscurantist as these initiatives are, there is probably worse to come at the state level, where school curricula are established (if you think the House of Representatives is bad, that institution resembles the National Academy of Sciences compared to some state legislatures). Already, Louisiana has a law on the books encouraging teachers to teach the (imaginary) controversy about evolution, and several other state legislatures have followed with similar bills. Some other advanced democracies such as the United Kingdom forbid teaching creationism in schools, even private ones, because to them it is not a matter of religious or academic freedom, but rather consumer fraud: they believe it should be illegal to harm minors by systematically impairing their education. Should the type of driving intellectual curiosity that has characterized Tea Party Republicans and their fellow travelers become any more widespread in American society, we can look forward to the sort of rigid, epistemic closure that bans heretical ideas in the same way that Catholic prelates placed an interdict upon Galileo Galilei for teaching the heliocentric model of the solar system.

The Deep State: Evolving Toward Extinction?

The mortal danger of wildfire to a herd of deer is what a half century of disastrous involvement in the Middle East ought to represent to American policy makers. But it does not. Being in favor of the Iraq War may have been objectively wrong, but it was an astute career move for many government operatives and contractors. Wall Street CEOs failed to understand that leveraging their portfolios with derivatives contracts was the equivalent of giving a child a loaded pistol, but with the exception of a handful of people like Richard Fuld, the main Wall Street players are still in their jobs, leveraging up for the next financial bubble.

Nature provides numerous examples of species whose traits have evolved such that they become maladapted to their environments. The extinct Irish elk's outsized antlers became more of a hindrance to its survival than a benefit: during periods of peak antler growth, the animal experienced osteoporosis. In a similar fashion, the military-industrial complex's pampered, privileged position in society and its cost-is-no-object mentality, along with its rigid and bureaucratized hierarchy, have made it a less effective force in accomplishing its overriding purpose: fighting and winning wars. That goal has become subsidiary to mastering Washington politics, maintaining the cash flow to contractors, and offering senior personnel second careers in industry. These maladaptations affect the quality both of personnel and equipment. This lengthy catalog of dysfunctions in our governing institutions both public and private, and in the elites that control them, points to a system that is not sustainable in the long term. It is also not that unusual in light of history. The normal way mature power structures try to maintain themselves is by redefining their vices as virtues and their mistakes as harmless mulligans that should not be counted on the scorecard. Disasters like Vietnam and Iraq no more undermine the legitimacy of the elites who engineered them, at least in their own eyes, than the sinking of the Spanish Armada undermined Philip II's unshakable belief that he was on the throne by the grace of God. It is the strategy of deny and move on. But it cannot go on.

15

IS THERE AN ALTERNATIVE?

I am not an advocate for frequent changes in laws and constitutions.
But laws and institutions must go hand in hand with the progress of
the human mind.
—Thomas Jefferson, letter to Samuel Kercheval, July 12, 1816

Overcoming Our New Gilded Age

There is an alternative strategy to the one habitually employed by great
powers in crisis. It was embraced to varying degrees and with differing
goals by figures of such contrasting personalities as Mustafa Kemal
Atatürk, Franklin D. Roosevelt, Charles de Gaulle, and Deng Xiaoping.
They were certainly not revolutionaries by temperament; if anything,
their natures were conservative. But they understood that the political
cultures in which they operated were fossilized and incapable of adapting
to the times. In their drive to reform and modernize the political systems
they inherited, their first obstacles to overcome were the outworn myths
that encrusted the thinking of the elites.

As the United States confronts its future after experiencing two
failed wars, a financial meltdown, and $17 trillion in accumulated debt,
the punditry has split into two camps: the first, the declinist camp, sees a
broken, dysfunctional political system incapable of reform and an economy soon to be overtaken by China. *New Yorker* writer George Packer is
one such voice, who sees our leadership class's breaking of the implicit
social compact more than three decades ago as the beginning of a great
"unwinding" process that has set the country on a downward trajectory.[1]
The other camp, the reformers, offers a profusion of individual nostrums

to turn the nation around: electoral reform, banking reform, military reform, and so on, without any real expectation they will be enacted before the Second Coming. Entrenched interests will fight tooth and nail against such proposals; that is why they are entrenched. But American history has many examples of reform occurring because the public demanded it and would not be silenced.

After the Civil War, the American political system was as locked down as it is now. Corporations owned the state legislatures and got what they wanted. It was during the 1880s, at the height of the Gilded Age, that the courts began accepting the notion of corporate personhood. Railroads could bankrupt farmers with discriminatory freight rates, while oil tycoons like John D. Rockefeller sought to drive every last competitor out of business (the railroads that overcharged the farmer gave steep freight discounts to Rockefeller for the privilege of transporting his oil). Our national economic policy was effectively being run by J. P. Morgan and a handful of his banking cronies. Striking workers were routinely massacred by corporate security guards.

Yet somehow, by dint of sustained agitation by prairie populists and urban progressives alike, conditions began to change. Congress passed the Sherman and Clayton antitrust measures and pure food and drug laws; states began to regulate the conditions of labor; child labor was gradually abolished; some states granted their citizens the power of initiative, referendum, and recall. Women finally received the vote. A couple of decades later, the New Deal completed the agenda with wage and hour laws, collective bargaining rights, banking reform, old age and disability insurance, and several other innovations—and this occurred during the biggest global economic catastrophe of the modern age.

Our forebears have shown that reforming the American political system, while likely to be difficult and protracted (it may take decades to accomplish) is not impossible. The Snowden revelations, whose impact has been surprisingly strong; the derailed drive for military intervention in Syria; a fractious Congress whose dysfunctions have begun to be an inconvenience to the Deep State; and the record level of popular dissatisfaction with the political status quo all show that there is now a deep but as yet inchoate hunger for change.

What would a platform for political change look like? Many reformers have studied their own pet issue for so long that they have developed a tunnel vision when it comes to the bigger picture. Accordingly, they offer single-issue reforms as a kind of panacea. Those on the Left, like Elizabeth Warren, who have looked long and hard at the financial industry, have begun to sound as if they think it is the source of all our problems, and that breaking up the big banks and implementing some other financial reforms will solve everything. Their view is perhaps more realistic than those on the Right who believe reintroducing the gold standard will cure every ailment from monetary inflation to the heartbreak of psoriasis, but neither one gets to the root of the problem.

We have many creative minds writing persuasively about a variety of American domestic issues, but they tend to see foreign and national security policy as a mysterious black box whose contents they are not qualified to comment on. I experienced this professionally, as colleagues and supervisors tended to regard national defense as something exotic and mysterious. That was fine with me—it reduced micromanagement, as I was the guy who supposedly knew about it—but it occurred to me that they didn't grasp the fact that defense was just one more government program paid for by funds drawn from the Treasury. Defense and domestic policy are intimately related. The business models of the military-industrial complex and the health care complex are identical in essence—their overriding output goal is cost, as third parties—either the taxpayer or the insurer—always foot the bill.

No one can talk about distortions in the American economy such as poor infrastructure or persistent unemployment, or make sense of civil liberties issues here at home, without understanding the high price exacted upon them by America's foreign policy and the national security state. The problems we sow overseas we will reap here, and not just in some metaphorical sense: everything has an opportunity cost, whether it is the dollars extracted from road and bridge repair and funneled into graft in the Middle East, or the moral and human cost of sending troops to fight and be wounded in protracted wars and offering our police fourteen-ton armored cars in case returning veterans with combat skills go crazy.

Those who decry too-big-to-fail banks often do not understand that they are the price of globalization and our drive to keep the dollar as the world reserve currency despite an eroding domestic industrial base. An explicit rationale for repealing Glass-Steagall was the alleged need for megabanks to compete with overseas institutions. A more tacit rationale was the efficiency of big banks at recycling back into the New York financial market the huge dollar surpluses of the Middle East and East Asia.

To think that one discrete reform will measurably change the system is like imagining that one could paint a pointillist picture from three inches away. One must step back and see the canvas whole, just as one must recognize that our economic system, approach to criminal justice, corporate privileges, and propensity to get into wars are not separate problems. They all spring from a complex of incentives in our system as it exists today. They will all have to be tackled if the country is to reverse the decay of its constitutionally established institutions and the transformation of its once-formidable manufacturing economy into a winner-take-all plutocracy. What follows are reforms that I believe could begin to stop the rot and put the United States back on track.

1. **Eliminate private money from public elections.** This is the first recommendation, because it is the key reform without which none of the other policy changes will happen. We can't afford to nibble around the edges with another McCain-Feingold Act or other marginal changes that can easily be bypassed. The only rational response after decades of ever more arcane laws and regulations and ever more creative evasions is to scrap the whole system and start from square one. We must get money out of our elections—that means *all* private money. Federally funded campaigns will undoubtedly create new problems, but can they be remotely as bad as the auctioning of candidates

that occurs today? With a small, guaranteed sum of money during a limited campaigning season (perhaps from Labor Day until the November election, a generous campaign season compared to election campaigns in the United Kingdom, which last less than a month, or Australia, where they last about six weeks) against an opponent who would get the same amount, but no more, we could finally end the interminable campaign season (which in the House begins the day a new member is sworn in), and incumbents could at last spend time governing rather than going to fund-raisers and dialing for dollars outside their congressional offices.

Public funding would be a cost-effective investment in the long run. Let us bear in mind that a few hundred thousand dollars in bundled contributions led to a $550 million loss to taxpayers in the Solyndra alternative energy case, and a few million dollars in Halliburton contributions led to billions in waste, fraud, and abuse in Iraq. A politician is a hog grateful to whoever is rattling the stick inside the swill bucket. It is time to take the swill bucket away.

2. **Sensibly redeploy and downsize the military and intelligence complex.** Evacuating most of our nearly six hundred overseas bases would save tens of billions of dollars annually. Remember South Korea, where the garrisoning of U.S. troops for sixty years rewarded us with the blessing of the Samsung smartphone? We now have a $20 billion annual trade deficit with South Korea, whose own gross domestic product is roughly one hundred times that of its North Korean rival. Our trade deficit with South Korea is larger in dollars than North Korea's entire economy. It is time for our allies to take up the slack. With somewhat less yawning disparities, the same lopsided economic comparisons apply elsewhere: the European Union has an economy eight times that of Russia, so why does the United States have to make military demonstrations in Poland to impress the Kremlin?

The "stability" that U.S. military power provides is dubious, comes at a high economic cost not borne by those allies who benefit, and could easily be replaced by slightly greater exertions from the host countries. A military sized to defend legitimate U.S. interests could make economies without losing capability. Indeed, it would gain combat power by jettisoning its gold-plated weapon systems whose intricate design is mainly intended to enrich contractors. The U.S. intelligence complex could also be rightsized to provide higher quality and more objective political intelligence on foreign events (the true purpose of foreign intelligence) rather than abusing U.S. citizens' Fourth Amendment rights. The surveillance state makes a mockery of all the pathetic compensatory braying we hear in some quarters about our being the land of the free and the home of the brave. The CIA must also jettison its legion of contract paramilitary gangs and covert troublemakers, whose activities are not worth the blowback that invariably results—as our last thirty years' experience in the Middle East and South Asia has made painfully evident.

3. **Stay out of the Middle East.** As should be evident from our decades-long fatal embrace of that troubled part of the world, the United States seems to have a reverse Midas touch: virtually everything we have touched has gone badly. Americans have arrogance aplenty, but it is clear they possess neither the intellectual discipline nor the wisdom to micromanage that volatile region. I suspect no one else has: although the British Empire is supposed in some circles to be a model for how to handle world power, the British made an appalling hash of the Middle East during World War I, creating problems that fester still. The time has come for some brave, farsighted American statesman to say, "Enough."

Our repeated interventions have not assured our security; they have impaired it at ruinous expense and created more enemies than our armed forces can kill. ISIS is undeniably a toxic gang of murderers, but our own disastrous intervention in Iraq formed the petri dish in which its diseased ideology could evolve. These and other failed interventions have necessitated or (more likely) furnished the Deep State with a convenient rationale for a huge military and an intrusive surveillance system. Protecting energy supplies is no excuse: the invasion of Iraq pulled much of that country's oil production off world markets for years, and the Iranian embargo has not increased world supplies of energy; it has reduced them. In any case, America could develop its own fossil and alternative energy supplies and institute sensible conservation incentives and efficiency standards for a fraction of the cost of our ruinous romance with the Middle East. Any politician, pundit, or academic who advocates American military intervention in the Middle East should be given antipsychotic medication for his or her own good—but mostly for ours.

4. **Redirect the peace dividend to domestic infrastructure improvement.** John Kerry is right—we do act like a poor country. That's because in some respects we are one. Domestic infrastructure of all kinds, not only transportation, but the power grid, public transportation, clean water, sewers, and dams, is increasingly rickety. Even our airports are no longer up to the standards being set by newer facilities like Singapore, Beijing, or Incheon. It is time to sweep aside opposition to building our internal infrastructure that has periodically hobbled this country since its founding: the politicians, now mainly on the Right, who resist infrastructure upgrades bear an uncomfortable resemblance to the antebellum Southern politicians who refused to agree to build canals and railroads. An added benefit of a comprehensive infrastructure program would be the jobs created. A paper titled "The Way Forward: Moving from the Post-Bubble, Post-Bust Economy to Renewed Growth and Competitiveness" by Nouriel Roubini, Daniel Alpert, and Robert Hockett proposes a five-year $1.2 trillion infrastructure investment program designed to create 23,000 jobs for every $1 billion of investment, or 27 million total jobs.

5. **Start enforcing our antitrust laws again.** Since the early 1980s, the doctrine of "efficiency" has trumped all else in judging antitrust cases.

During the George W. Bush administration, the antitrust division of the Justice Department actually argued, with only one exception, on behalf of antitrust defendants, not plaintiffs. It even declined to support the Federal Trade Commission in arguing against monopolistic pharmaceutical patent settlements before the Supreme Court. The Court itself has often taken a strongly anticonsumer line. As a result, price-fixing has become common, as millions of cable subscribers in allocated markets have discovered from their sky-high bills. Market-dominant firms also practice bid rigging when they tender bids for federal, state, and local government contracts. The DOD's encouragement of defense company mergers in the mid-1990s resulted in whole defense sectors in which there is little if any competition. Companies with dominance in a market sector are also in a position to squeeze dependent suppliers and subcontractors into unprofitability, as Walmart has done. Conservatives believe in the Jeffersonian doctrine of small government, but forget that Jefferson combined that with an abhorrence of the monopolistic dominance of the corporations of his day, such as the British East India Company or the Hudson's Bay Company.

6. **Reform tax policy.** "Comprehensive tax reform" is something of a misnomer. What its ardent proponents want is to reduce the nominal corporate income tax rate. The bait is supposed to be a simultaneous reduction of corporate loopholes, but past experience suggests that tax legislation in the hands of these people will lower the top rate (which few corporations with competent tax lawyers pay in any case) but never get around to closing the loopholes. Proposals to eliminate even obvious abuses like the corporate deduction for company aircraft have gone nowhere. It is no surprise that corporate tax collections have fallen to barely more than one-third of their level in 1950 as a percentage of federal revenue. The same problem applies to individual income taxes: hedge fund managers paying taxes at lower personal rates than firemen or nurses is a travesty. But why would a Congress dependent on corporations and the wealthy enact such a change?

If there is enough public outrage, it does bear results: Walgreens drugstores planned in 2014 to move its headquarters to Switzerland. The stores would remain in the United States, but Walgreens would no longer pay U.S. corporate taxes, because of a tax scam called corporate inversion, despite receiving about $17 billion a year from the U.S. taxpayer for filling Medicare and Medicaid prescriptions. Yet popular protests and citizen pressure on Congress caused Walgreens to reverse its decision. It would require a much stronger, sustained level of popular outrage to effect sweeping change in the tax code, but it is not impossible: the late-nineteenth-century populist uprising led to the passage of antitrust laws and other reforms.

7. **Reform immigration policy.** One of the most polarized social issues these days is immigration. Typically, Democrats piously think more immigration is self-evidently marvelous on some principle called diversity, which they can't rationally explain, and that anyone who disagrees is a racist and a xenophobe. The Republicans are split: the foot soldiers hate immigration more than the plague, while business Republicans quietly lobby for as many H-1B work visas as possible in order to depress domestic wages so as to employ a low-paid group of indentured servants (in an outrageous recent case, Disney fired 250 IT workers, replacing them with imported labor, and required the fired employees to train their replacements as a condition of getting severance pay). The culture war that erupted over a recent immigration bill called the Dream Act showed the absurdity of the squabble: 95 percent of the controversy surrounded the parts of the bill providing for a path to citizenship—clearly something constructive must be done to change the status of current undocumented aliens—yet most of the bill's provisions, heavily lobbied for by the technology companies, opened the floodgates both for the H-1B temporary worker visa program and other legal immigration avenues, and these provisions hardly received comment.

Far too many U.S. citizens are unemployed or underemployed in a variety of professions, including highly skilled ones like computer programming. Corporate CEOs perpetually complain that they cannot find American workers educated enough to fill vacant positions, although they do everything possible to dodge the taxes that fund education and their companies have virtually eliminated the apprenticeship programs that once were common. Work visas should be granted only in limited circumstances, not as a blanket policy to make the labor supply exceed demand at a time of persistent high unemployment. In effect, Washington has allowed corporations to act as human traffickers. Our immigration policy must not be based on spite, but neither should it rest on sentimentality: national interest ought to dictate first what is good for our own people. If America should not colonize the world with its military power, neither should the world colonize America at the behest of corporate interests who don't want to pay our own citizens a living wage.

8. **Adopt a single-payer health care system.** Free-market proponents demand efficiency, whether as the sole criterion for determining an antitrust case, in time-motion studies for hurrying along employees on an assembly line, or in cost-benefit analysis for pollution control. Yet their calls for efficiency fall silent when it comes to a sector that makes up 17.9 percent of our economy: the U.S. health care system. There are many reasons why medicine is simply not amenable to a laissez-faire market system of distribution in the way automobiles or refrigerators are. When the Big One hits you in the chest at three in the morning, and you are hauled away unconscious in the ambulance, it is a bit tricky to shop just then for the highest-quality, lowest-cost hospital.

The reality of health care also refutes Chicago school ideologues who fantasize about the existence of markets based on transparency and "perfect information": hospitals, clinics, and practitioners do not post a price list the way a restaurant posts a menu. In fact, they charge whatever they're able to con the insurer or Medicare into paying—everyone who has been in a hospital can tell an anecdote about a hundred-dollar Q-tip or some similar outrage on their bill. Pharmaceutical companies, assisted by Congress, collude in price-fixing. This all comes at a cost: the advanced economies of Western Europe generally spend only half to two-thirds of what the United States spends on health care as a percentage of gross domestic product—with better outcomes, to judge from their superior life-expectancy statistics. And these are generally government-run, single-payer systems. But since that solution is anathema to the free-market crowd, we are stuck with a monstrous hybrid that has neither free-market efficiency and competition nor the inclusiveness and standardization of a national system. A single-payer system would be more efficient and lead to an additional benefit: the 5 or 6 percent of the economy freed up by true health care reform (close to a trillion dollars annually) could go to more worthwhile things than paying for sheer waste in health care, such as research or infrastructure, or could revert back to the long-suffering consumer's pocket.

9. **Abolish corporations' personhood status, or else treat them exactly like persons.** Corporations in America now have it both ways: *Citizens United, Hobby Lobby,* and other rulings now give them virtually all the constitutional attributes of a U.S. citizen: their political bribery is protected as First Amendment speech and their corporate officers' "right" to impose their personal views on their employees is safeguarded by the "free exercise of religion" clause of that amendment. Yet the bedrock legal purpose of a corporation has always been to shield its executives and directors from civil or criminal liability for the firm's wrongdoing—liability that a real person could never dodge. Corporations also enjoy a myriad of tax advantages that actual human beings do not have: can an individual claim personal depreciation as he ages? Of course not. Corporations also benefit from corporate inversion rules that exempt a company from U.S. taxes if it merges with a foreign company and moves its headquarters abroad, even if it continues to generate the vast bulk of its revenue in the United States.

U.S. citizens are still subject to federal tax laws when they reside in a foreign country. The recently passed Foreign Account Tax Compliance Act contains onerous and intrusive reporting requirements on U.S persons living abroad, with stiff penalties for noncompliance. Corporations are exempt from this law—the same corporations that squirrel away hundreds of billions of dollars in overseas tax havens. Corporate executives need to stop their whining about how the United States, a nation that has historically coddled business interests, is some sort of incipient Bolshevik people's republic. They must face a choice: if they want corporate personhood, accept all the legal burdens of a person; if not, agree to the tax reform in our previous recommendation, which does not grant them aggregate tax benefits greatly exceeding those of a middle-income wage earner. Otherwise, they may want to entertain their libertarian fantasies by incorporating in the laissez-faire playground of Somalia while contemplating how to make up for their lost revenue from being shut out of the U.S. market.

What I have just suggested sounds utopian, even unworldly. But the United States has done more surprising things in its history. One of the most astonishing events of my life was the rapid collapse of the Soviet Union and its empire in Eastern Europe. The Wise Men of Washington, Bob Gates and the rest of his tribe, assumed it to be a well-functioning totalitarian system, cold as ice and unyielding as steel. Yet it crumbled not because of military force or violent revolution. The people who lived there and bore its burdens simply gave up believing in its myths. The United States is far better situated than the Soviet Union ever was, despite our many institutional flaws and the accretion of ideological myths that have impaired our ability to see the world as it is and live sensibly and peaceably within it. The path to a better America will come surprisingly easily when, to paraphrase Abraham Lincoln, we "disenthrall ourselves" from worn-out myths and the fears that underlie them.

NOTES

Chapter One. Beltwayland

1. David Brinkley, *Washington Goes to War,* New York: Knopf, 1988.
2. "How the Most Ideologically Polarized Americans Live Different Lives," Pew Research Center, June 13, 2014. http://www.pewresearch.org/fact-tank/2014/06/13/big-houses-art-museums-and-in-laws-how-the-most-ideologically-polarized-americans-live-different-lives.
3. "Ideology and Brand Consumption," *Psychological Science,* March 15, 2013. http://pss.sagepub.com/content/24/3/326.
4. Author interview with Andrew Feinstein, London, April 29, 2014. Feinstein is the author of *The Shadow World: Inside the Global Arms Trade,* New York: Farrar, Straus & Giroux, 2011.
5. "Khalifa Hiftar, the Ex-General Leading a Revolt in Libya, Spent Years in Exile in Northern Virginia," *Washington Post,* May 20, 2014. http://www.washingtonpost.com/world/africa/rival-militias-prepare-for-showdown-in-tripoli-after-takeover-of-parliament/2014/05/19/cb36acc2-df6f-11e3-810f-764fe508b82d_story.html.

Chapter Two. What Is the Deep State?

1. "Exclusive: NSA Pays £100m in Secret Funding for GCHQ," *The Guardian,* August 1, 2013. http://www.theguardian.com/uk-news/2013/aug/01/nsa-paid-gchq-spying-edward-snowden.
2. "Top Secret America: A *Washington Post* Investigation," *Washington Post,* updated September 2010. http://projects.washingtonpost.com/top-secret-america/.
3. Irving L. Janis, *Groupthink: Psychological Studies of Policy Decisions and Fiascoes,* 2nd ed., New York: Houghton Mifflin, 1982.
4. "U.S. Stock Ownership Stays at Record Low," Gallup, May 8, 2013. http://www.gallup.com/poll/162353/stock-ownership-stays-record-low.aspx.
5. "Executive Compensation Data Firm Equilar Releases Annual CEO Pay

Study," Equilar, April 13, 2014. http://www.equilar.com/press-releases/23-annual-ceo-pay-study.html.

6. "Median Income Rises, but Is Still 6% Below Level at Start of Recession in '07," *New York Times,* August 21, 2013. http://www.nytimes.com/2013/08/22/us/politics/us-median-income-rises-but-is-still-6-below-its-2007-peak.html?

Chapter Three. Bad Ideas Have Consequences

1. Robert Mann, *A Grand Delusion: America's Descent into Vietnam,* New York: Basic Books, 2001.

2. The memorandum is available on the website of the Washington and Lee University School of Law. http://law.wlu.edu/powellarchives/page.asp?pageid=1251.

3. "Business: Ford's Rolls-Royces," *Time,* July 8, 1940. http://content.time.com/time/magazine/article/0,9171,795076,00.html.

4. Dan Avnon and Avner de-Shalit, *Liberalism and Its Practice,* London and New York: Routledge, 1998.

5. "U.S. Manufacturing Surges Ahead—but Don't Look for a Factory Job," *Forbes,* August 22, 2011. http://www.forbes.com/sites/jonbruner/2011/08/22/u-s-manufacturing-surges-ahead-but-dont-look-for-a-factory-job-infographic/.

6. Simon Johnson and James Kwak, *13 Bankers: The Wall Street Takeover and the Next Financial Meltdown,* New York: Vintage, 2011.

7. Madeleine Albright, *Madam Secretary: A Memoir,* New York: Miramax, 2003.

8. "Transcript: Albright Interview on NBC-TV," February 19, 1998. http://www.fas.org/news/iraq/1998/02/19/98021907_tpo.html.

Chapter Four. Do Elections Matter?

1. "West Virginia Puzzled, Outraged over Chemical Leak," *Los Angeles Times,* January 16, 2014. http://articles.latimes.com/2014/jan/16/nation/la-na-chemical-danger-20140117.

2. "With Bags of Cash, C.I.A. Seeks Influence in Afghanistan," *New York Times,* April 28, 2013. http://www.nytimes.com/2013/04/29/world/asia/cia-delivers-cash-to-afghan-leaders-office.html.

3. "80 Percent of Americans Don't Trust the Government. Here's Why," *The Atlantic,* April 19, 2010. http://www.theatlantic.com/business/archive/2010/04/80-percent-of-americans-dont-trust-the-government-heres-why/39148/.

4. "Congress Less Popular than Cockroaches, Traffic Jams," Public Policy Poll-

ing, January 8, 2013. http://www.publicpolicypolling.com/main/2013/01/
congress-less-popular-than-cockroaches-traffic-jams.html.

5. "A Long, Steep Drop for Americans' Standard of Living," *Christian Science Monitor,* October 19, 2011. http://www.csmonitor.com/Business/2011/1019/A-long-steep-drop-for-Americans-standard-of-living.

6. "US Election: How Can It Cost $6bn?" BBC News, August 2, 2012. http://www.bbc.com/news/magazine-19052054.

7. "Scholar Behind Viral 'Oligarchy' Study Tells You What It Means," *Talking Points Memo,* April 22, 2014. http://talkingpointsmemo.com/dc/princeton-scholar-demise-of-democracy-america-tpm-interview.

8. Kenneth P. Vogel, *Big Money: 2.5 Billion Dollars, One Suspicious Vehicle, and a Pimp—On the Trail of the Ultra-Rich Hijacking American Politics,* New York: Public Affairs, 2014.

9. "Alan Grayson Lets Both Parties Have It: 'People's Lives Are Circling the Drain, and Nobody's Even Talking About It,'" *Salon,* July 9, 2015. http://www.salon.com/2015/07/09/alan_grayson_lets_both_parties_have_it_peoples_lives_are_circling_the_drain_and_nobodys_even_talking_about_it/.

10. "The Big Lobotomy: How Republicans Made Congress Stupid," *Washington Monthly,* June/July/August 2014. http://www.washingtonmonthly.com/magazine/junejulyaugust_2014/features/the_big_lobotomy050642.php.

11. "House Press Offices Expand as Other Staffs Shrink," *USA Today,* July 1, 2014. http://www.usatoday.com/story/news/politics/2014/07/01/house-staff-cuts-communications-press/11425389/.

12. Joshua L. Kalla and David E. Broockman, "Congressional Officials Grant Access to Individuals Because They Have Contributed to Campaigns: A Randomized Field Experiment," 2014. http://web.archive.org/web/20150708051134.

13. "What Israel's Chief of Staff Is Worried About—No, It's Not Iran," *Forward,* May 26, 2015. http://forward.com/opinion/israel/308757/the-top-priority-of-israels-chief-of-staff-and-no-its-not-bombing-iran/.

14. "How the GOP Became the Israel Party," *American Conservative,* April 8, 2015. http://www.theamericanconservative.com/articles/how-the-gop-became-the-israel-party/.

15. "Senator Lindsey Graham Meeting in Israel with PM Netanyahu," Fox News, December 27, 2014. http://gretawire.foxnewsinsider.com/2014/12/27/senator-lindsey-graham-meeting-in-israel-with-pm-netanyahu-click-for-transcript/.

16. "Adelson to Keep Betting on the GOP," *Wall Street Journal,* December 4, 2012. http://www.wsj.com/articles/SB10001424127887323717004578159570568104706.

17. "Paul Singer: This Is the New 'Big Short,'" CNBC, May 28, 2015. http://www.cnbc.com/id/102715625.

18. "G.O.P.'s Israel Support Deepens as Political Contributions Shift," *New York Times*, April 4, 2015. http://www.nytimes.com/2015/04/05/us/politics/gops-israel-support-deepens-as-political-contributions-shift.html.

19. "McAllister Admits to Casting Vote for Money," *Ouachita Citizen*, June 6, 2014. http://www.hannapub.com/ouachitacitizen/news/local_state_headlines/article_8a017c20-ed41-11e3-b622-0017a43b2370.html.

20. "Bernanke Cashes In," CNBC, May 22, 2014. http://video.cnbc.com/gallery/?video=3000278038.

21. "Transformation, Like Reagan," *Politico*, January 16, 2008. http://www.politico.com/blogs/bensmith/0108/Transformation_like_Reagan.html.

22. "A Fisher King in the White House," *Full Stop*, July 9, 2013. http://www.full-stop.net/2013/07/09/blog/meagan-day/a-fisher-king-in-the-white-house/.

23. "The Making of Hillary 5.0: Marketing Wizards Help Re-Imagine Clinton Brand," *Washington Post*, February 21, 2015. http://www.washingtonpost.com/politics/the-making-of-hillary-50-marketing-wizards-help-reimagine-clinton-brand/2015/02/21/bfb01120-b919-11e4-aa05-1ce812b3fdd2_story.html.

24. Bob Woodward, *The Agenda: Inside the Clinton White House*, New York: Simon & Schuster, 1994.

25. "Why I Am Cancelling My Documentary on Hillary Clinton," *Huffington Post*, September 30, 2013. http://www.huffingtonpost.com/charles-ferguson/hillary-clinton-documentary_b_4014792.html.

26. "The Bill and Hillary Clinton Money Machine Taps Corporate Cash," *Wall Street Journal*, July 1, 2014. http://www.wsj.com/articles/the-bill-and-hillary-clinton-money-machine-taps-corporate-cash-1404268205.

27. Lou Dubose and Jake Bernstein, *Vice: Dick Cheney and the Hijacking of the American Presidency*, New York: Random House, 2006.

28. James Mann, *Rise of the Vulcans: The History of Bush's War Cabinet*, New York: Penguin, 2004.

29. "'Torture Report': A Closer Look at When and What President Bush Knew," National Public Radio, December 16, 2014. http://www.npr.org/sections/thetwo-way/2014/12/16/369876047/torture-report-a-closer-look-at-when-and-what-president-bush-knew.

30. "The Golf Address," *New York Times*, August 23, 2014. http://www.nytimes.com/2014/08/24/opinion/sunday/maureen-dowd-the-golf-address.html.

31. "Gates Conceals Real Story of 'Gaming' Obama on Afghan War," Inter Press Service, January 10, 2014. http://www.ipsnews.net/2014/01/gates-conceals-real-story-gaming-obama-afghan-war/.

32. Ibid.
33. "U.S. Model for a Future War Fans Tensions with China and Inside Pentagon," *Washington Post,* August 1, 2012. http://www.washingtonpost.com/world/national-security/us-model-for-a-future-war-fans-tensions-with-china-and-inside-pentagon/2012/08/01/gJQAC6F8PX_story.html.
34. "The Trillion Dollar Nuclear Triad," James Martin Center for Nonproliferation Studies, January 2014. http://cns.miis.edu/opapers/pdfs/140107_trillion_dollar_nuclear_triad.pdf.
35. "This Could Be the Most Dominant Republican Congress Since 1929," *Washington Post,* November 3, 2014. http://www.washingtonpost.com/blogs/the-fix/wp/2014/11/03/this-could-be-the-most-dominant-republican-congress-since-1929.
36. "Stop Whining, I'm Your Friend," *The Economist,* August 9, 2014. http://www.economist.com/news/united-states/21611140-president-wants-ceos-play-ball-he-might-have-change-his-own-language-stop.

Chapter Five. Does Our Defense Actually Defend America?

1. "A Review of FBI Security Programs," Commission for Review of FBI Security Programs, v.s. Department of Justice, March 2002. http://www.fas.org/irp/agency/doj/fbi/websterreport.html.
2. "The Golden Age of Black Ops," *Huffington Post,* January 20, 2015. http://www.huffingtonpost.com/nick-turse/black-ops_b_6507142.html.
3. "America's $1 Trillion National Security Budget," Project on Government Oversight, March 13, 2014. http://www.pogo.org/our-work/straus-military-reform-project/defense-budget/2014/americas-one-trillion-national-security-budget.html.
4. "U.S. Military Spending Dwarfs Rest of World," NBC News, February 24, 2014. http://www.nbcnews.com/storyline/military-spending-cuts/u-s-military-spending-dwarfs-rest-world-n37461.
5. "How Much Does the Pentagon Pay for a Gallon of Gas?" *National Defense,* April 2010. http://www.nationaldefensemagazine.org/archive/2010/April/Pages/HowMuchforaGallonofGas.aspx.
6. "U.S., Djibouti Reach Agreement to Keep Counterterrorism Base in Horn of Africa Nation," *Washington Post,* May 5, 2014. http://www.washingtonpost.com/politics/us-djibouti-reach-agreement-to-keep-counterterrorism-base-in-horn-of-africa-nation/2014/05/05/0965412c-d488-11e3-aae8-c2d44bd79778_story.html.
7. "Chaos in Tower, Danger in Skies at Base in Africa," *Washington Post,* April 30, 2015. http://www.washingtonpost.com/world/national-security/miscues

-at-us-counterterrorism-base-put-aircraft-in-danger-documents-show/2015/04/30/39038d5a-e9bb-11e4-9a6a-c1ab95a0600b_story.html.

8. "Billions from Beijing: Africans Divided over Chinese Presence," *Der Spiegel,* November 29, 2013. http://www.spiegel.de/international/world/chinese-investment-in-africa-boosts-economies-but-worries-many-a-934826.html.

9. "China and Africa: What the U.S. Doesn't Understand," CNN, July 2, 2013. http://management.fortune.cnn.com/2013/07/02/china-africa-us/.

10. David E. Brown, *AFRICOM at 5 Years: The Maturation of a New U.S. Combatant Command,* Strategic Studies Institute, U.S. Army War College, August 2013. http://www.strategicstudiesinstitute.army.mil/pdffiles/PUB1164.pdf.

11. Thomas E. Ricks, *The Generals: American Military Command from World War II to Today,* New York: Penguin, 2012.

12. *Alternatives for Modernizing U.S. Fighter Forces,* Congressional Budget Office, May 2009. http://www.cbo.gov/sites/default/files/cbofiles/ftpdocs/101xx/doc10113/05-13-fighterforces.pdf.

13. "The Troubled F-35," *The Week,* August 8, 2014 (print edition).

14. "Before Shooting in Iraq, a Warning on Blackwater," *New York Times,* June 29, 2014. http://www.nytimes.com/2014/06/30/us/before-shooting-in-iraq-warning-on-blackwater.html.

15. Seymour Melman, *Profits without Production,* New York: Knopf, 1983.

16. "Rationalizing America's Defense Industry: Renewing Investor Support for the Defense Industrial Base and Safeguarding National Security," address by William Anders, Washington, DC: October 30, 1991.

17. Winslow T. Wheeler, ed., *The Pentagon Labyrinth: 10 Short Essays to Help You Through It, Defense Week,* Center for Defense Information, 2011.

18. "Over 350,000 Killed by Violence, $4.4 Trillion Spent and Obligated," Watson Institute for International Studies, 2011. http://costsofwar.org/.

Chapter Six. Economic Warfare:
Big Banks and the National Security State

1. *Defense Strategy for the 1990s: The Regional Defense Strategy,* prepared for Secretary of Defense Dick Cheney, January 1993. http://www.informationclearinghouse.info/pdf/naarpr_Defense.pdf.

2. *The National Security Strategy of the United States of America,* September 2002. http://georgewbush-whitehouse.archives.gov/nsc/nss/2002/.

3. "Iraq: Baghdad Moves to Euro," Radio Free Europe/Radio Liberty, November 1, 2014. http://www.rferl.org/content/article/1095057.html.

4. Ron Suskind, *The Price of Loyalty: George W. Bush, the White House, and the Education of Paul O'Neill*, New York: Simon & Schuster, 2004.

5. "Saving the World Economy from Gaddafi," *RT News,* May 5, 2011. http://rt.com/news/economy-oil-gold-libya/.

6. "New Details on F.B.I. Aid for Saudis After 9/11," *New York Times*, March 27, 2005. http://www.nytimes.com/2005/03/27/politics/27exodus.html.

7. "9/11 Link to Saudi Arabia Is Topic of 28 Redacted Pages in Government Report; Congressmen Push for Release," *International Business Times*, December 9, 2013. http://www.ibtimes.com/911-link-saudi-arabia-topic-28-redacted-pages-government-report-congressmen-push-release-1501202.

8. "Fossil Fuel Exploration Subsidies: Saudi Arabia," Oil Cange International Country Study, November 2014. http://www.odi.org/sites/odi.org.uk/files/odi-assets/publications-opinion-files/9268.pdf.

9. Barbara Salazar Torreon, *Instances of Use of United States Armed Forces Abroad, 1798–2014*, Congressional Research Service, January 13, 2014. http://fas.org/sgp/crs/natsec/R42738.pdf.

10. Juan Zarate, *Treasury's War: The Unleashing of a New Era of Financial Warfare,* New York: Public Affairs, 2013.

11. Author interview with Andrew Cockburn, April 8, 2014.

12. "Why Sanctions Don't Really Work," *Los Angeles Times*, March 19, 2014. http://articles.latimes.com/2014/mar/19/opinion/la-oe-cockburn-sanctions-20140320.

13. "Obama Gives the Castro Regime in Cuba an Undeserved Bailout," *Washington Post*, December 17, 2014. http://www.washingtonpost.com/opinions/the-obama-administration-extends-the-castro-regime-in-cuba-a-bailout-it-doesnt-deserve/2014/12/17/a25a15d4-860c-11e4-9534-f79a23c40e6c_story.html.

14. "Pros and Cons of U.S. Sanctions Against Venezuela," NBC News, December 17, 2014. http://www.nbcnews.com/news/latino/globalpost-pros-cons-u-s-sanctions-against-venezuela-n269221.

Chapter Seven. The Commanding Heights

1. "Norquist Compares Sen. Schumer's Tax-Dodger Bill to the Nazis, Communists," *The Hill*, May 19, 2012. http://thehill.com/policy/finance/228427-norquist-compares-schumers-tax-dodger-bill-to-the-nazis.

2. "The Education of Lord Bloomberg," *New York Review of Books,* April 7, 2011. http://www.nybooks.com/blogs/nyrblog/2011/apr/11/mayor-bloomberg-lord-schools/.

3. "The Plight of the 1%," Reuters, December 20, 2011. http://blogs.reuters.com/felix-salmon/2011/12/20/the-plight-of-the-1/.

4. "For the Love of Money," *New York Times*, January 18, 2014. http://www
.nytimes.com/2014/01/19/opinion/sunday/for-the-love-of-money.html.

5. "Bankers Join Billionaires to Debunk 'Imbecile' Attack on Top 1%,"
Bloomberg Businessweek, December 20, 2011. http://www.bloomberg.com/
news/articles/2011-12-20/bankers-join-billionaires-to-debunk-imbecile
-attack-on-top-1-.

6. "Policy Basics: Where Do Federal Tax Revenues Come From?" Center for
Budget and Policy Priorities, March 11, 2015. http://www.cbpp.org/cms/?
fa=view&id=3822.

7. Thomas Saez, "Striking It Richer: The Evolution of Top Incomes in the United
States," September 3, 2013. http://eml.berkeley.edu/~saez/saez-UStopincomes
-2012.pdf.

8. Gabriel Zucman, "Taxing across Borders: Tracking Personal Wealth and
Corporate Profits," *Journal of Economic Perspectives*, Fall 2014. http://gabriel
-zucman.eu/files/Zucman2014JEP.pdf.

9. Text reprinted by History Matters, an online survey course of George Mason University. http://historymatters.gmu.edu/d/5769.

10. Smedley D. Butler, *War Is a Racket: The Antiwar Classic by America's Most
Decorated Soldier*, Los Angeles: Feral House, 2003.

11. Noam Chomsky, *Deterring Democracy*, London and New York: Verso,
1991.

12. Author interview with Marshall Auerback, research associate at the Levy
Economics Institute of Bard College and consulting economist for PIMCO,
June 25, 2014.

13. "Treasury Lost $78 Billion Due to Overpayment of TARP Funds, Panel
Says," Yahoo, February 6, 2009. http://voices.yahoo.com/treasury-lost-78
-billion-due-overpayment-tarp-2618149.html?cat=9.

14. "Banks Seen Dangerous Defying Obama's Too-Big-to-Fail Move,"
Bloomberg News, April 16, 2012. http://www.bloomberg.com/news/2012
-04-16/obama-bid-to-end-too-big-to-fail-undercut-as-banks-grow.html.

Chapter Eight. The Deep State, the Law, and the Constitution

1. "HSBC Annual Profits Reach £13.8bn," BBC News, February 27, 2012.
http://www.bbc.co.uk/news/business-17176332.

2. "SEC's White Feels BlackRock's Pain Over Systemic Label," Bloomberg
News, May 23, 2014. http://www.bloomberg.com/news/2014-05-22/sec-s
-white-feels-blackrock-s-pain-over-systemic-label.html.

3. "Kids Doing Time for What's Not a Crime: The Over-Incarceration of Status
Offenders," Texas Public Policy Foundation, March 2014. http://www.texas

policy.com/sites/default/files/documents/2014-03-PP12-Juvenile
JusticeStatusOffenders-CEJ-DerekCohenMarcLevin.pdf.

4. "Cops or Soldiers?," *The Economist*, March 22, 2014. http://www.economist
.com/news/united-states/21599349-americas-police-have-become-too-
militarised-cops-or-soldiers.

5. "War Gear Flows to Police Departments," *New York Times*, June 8, 2014.
http://www.nytimes.com/2014/06/09/us/war-gear-flows-to-police
-departments.html.

6. "Turn Off That Camera! Animal Cruelty Exposés Being Blocked," ABC
News, February 5, 2013. http://abcnews.go.com/Blotter/ag-gag-laws-animal
-cruelty-exposes-blocked/story?id=18337864.

7. "North Carolina GOP Pushes Unprecedented Bill to Jail Anyone Who
Discloses Fracking Chemicals," *Mother Jones*, May 19, 2014. http://www
.motherjones.com/blue-marble/2014/05/north-carolina-felony-fracking
-chemicals-disclosure.

8. "An Offer You Can't Refuse," Human Rights Watch, December 5, 2013.
http://www.hrw.org/node/120933.

9. "Eric Holder: A 'State of Crisis' for the Right to Counsel," *The Atlantic*,
March 15, 2013. http://www.theatlantic.com/national/archive/2013/03/
eric-holder-a-state-of-crisis-for-the-right-to-counsel/274074/.

10. "Stop and Seize: Aggressive Police Take Hundreds of Millions of Dollars
from Motorists Not Charged with Crimes," *Washington Post*, September 6,
2014.   http://www.washingtonpost.com/sf/investigative/2014/09/06/stop
-and-seize/.

11. "Prison Economics Help Drive Ariz. Immigration Law," National Public
Radio, October 28, 2010. http://www.npr.org/2010/10/28/130833741/
prison-economics-help-drive-ariz-immigration-law.

12. *United States v. Reynolds,* 345 U.S. 1 (1953) (Supreme Court opinion).
http://caselaw.lp.findlaw.com/scripts/getcase.pl?court=us&vol=345&
invol=1.

13. "ACLU v. National Security Agency: Why the 'State Secrets Privilege'
Shouldn't Stop the Lawsuit Challenging Warrantless Telephone Surveillance of Americans," FindLaw, June 16, 2006. http://writ.news.findlaw
.com/dean/20060616.html.

14. "Department of Justice White Paper" (undated), leaked to NBC News.
http://msnbcmedia.msn.com/i/msnbc/sections/news/020413_DOJ
_White_Paper.pdf.

15. "More than 2,400 Dead as Obama's Drone Campaign Marks Five Years," Bureau of Investigative Journalism, January 23, 2014. http://www.thebureau

investigates.com/2014/01/23/more-than-2400-dead-as-obamas-drone
-campaign-marks-five-years/.

16. "Cynicism-in-Public-Life Contest, John Roberts Edition," *The Atlantic*,
April 4, 2014. http://www.theatlantic.com/politics/archive/2014/04/cynicism-
in-public-life-contest-john-roberts-edition/360135/.

17. "How the Heritage Foundation, a Conservative Think Tank, Promoted the
Individual Mandate," *Forbes*, October 20, 2011. http://www.forbes.com/
sites/theapothecary/2011/10/20/how-a-conservative-think-tank-invented
-the-individual-mandate.

18. "Dems Who Flipped on FISA Immunity See More Telecom Cash," CBS
News, June 24, 2008. http://www.cbsnews.com/news/dems-who-flipped
-on-fisa-immunity-see-more-telecom-cash/.

19. "Obama's FISA Shift," ABC News, July 9, 2008. http://abcnews.go.com/
blogs/politics/2008/07/obamas-fisa-shi/.

20. "As Obama Makes Case, Congress Is Divided on Campaign Against Mili-
tants," *New York Times*, September 8, 2014. http://www.nytimes.com/2014/
09/09/us/as-obama-makes-case-congress-is-divided-on-campaign-against
-militants.html.

21. "Condi Rice Blasts Obama on Weakness, Leadership," *Weekly Standard*,
March 27, 2014. http://www.weeklystandard.com/blogs/condi-rice-blasts
-obama-weakness-leadership_786123.html.

Chapter Nine. Silicon Valley and the American Panopticon

1. "Jailed for Jailbreaking: The New Law Could Land You in the Slammer,"
Network World, January 30, 2013. http://www.networkworld.com/article/
2163148/software/jailed-for-jailbreaking--the-new-law-could-land-you
-in-the-slammer.html.

2. "Microsoft, IBM Top List of U.S. Tech Firms with Biggest Overseas Profit
Hauls," Bloomberg News, August 13, 2013. http://www.bloomberg.com/
news/2013-08-13/microsoft-ibm-top-list-of-u-s-tech-firms-with-biggest
-overseas-profit-hauls.html.

3. "Das amerikanische System hat Krebs" (interview with George Packer),
Basler Zeitung, September 6, 2014. http://bazonline.ch/leben/gesellschaft/
Das-amerikanische-System-hat-Krebs/story/28898212.

4. "Cash-Rich Spending Spree Is Sign of a Growing Tech Bubble," *MarketWatch*,
August 7, 2014. http://www.marketwatch.com/story/cash-rich-spending
-spree-is-sign-of-a-growing-tech-bubble-2014-08-07.

5. "The Real Story on Apple's Tax Avoidance: How Ordinary It Is," *Forbes*,
May 21, 2013. http://www.forbes.com/sites/beltway/2013/05/21/the-real
-story-about-apples-tax-avoidance-how-ordinary-it-is/.

6. "Microsoft, IBM Top List of U.S. Tech Firms with Biggest Overseas Profit Hauls," Bloomberg News, August 13, 2013. http://www.bloomberg.com/news/2013-08-13/microsoft-ibm-top-list-of-u-s-tech-firms-with-biggest-overseas-profit-hauls.html.

7. "Most Untaxed Overseas Profits in U.S. Technology," Bloomberg.com (chart). http://www.bloomberg.com/visual-data/best-and-worst/most-untaxed-overseas-profits-in-us-technology-companies.

8. "The Education of a Libertarian," *Cato Unbound*, April 13, 2009. http://www.cato-unbound.org/2009/04/13/peter-thiel/education-libertarian.

9. "ChamberLeaks: Military Contractors Palantir and Berico Under Scrutiny," ThinkProgress, March 19, 2011. http://thinkprogress.org/economy/2011/03/19/144160/chamberleaks-berico-palantir/.

10. "How a 'Deviant' Philosopher Built Palantir, a CIA-Funded Data-Mining Juggernaut," *Forbes*, September 2, 2013. http://www.forbes.com/sites/andygreenberg/2013/08/14/agent-of-intelligence-how-a-deviant-philosopher-built-palantir-a-cia-funded-data-mining-juggernaut/.

11. "Tech's Toxic Political Culture: The Stealth Libertarianism of Silicon Valley Bigwigs," *Salon*, June 6, 2014. http://www.salon.com/2014/06/06/techs_toxic_political_culture_the_stealth_libertarianism_of_silicon_valley_bigwigs/.

12. "Statement by the Office of the Director of National Intelligence and the U.S. Department of Justice on the Declassification of Documents Related to the Protect America Act Litigation," Office of the Director of National Intelligence, September 11, 2014. http://icontherecord.tumblr.com/post/97251906083/statement-by-the-office-of-the-director-of.

13. Glenn Greenwald, *No Place to Hide: Edward Snowden, the NSA, and the U.S. Surveillance State*, New York: Metropolitan Books, 2014.

14. "Exclusive: Emails Reveal Close Google Relationship with NSA," Aljazeera America, May 6, 2014. http://america.aljazeera.com/articles/2014/5/6/nsa-chief-google.html.

15. "Could Big Data Have Prevented the Fort Hood Shooting?," *Defense One*, April 9, 2014. http://www.defenseone.com/ideas/2014/04/could-big-data-have-prevented-fort-hood-shooting/82249/.

16. "In NSA-Intercepted Data, Those Not Targeted Far Outnumber the Foreigners Who Are," *Washington Post*, July 5, 2014. http://www.washingtonpost.com/world/national-security/in-nsa-intercepted-data-those-not-targeted-far-outnumber-the-foreigners-who-are/2014/07/05/8139adf8-045a-11e4-8572-4b1b969b6322_story.html.

17. Author interview with Thomas Drake, former senior executive of the National Security Agency, July 8, 2014.

18. *Net Losses: Estimating the Global Cost of Cybercrime,* Center for Strategic and International Studies, June 2014. http://www.mcafee.com/us/resources/reports/rp-economic-impact-cybercrime2.pdf.

19. Author correspondence with William Edward Binney, former official of the National Security Agency, August 8, 2014.

20. "Exclusive: Secret Contract Tied NSA and Security Industry Pioneer," Reuters, December 20, 2014. http://www.reuters.com/article/2013/12/20/us-usa-security-rsa-idUSBRE9BJ1C220131220.

21. "C.I.A. Is Said to Pay AT&T for Call Data," *New York Times,* November 7, 2013. http://www.nytimes.com/2013/11/07/us/cia-is-said-to-pay-att-for-call-data.html.

22. "In Surveillance Debate, White House Turns Its Focus to Silicon Valley," *New York Times,* May 2, 2014. http://www.nytimes.com/2014/05/03/us/politics/white-house-shifts-surveillance-debate-to-private-sector.html.

23. "FTC Recommends Congress Require the Data Broker Industry to Be More Transparent and Give Consumers Greater Control over Their Personal Information," Federal Trade Commission press release, May 27, 2014. http://www.ftc.gov/news-events/press-releases/2014/05/ftc-recommends-congress-require-data-broker-industry-be-more.

Chapter Ten. Personnel Is Policy

1. "President Obama on 'House of Cards': Frank Underwood is 'Getting a Lot of Things Done,'" *The Wrap,* December 17, 2013. http://www.thewrap.com/president-obama-house-cards-frank-underwood-getting-lot-things-done/.

2. "One Documentary Later, Rumsfeld's Inner World Remains 'Unknown,'" National Public Radio, March 30, 2014. http://www.npr.org/2014/03/30/294825234/one-documentary-later-rumsfelds-inner-world-remains-unknown.

3. "Bob Rubin's House of Cards," *Daily Beast,* November 29, 2008. http://www.thedailybeast.com/articles/2008/11/29/bob-rubinrsquos-house-of-cards.html.

4. "Former NSA Chief Is Working for Wall Street Now," *The Huffington Post,* July 8, 2014. http://www.huffingtonpost.com/2014/07/08/wall-street-cyber-council_n_5568142.html.

5. "Banks Dreading Computer Hacks Call for Cyber War Council," Bloomberg News, July 8, 2014. http://www.bloomberg.com/news/2014-07-08/banks-dreading-computer-hacks-call-for-cyber-war-council.html.

6. Ibid.

7. "Robert Gates and Iran/Contra," *Counterpunch,* November 8, 2006. http://www.counterpunch.org/2006/11/08/robert-gates-and-iran-contra/.

8. Author interview with Raymond L. McGovern, January 19, 2014.

9. Robert E. Moffit, Ph.D., George Nesterczuk, and Donald J. Devine, "Taking Charge of Federal Personnel," Heritage Foundation, January 10, 2001. http://www.heritage.org/research/reports/2001/01/taking-charge-of -federal-personnel.

10. "Ties to GOP Trumped Know-How Among Staff Sent to Rebuild Iraq," *Washington Post*, September 17, 2006. http://www.washingtonpost.com/ wp-dyn/content/article/2006/09/16/AR2006091600193.html.

11. Bob Woodward, *State of Denial: Bush at War, Part III*, New York: Simon & Schuster, 2006.

12. "Requirements for the TRAILBLAZER and THINTHREAD Systems," Office of the Inspector General, Department of Defense, December 13, 2004, redacted copy archived by the Federation of American Scientists. https://www.fas.org/irp/agency/dod/ig-thinthread.pdf.

13. "The Kasich Case: From Congressman to Businessman: John Kasich Cuts a New Deal," *New York Observer*, September 17, 2001. http://observer.com/ 2001/09/the-kasich-case-from-congressman-to-businessman-john -kasich-cuts-a-new-deal/.

14. "Lehman Brothers Collapse Haunts John Kasich in Ohio Governor's Race," ABC News, May 12, 2010. http://abcnews.go.com/Politics/2010-election -wall-street-factor-ohio-governors-race/story?id=10586618.

15. "10 Questions with Ohio Gov. John Kasich," CNBC, July 14, 2015. http:// www.cnbc.com/2015/07/14/s-with-ohio-gov-john-kasich.html.

16. "The Disturbing Link Between Psychopathy and Leadership," *Forbes*, April 25, 2013. http://www.forbes.com/sites/victorlipman/2013/04/25/the-disturbing -link-between-psychopathy-and-leadership/.

17. Andrew Cockburn, *Rumsfeld: His Rise, Fall, and Catastrophic Legacy*, New York: Scribner, 2007.

18. "Attitudes to Torture," Amnesty International, May 2014. http://www .amnestyusa.org/pdfs/GlobalSurveyAttitudesToTorture2014.pdf.

Chapter Eleven. Austerity for Thee but Not for Me

1. "John Kerry Slams 'New Isolationism' and Says US Behaving Like Poor Nation," *The Guardian*, February 27, 2014. http://web.archive.org/web/ 20140228160343.

2. *Social Justice in the OECD—How Do the Member States Compare?* Bertelsmann Foundation, October 2011. http://www.sgi-network.org/uploads/ tx_amsgistudies/SGI11_Social_Justice_OECD.pdf.

3. "Maternal Mortality Rates Up in the U.S.," UPI, May 2, 2014. http://www .upi.com/Health_News/2014/05/02/Maternal-mortality-rates-up-in-the -US/4671399049359/.

4. "2010 Mortality," Texas Department of State Health Services. http://www
.dshs.state.tx.us/chs/vstat/vs10/nmortal.shtm.

5. "U.S. Foreign Aid to Israel," Congressional Research Service, June 10, 2015.
http://www.fas.org/sgp/crs/mideast/RL33222.pdf.

6. "Life Expectancy: Data by Country," World Health Organization, 2013.
http://apps.who.int/gho/data/node.main.688?lang=en.

7. "The Sorry State of Amtrak's On-Time Performance, Mapped," *Washington
Post*, July 10, 2014. http://www.washingtonpost.com/blogs/wonkblog/wp/
2014/07/10/the-sorry-state-of-amtraks-on-time-performance-mapped/.

8. "Roads to Ruin: Towns Rip Up the Pavement," *Wall Street Journal*, July 17,
2010. http://online.wsj.com/news/articles/SB1000142405274870491330
4575370950363737746.

9. Author interview with Brian J. O'Malley, July 12, 2014.

10. "The Rockets from Hamas, and the Iron Dome That Could Use Patching,"
National Public Radio, *All Things Considered,* July 9, 2014. http://www.npr
.org/2014/07/09/330183774/the-rockets-from-hamas-and-the-iron-dome
-that-could-use-patching.

11. "Congress Backs Aid to Israel," *Politico*, August 1, 2014. http://www.politico
.com/story/2014/08/senate-approves-israel-aid-109642.html.

12. "This Is Why Washington Is Awful: Senators Congratulate Themselves for
Giving Israel More Money," *Salon*, August 4, 2014. http://www.salon.com/
2014/08/04/this_is_why_washington_is_awful_senators_congratulate
_themselves_for_giving_israel_more_money.

13. "Prison Construction Boom Reaches 3 in 10 Counties," Urban Institute,
April 29, 2004. http://www.urban.org/publications/900710.html.

14. Frank Schmalleger and John Smykla, *Corrections in the 21st Century,* New
York: McGraw-Hill, 2011.

15. "Detroit's Latest Pension Disgrace: A Gaudy New Arena at Retirees' Expense," *Salon,* July 24, 2014. http://www.salon.com/2014/07/24/detroits
_pension_disgrace_a_gaudy_new_stadium_at_retirees_expense_partner.

16. "Isolation Isn't an Option," *Washington Post,* May 4, 2014 (print edition).

17. "Dethrone 'King Dollar,'" *New York Times*, August 27, 2014. http://www
.nytimes.com/2014/08/28/opinion/dethrone-king-dollar.html.

18. "Poverty Rate Is Up in New York City, and Income Gap Is Wide, Census
Data Show," *New York Times*, September 19, 2013. http://www.nytimes
.com/2013/09/19/nyregion/poverty-rate-in-city-rises-to-21-2.html.

19. "Afghans Worry as U.S. Spending Boom Comes to an End," *Washington
Post*, June 9, 2014. https://www.washingtonpost.com/world/afghans-worry
-as-us-spending-boom-comes-to-an-end/2014/06/08/ec9645a0-e995
-11e3-9f5c-9075d5508f0a_story.html.

20. "America's Global Image Remains More Positive Than China's," Pew Research Global Attitudes Project, July 18, 2013. http://www.pewglobal.org/2013/07/18/americas-global-image-remains-more-positive-than-chinas.

Chapter Twelve. A Stopped Clock Is Right Twice a Day

1. "As Candidate for Congress, Ted Yoho Suggested Limiting the Right to Vote to Property Owners," Right Wing Watch, May 20, 2014. http://www.rightwingwatch.org/content/candidate-congress-ted-yoho-suggested-limiting-right-vote-property-owners.
2. "Tim Geithner's Principal Hypocrisy," Reuters, August 6, 2012. http://blogs.reuters.com/great-debate/2012/08/06/tim-geithner%E2%80%99s-principal-hypocrisy/.
3. "George Will: Colleges Become the Victims of Progressivism," *Washington Post,* June 6, 2014. http://www.washingtonpost.com/opinions/george-will-college-become-the-victims-of-progressivism/2014/06/06/e90e73b4-eb50-11e3-9f5c-9075d5508f0a_story.html.
4. "The Nonprofit Sector in Brief 2014," Urban Institute, October 2014. http://www.urban.org/sites/default/files/alfresco/publication-pdfs/413277-The-Nonprofit-Sector-in-Brief--.PDF.
5. "$105 Million in 5 Years," CNN Money, September 12, 2014. http://money.cnn.com/2014/09/12/news/companies/goodell-pay.
6. "The Red Line and the Rat Line," *London Review of Books,* April 17, 2014. http://www.lrb.co.uk/v36/n08/seymour-m-hersh/the-red-line-and-the-rat-line.
7. "Conservatives Seek to Regain Control of Republican Agenda," *Washington Post,* May 15, 2014. http://www.washingtonpost.com/politics/conservatives-seek-to-regain-control-of-republican-agenda/2014/05/15/aaa20c80-dc6e-11e3-bda1-9b46b2066796_story.html.
8. "Republican Civil War Erupts: Business Groups v. Tea Party," Bloomberg News, October 8, 2013. http://www.bloomberg.com/news/2013-10-18/republican-civil-war-erupts-business-groups-v-tea-party.html.
9. "No, the 113th Congress Wasn't the Least Productive Ever," *National Journal,* December 23, 2014. http://www.nationaljournal.com/congress/no-the-113th-congress-wasn-t-the-least-productive-ever-20141223.
10. Author correspondence, May 29, 2015.
11. "This Map Shows Why the F-35 Has Turned into a Trillion-Dollar Fiasco," *Business Insider Australia,* August 20, 2014. http://www.businessinsider.com.au/this-map-explains-the-f-35-fiasco-2014-8.
12. "The Royals of Capitol Hill," *The Economist,* July 19, 2014. http://www.econ

omist.com/news/united-states/21607878-house-members-have-too-much-job-security-makes-bad-government-royals.

13. "Lack of Earmarks, Appropriations Bills Forces Lobbying Firm Van Scoyoc to Change Approach," *Washington Post*, May 9, 2014. http://www.washington post.com/business/lack-of-earmarks-appropriations-bills-forces-lobbying -firm-van-scoyoc-to-change-approach/2014/05/09/9bebc310-be74-11e3 -b195-dd0c1174052c_story.html.

14. "Dow Posts Biggest Loss in Three Weeks," *Wall Street Journal*, June 11, 2014. http://online.wsj.com/articles/u-s-stocks-trade-lower-1402489039.

15. "The Plight of the 1%," Reuters, December 20, 2011. http://blogs.reuters .com/felix-salmon/2011/12/20/the-plight-of-the-1/.

Chapter Thirteen. Signs of Change?

1. "As Syria War Escalates, Americans Cool to U.S. Intervention: Reuters/Ipsos Poll," Reuters, August 24, 2013. http://www.reuters.com/article/2013/08/25/ us-syria-crisis-usa-poll-idUSBRE97O00E20130825.

2. "I'm Still Tortured by What I Saw in Iraq," *Washington Post*, November 30, 2008. http://www.washingtonpost.com/wp-dyn/content/article/2008/11/28/ AR2008112802242.html.

3. "WikiLeaks' Trove Is a Mere Drop in Ocean of US Classified Documents," *Christian Science Monitor*, December 21, 2010. http://www.csmonitor.com/ USA/DC-Decoder/Decoder-Buzz/2010/1221/WikiLeaks-trove-is-a -mere-drop-in-ocean-of-US-classified-documents.

4. "President Gives Vote of Confidence to CIA Chief," *The Hill*, August 1, 2014. http://thehill.com/policy/technology/214100-obama-stands-behind -cia-leader.

5. "Senate, CIA Clash over Redactions in Interrogation Report," *Washington Post*, August 5, 2014. http://www.washingtonpost.com/world/national -security/senate-cia-clash-over-redactions-in-interrogation-report/ 2014/08/05/2f904f04-1ce0-11e4-ab7b-696c295ddfd1_story.html.

6. "For Kitchen Staff at Federal Agencies, Background Checks Are a Must-Order Item," *Washington Post*, August 9, 2014. http://www.washingtonpost .com/politics/for-kitchen-staff-at-federal-agencies-background-checks-are -a-must-order-item/2014/08/09/fefa1fe6-1c08-11e4-ae54-0cfe1f974f8a _story.html.

7. "The NSA Is Crippling America's Economy," *Salon*, November 27, 2013. http:// www.salon.com/2013/11/27/the_nsa_is_hurting_americas_economy _partner.

8. "Microsoft, Suspecting NSA Spying, to Ramp Up Efforts to Encrypt Its Internet Traffic," *Washington Post*, November 26, 2013. http://www.washington

post.com/business/technology/microsoft-suspecting-nsa-spying-to-ramp
-up-efforts-to-encrypt-its-internet-traffic/2013/11/26/44236b48-56a9
-11e3-8304-caf30787c0a9_story.html.

9. "The FBI and NSA Hate Apple's Plan to Keep Your iPhone Data Secret,"
   Time, September 27, 2014. http://time.com/3437222/iphone-data-encryp
   tion/.

Chapter Fourteen. America Confronts the World

1. "Kerry Condemns Russia's 'Incredible Act of Aggression' in Ukraine," Reuters, March 2, 2014. http://www.reuters.com/article/2014/03/02/us-ukraine
   -crisis-usa-kerry-idUSBREA210DG20140302.

2. "Kerry Sees Ukraine Crisis as Uniquely Putin's," *Wall Street Journal,*
   April 29, 2014. http://online.wsj.com/news/articles/SB100014240527023
   04163604579530141321140198.

3. "Hillary Clinton: 'Failure' to Help Syrian Rebels Led to the Rise of ISIS,"
   The Atlantic, August 10, 2014. http://www.theatlantic.com/international/
   archive/2014/08/hillary-clinton-failure-to-help-syrian-rebels-led-to-the
   -rise-of-isis/375832/.

4. "Stopping Russia Starts in Syria," CNBC, April 23, 2014. http://www.cnbc
   .com/id/101605835.

5. "Blackstone Chief Schwarzman Likens Obama to Hitler over Tax Rises,"
   Daily Telegraph, August 16, 2010. http://www.telegraph.co.uk/finance/
   newsbysector/banksandfinance/7949062/Blackstone-chief-Schwarzman
   -likens-Obama-to-Hitler-over-tax-rises.html.

6. "Progressive Kristallnacht Coming?" (letter), *Wall Street Journal,* January 24, 2014. http://online.wsj.com/news/articles/SB10001424052702304
   549504579316913982034286.

7. "Obama Asks for Authorization to Provide Direct Military Training to Syrian Rebels," *Washington Post,* June 26, 2014. http://www.washingtonpost
   .com/world/national-security/obama-backs-us-military-training-for-syrian
   -rebels/2014/06/26/ead59104-fd62-11e3-932c-0a55b81f48ce_story.html.

8. "Lindsey Graham: We Need Troops to Fight Islamic State 'Before We All Get
   Killed Here at Home,'" *Washington Post,* September 14, 2014. http://www
   .washingtonpost.com/blogs/post-politics/wp/2014/09/14/lindsey-graham
   -we-need-troops-to-fight-islamic-state-before-we-all-get-killed-here-at
   -home/.

9. "Iraq Crisis: How Saudi Arabia Helped Isis Take Over the North of the
   Country," *The Independent,* July 13, 2014. http://www.independent.co.uk/
   voices/comment/iraq-crisis-how-saudi-arabia-helped-isis-take-over-the
   -north-of-the-country-9602312.html.

10. "Public Acceptance of Evolution," *Science*, August 11, 2006. http://www
.sciencemag.org/content/313/5788/765.

11. Bernard Lewis, *Islam and the West*, New York: Oxford University Press,
1993.

12. "Michele Bachmann: The Rapture Is Coming and It's Obama's Fault," *Huffington Post*, April 20, 2015. http://www.huffingtonpost.com/2015/04/20/
michele-bachmann-obama-rapture_n_7104136.html.

13. "Bush's Shocking Biblical Prophecy Emerges: God Wants to 'Erase' Mid-
East Enemies 'Before a New Age Begins,'" *Alternet*, May 24, 2009. http://
www.alternet.org/story/140221/bush%27s_shocking_biblical_prophecy_
emerges%3A_god_wants_to_%22erase%22_mid-east_enemies_%22be
fore_a_new_age_begins%22.

Chapter Fifteen. Is There an Alternative?

1. "Decline and Fall: How American Society Unravelled," *The Guardian*,
June 19, 2013. http://www.theguardian.com/world/2013/jun/19/decline
-fall-american-society-unravelled.

INDEX